W9-AUE-425

"David Fisher replays a journey from Norway to Siberia via the North Pole with irreverence, wit and frequent forays into history."

—USA Today

OCTOBER 28, 1873
TWO DOZEN SAILORS
BOUND FOR THE POLE

"They spent the winter there, their second winter since leaving home. Temperatures dropped to 59 degrees below zero. Their eyelids froze shut and had to be carefully warmed in order to open their eyes; panic and haste meant eyelids torn loose from their faces. They discovered that intense cold somehow generated an overwhelming thirst, and despite the presence of snow and ice everywhere there was a great scarcity of water, for the snow and ice were of such a low temperature that it couldn't be put into their mouths.

"When spring came once again von Payer took a party of ten men and three dogs, and left the *Tegetthoff* —not heading south in hope of rescue, but north to complete his mission of finding a route to the pole."

KEY

1. 78'37N, 70W, where Kane tells his tale.
2. Archangel, where Chancellor landed. *July 27.*
3. Cook's *Miranda* founders on a reef, and he seeks help. *July 27.*
4. Hudson's mermaid is sighted. *July 28.*
5. Disko Bay, where Franklin was last seen. *July 28.*
6. Boóthia Peninsula, containing the first clue to Franklin's disappearance. *July 28.*
7. Victory Point: McClintock finds Franklin's message. *July 28.*
8. Beechey Island, where the Franklin expedition wintered. *July 28.*
9. Julius von Payer's furthest north. *July 29.*
10. King Oscar Land (mirage). *July 29.*
11. Petermann Land (mirage). *July 29.*
12. Jeannette Island (De Long). *July 29.*
13. Lena Delta, where De Long died. *July 29.*
14. White Island (now called *Kvitoya*), where Andrée's body was found. *July 30.*
15. Melville Bay, where Parry discovered the Eskimos. *July 31.*
16. Parry's furthest north, 1827.
17. George Nares's furthest north, 1875. *August 1.*
18. McCormick Bay, Peary's 1891 base. *August 3.*
19. Independence Bay, summit of Peary's 1891 trip. *August 3.*
20. Peary Land, discovered by Peary in 1891. *August 3.*
21. Etah, Peary's 1905 base. *August 3.*
22. Mount McKinley, "climbed" by Cook. *August 3.*
23. Cape Sheridan, Peary's 1908 base. *August 4.*
24. The islands that Cook didn't see. *August 4.*
25. Roald Amundsen's crash landing. *August 6.*
26. Foyn Island (now called *Foynoya*), where Nobile's *Italia* crashed. *August 6.*
27. Crocker Land (mirage). *August 8–11.*

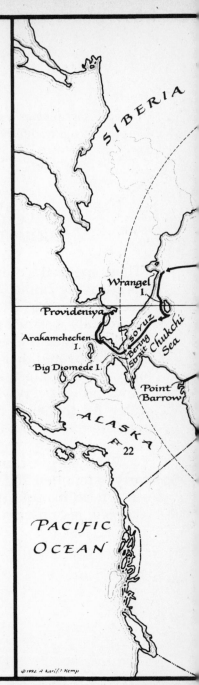

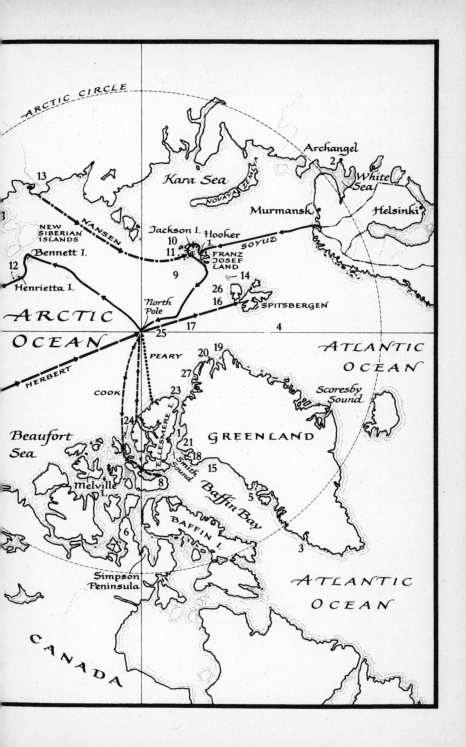

ACROSS THE TOP OF THE WORLD

TO THE NORTH POLE
BY SLED, BALLOON, AIRPLANE
AND NUCLEAR ICEBREAKER

DAVID E. FISHER

DELTA
EXPEDITION

A Delta Book
Published by
Dell Publishing
a division of
Bantam Doubleday Dell Publishing Group, Inc.
1540 Broadway
New York, New York 10036

Copyright © 1992 by David E. Fisher

All rights reserved. No part of this book may be reproduced or transmitted in
any form or by any means, electronic or mechanical, including photocopying,
recording, or by any information storage and retrieval system, without the
written permission of the Publisher, except where permitted by law. For
information address Random House, Inc., New York, New York.

The trademark Delta® is registered in the U.S. Patent and Trademark Office.

ISBN: 0-385-31223-7

Reprinted by arrangement with Random House, Inc.

Manufactured in the United States of America

Published simultaneously in Canada

July 1994
10 9 8 7 6 5 4 3 2 1

RRH

THIS BOOK IS FOR MARSHALL

Beyond this flood a frozen continent
Lies dark and wild, beat with perpetual storms
Of whirlwind and dire hail, which on firm land
Thaws not, but gathers heap, and ruin seems
Of ancient pile; all else deep snow and ice,
A gulf profound as that Serbonian bog
Betwixt Damiata and Mount Casius old,
Where armies whole have sunk; the parching air
Burns frore, and cold performs th' effect of
    fire.

—MILTON, *Paradise Lost*

"What *is* the North Pole?" Pooh asked.
"It's just a thing you discover," said Christopher Robin carelessly.

—A. A. MILNE, *Winnie-the-Pooh*

AUTHOR'S NOTE

All historical names and places in this book are accurate, but for reasons of privacy the names and identifiable characteristics of some of the passengers on the *Soyuz* have been changed.

ACKNOWLEDGMENTS

I am indebted to Wally Herbert and John Tolson for informative discussions about polar exploration and navigation, and to Herbert for guidance into the past; to Mike McDowell, Quark Expeditions, and Salen Lindblad for their graciousness and hospitality; and particularly to Kay Hale and Helen Albertson, librarians at the University of Miami's Rosenstiel School for Marine and Atmospheric Science, for their unfailing and cheerful help in tracking down obscure books and unintelligible questions. I also want to thank my lovely wife, Leila, for allowing me to abandon our vacation at the last minute in order to run off to the North Pole.

THE BEGINNING

SOVETSKIY SOYUZ

‧‖‖‧

I saw that we had passed upon a new belt of ice that was obviously unsafe. To the right and left and front was one great expanse of snow-flowered ice. The nearest solid floe was a mere lump, which stood like an island in the white level. To turn was impossible: we had to keep up our gait. We urged on the dogs with whip and voice, the ice rolling like leather beneath the sledge-runners: it was more than a mile to the lump of solid ice. Fear gave to the poor beasts their utmost speed, and our voices were soon hushed to silence.

The suspense, unrelieved by action or effort, was intolerable: we knew that there was no remedy but to reach the floe, and that every thing depended upon our dogs, and our dogs alone. A moment's check would plunge the whole concern into the rapid tideway: no presence of mind or resource bodily or mental could avail us. The seals were looking at us with that strange curiosity which seems to be their characteristic expression: we must have passed some fifty of them, breast-high out of water, mocking us by their self-complacence.

This desperate race against fate could not last: the rolling of the tough salt-water ice terrified our dogs; and when within fifty paces from the floe they paused. The left-hand runner went through: our leader "Toodlamick" followed, and in one second the entire left of the sledge was submerged. I leaned forward to cut poor Tood's traces, and the next minute was swimming in a little circle of pastry ice and water alongside him. Hans, dear good fellow, drew near to help me, uttering piteous expressions in broken English; but I ordered him to throw himself on his belly, with his hands and legs extended, and to make for the island by cogging himself forward with his Jack-knife. In the mean time—a mere instant—I was floundering about with sledge, dogs, and lines in a confused puddle around me.

I succeeded in cutting poor Tood's lines and letting him scramble to the ice, for the poor fellow was drowning me with his piteous caresses, and made my way for the sledge; but I found that it would not buoy me, and that I had no resource but to try the circumference of the hole. Around this I paddled faithfully, the miserable ice always yielding when my hopes of a lodgement were greatest. During this process I enlarged my circle of operations to a very uncomfortable diameter, and was beginning to feel weaker after every effort. Hans meanwhile had reached the firm ice, and was on his knees, like a good Moravian, praying incoherently in English and Esquimaux; at every fresh crushing-in of the ice he would ejaculate "God!" and when I recommenced my paddling he recommenced his prayers.

I was nearly gone. My knife had been lost in cutting out the dogs; and a spare one which I carried in my trousers-pocket was so enveloped in the wet skins that I could not reach it. I owed my extrication at last to a newly-broken team-dog, who was still fast to the sledge and in struggling carried one of the runners chock against the edge of the circle. All my previous attempts to use the sledge as a bridge had failed, for it broke through, to the much greater injury of the ice. I felt that it was a last chance. I threw myself on my back, so as to lessen as much as possible my weight, and placed the nape of my neck against the rim or edge of the ice; then with caution slowly bent my leg, and, placing the ball of my moccasined foot against the sledge, I pressed steadily against the runner, listening to the half-yielding crunch of the ice beneath.

Presently I felt that my head was pillowed by the ice, and that my wet fur jumper was sliding up the surface. Next came my shoulders; they were fairly on. One more decided push, and I was launched up on the ice and safe. I reached the ice-floe, and was frictioned by Hans with frightful zeal. We saved all the dogs; but the sledge, kayack, tent, guns, snow-shoes, and every thing besides, were left behind. The thermometer at 8 degrees will keep them frozen fast in the sledge till we can come and cut them out.

On reaching the ship, after a twelve mile trot, I found so much comfort and warm welcome that I forgot my failure. The fire was lit up, and one of our few birds slaughtered forthwith. It is with real gratitude that I look back upon my escape, and bless the great presiding Goodness for the very many resources which remain to us.

That was written by Dr. Elisha Kent Kane in 1853 on his first voyage of Arctic exploration. One hundred and thirty-eight years later, I began my own first Arctic voyage. Dr. Kane's began with a search for the long-lost Franklin expedition to the North Pole, and mine began with Zafer Top's glum face.

The National Science Foundation had just bought me a new rare-gas mass spectrometer, and I had dropped in on Zafer, who is a colleague at the University of Miami's School of Marine and Atmospheric Sciences, to discuss what experiments we might do together with it. Zafer is a young Turk who got his Ph.D. in Canada and now works with us in Miami. His specialty is measuring the lightest of the rare gases, helium-3, in ocean waters. Since helium-3 is formed from the radioactive decay of tritium, most of which was produced and flung into the air during the nuclear-testing epoch of the late 1950s, the amount of helium-3 in a body of water gives an accurate estimate of the last time the water was in contact with the atmosphere. Using this technique Top can trace oceanic circulations over periods of several decades, and this might give us an idea of how much carbon dioxide is being dissolved into the oceanic upper layers and circulated down into deep storage at depth. This is one of the largest unsolved problems about the severity and onslaught of the greenhouse effect: can the oceans possibly act as a sink, removing significant amounts of CO_2 from the atmosphere and thus delaying and mollifying the warming of the earth?

When I walked into his office Zafer was sitting glumly behind his desk, staring into space. I knew that look all too well; it's become a common one in academic scientists' circles lately.

"I see you've had a proposal rejected," I guessed, feeling like Sherlock Holmes.

He was not in a mood to play games. He merely nodded.

"Not the end of the world," I said. "Will you resubmit?"

This is the normal game we play lately with the NSF. If a proposal comes back with bad reviews from our peers we normally shut it away in a drawer and try to forget it. But we're good scientists, and we don't write many bad proposals. The more usual thing these days is for a proposal to come back with good reviews and still be rejected because there isn't enough money to go around, in which case we try to modify it and resubmit.

My mass spectrometer proposal had been rejected on its first submission with fairly rough reviews. I managed to rewrite it and submit it again, and again it was rejected, even though this time all the reviews were very positive. Thinking that a proposal with good reviews ought to be funded, I had gone up to Washington to talk about it.

"When we say no these days," the NSF program director told me, "it doesn't necessarily mean that we don't like the project. Sometimes it's just that we can't afford it right away. Everyone agrees you ought to get a mass spec," he continued. "But we don't have the money to fund it. It's a quarter of a million bucks, after all, and that's not easy to come by. We don't have the money to fund more than a small percentage of the proposals that deserve funding. So getting the good reviews doesn't get you the money, it just puts you on our ladder. If you keep resubmitting, and if you keep getting good reviews, you'll gradually move up the ladder. In another year or two you ought to be in the top few percent, and then we'll be able to give you the money."

And that's what happened. But when I asked Zafer if he was going to resubmit he shook his head. "This was once in a lifetime," he said. "There's no opportunity to resubmit. I was going to go to the North Pole."

That sounded interesting, so I sat down and he told me about it. An Australian physicist, he said, had chartered a Russian nuclear-powered icebreaker to go to the North Pole on a combined scientific and luxury-cruise expedition. The NSF was going to fund twelve or thirteen scientists to go along and conduct research in the polar areas. Zafer had submitted a proposal to take water samples at various depths along the track of the ship, to be analyzed for helium-3. He had been turned down because the samples couldn't be obtained while the ship was moving; it would have to be stopped while bottles were lowered, and the cruise directors had replied that they couldn't afford to stop for the several hours necessary for each sample.

I left Zafer sitting glumly at his desk, and walked away

on air. This was the first time a gift from the gods had been dropped into my lap. Less than a year before I had read an article in the *National Geographic* by Wally Herbert, an Arctic explorer, arguing that Admiral Robert Peary, acclaimed worldwide since 1909 as the discoverer of the North Pole, hadn't actually got there. The *Geographic* had followed up with a "scientific" commission that analyzed the lengths and angles of shadows in Peary's photographs to prove that he had. I had looked at the photos and decided that they proved nothing. An astronomer from Baltimore had written that not only hadn't Peary reached the pole, he had *known* he hadn't: the man was a fake and a liar. Fascinated by what looked like the beginnings of a story, I had read the account written by Dr. Frederick Cook of *his* purported discovery of the pole. Initially feted as the discoverer, Cook had since been repudiated by everyone as a faker. Reading his book, I believed him.

Only a handful of people had been to the pole since Peary and Cook claimed it. Wally Herbert, the British author of the *Geographic* article, had duplicated Peary's feat, reaching the pole by dogsled in 1969 and continuing on across the Arctic Sea to Norway. An American, Ralph Plaisted, had gone one way by snowmobile in 1968; he was supplied by air and flown out from the pole. Will Steger led a sledge expedition there in 1985, and Naomi Uemura went all by himself in 1978. Richard Byrd, of the Virginia Byrds, claimed to have flown over the pole in 1926, and the Norwegian Roald Amundsen actually did so in a dirigible the following year. The nuclear submarines *Skate* and *Nautilus* had gone under the ice in the late 1950s, but I couldn't find any record of a surface ship ever having broken through the ice to reach it.

But now here was the *Sovetskiy Soyuz*, a Russian nuclear-powered icebreaker, making a luxury cruise there. I couldn't go as a scientist—my research has nothing to do with the polar regions—but I've always wanted to be an expert on luxury. I called the cruise line and found that the fare was $30,000 for a three-week cruise, the first ever by a surface ship to cross the Arctic Ocean from one side to the other by way of the North Pole.

The combination of price and destination was irresistible. People paying $10,000 a week, I reasoned, would be treated to the ultimate in luxury, while any trip to the pole must be fraught with adventure. My fellow passengers would be the Indiana Jones type, young and athletic, yet rich and beautiful. Before I hung up the phone I had booked my passage.

The *Sovetskiy Soyuz* was to leave from Murmansk, USSR, on July 27, 1991. About half the passengers were Americans, and we were to fly Finnair from New York to Helsinki, thence to Rovaniemi and on to Murmansk. It seemed to me that to start a trip to the North Pole by simply flying from Miami to New York would be too plebeian; to get into the spirit of adventure I decided to take Amtrak instead. It was my first mistake.

Actually, it was my second. As I was driving across town to the Miami Amtrak station I heard on the radio an audience call-in show, and realized I was going on the wrong trip. The man being interviewed ran a travel tour company called Fantasy Tours. For only $3,750 a week—cheap compared to the $10,000 per week for the *Soyuz*—he takes men to Thailand where they live out their most excessive fantasies.

Which are?

Well, it starts out with big-game hunting from elephantback in the rain forest, but quickly accelerates from there. Evenings are spent in the Kangaroo Club, which has evidently been named by a New England newspaper as one of the five most sleazy bars in the world. Women of all persuasions are available for the taking, and they really don't need to be persuaded.

"Aren't some of these girls underage?" the host asked. "How do you handle that?"

"Absolutely no problem," the tour guide told him. "Actually that's a common misapprehension. The girls are *not* underage. There's no such concept in Thailand, no such thing as an age of consent, so you have nothing to worry about."

Aside from a rather nice point of morality there, it seemed like a wonderful tour. It was just my luck that I was going to the North Pole instead.

I hadn't been on a train journey of more than a few hours for forty years. I remembered it from when my father took our whole family on the train from Philadelphia to Miami for Christmas vacation. I remembered the berth as huge and comfortable, and the journey as pure pleasure. I had a book and a grandmother along, and the time sped faster than the trees zipping by outside our windows in which I searched for lurking Indians.

Times change. I still had a book for the trip, but everything else was different. Though it was July in Miami I was lugging with me two huge suitcases filled with double-lined Arctic snow boots, an immense parka, several sweaters, foul weather gear, two fur hats, three pairs of gloves and a laptop computer. The sleeping berth I had was a single, and incredibly small. As I lurched down the aisle and caught my first glimpse of it I was overwhelmed by a sudden flash of claustrophobia. I'll never get my bags in there, I thought, and if the door were to be closed I'd suffocate within minutes.

But the suitcases fit in, one jammed in over the folded bed and the other on the closed toilet. I couldn't see how I'd get into bed or use the toilet, but for now it seemed rather cozy. And the pleasure, as the train started, of sitting in a moving vehicle without wearing a seat belt was both lyrical and comforting.

As soon as we were on our way I left my compartment and walked through the train, looking around. Although it obviously was no longer a high-class form of transport, as in the '20s and '30s when the *wagons-lits* of the Orient Express rumbled in luxury across Europe and the Pullmans ran down the coast from New York to Palm Beach and Miami, and though the coach cars were jammed full of people who didn't look as if they'd mind missing the opportunity of washing for thirty-six hours, there was still a touch of the romance of the old days.

I headed to the club car for a cup of coffee. Forty years ago I had been too young to be admitted there, and since then I had seen such films as *Strangers on a Train* and knew what I had missed, so now it was the first thing I wanted to experience. It turned out to have changed about as much as the rest of the world in the past forty years: instead of deep chairs and carpeting and baritoned Negroes bringing drinks, it consisted of linoleumed tables with cheap plastic seats, one bored counterman behind a bar serving chips, beer and coffee, and children running up and down the aisle screeching with laughter as the train lurched and threw them into the grown-ups. They didn't even have to apologize, since it wasn't their fault. Paradise.

Trainmen have a life all their own. "Hey, Alex," Claude calls. "What train that was went all the way to Boston?"

Claude and a bunch of the other porters and kitchen people are relaxing in the nearly empty club car out of Philadelphia. The only thing they talk about when they get together is their life on the trains. No one ever mentions his wife or family, or troubles or sports or politics. All they talk about are trains.

"That Champion, that was."

"Yeah, right. The Champion."

"Shoot, I know the Champion," Roy says. "That Champion never went to Boston. No way."

"You telling me? I worked the sleeper lounge on that train, all the way to Boston."

"Some *cars* went to Boston, not the whole train. They put on some cars at D.C.—"

"No way! That train went to Boston, the *whole* train."

"Uh-uh. Not 'less there were two Champions."

"Yeah, that right! There was the Champion, and then there was the West *Coast* Champion."

"Well, no West Coast train ever went to Boston. We not talking San Francisco here—"

"I don't mean *that* west coast. I meanin' Tampa. You see, the Boston people they didn't go to Miami. That was the New York folks went to Miami. The Boston people went to Tampa."

"Why anyone go to Tampa?"

"I didn't mean they go to *Tampa*. I meanin' St. Petersburg, Sarasota, you know. The Boston people goin' there, the New York people they go to Miami. So we had this West Coast Champion go all the way from Tampa to Boston, no pickin' and cuttin' in D.C. No sir. The whole *train*."

"Yeah, I told you. I worked the sleeper lounge on that Champion, all the way to Boston. The whole train, it go there."

In *The Great Railway Bazaar*, Paul Theroux laments that the Orient Express is now unique among trains for its lack of food. Even "the poorest Madrasi train," he says, gives you an eatable lunch of vegetables and rice. Before he took the Orient Express he had thought Amtrak the worst railway in the world; I must now inform him that Amtrak has recaptured the title. The dining car is so called not only euphemistically but with sadism. My meal consisted of what was called turkey and peas. The turkey had been left to soak in lukewarm water for hours. I understand the chef's reasoning: one could drop the slices of predigested turkeyish meat into boiling water for one minute to heat them up; then perhaps two minutes at 50 degrees centigrade would do the same, or four minutes at 25 degrees. To be safe, let them soak for a few hours. Unfortunately, the second law of thermodynamics takes over and leaves the turkeyish stuff lukewarm and soggy. The peas . . . Well, never mind.

After the thirty-six-hour train trip, followed by a hideous voyage through New York's subway system at rush hour lugging two huge suitcases to Kennedy airport and a nine-hour flight across the Atlantic, Helsinki was strangely pleasant. Strolling through the town I had the curious illusion that I had never left Miami: it was sunny and warm, the streets were clean, there was a touristy bayside market, and no one on the streets spoke English.

At the hotel I met the American portion of our group, and was immediately disappointed. They were not a bunch of young, handsome people desperately seeking adventure, but a distinctly older group. My roommate—the $30,000 did not include private facilities—was a very old man, Howard Tetler from Minnesota. He was very old, but he had more energy than I had. After the stroll through town I was exhausted and jet-lagged, and went up to the room to sleep. He went out on the town.

As I opened the hotel door I realized I had the only key. We had asked at the desk for two keys but were told that the hotel policy in Helsinki is only one key per room. "Why?" I asked.

"It makes it easier for us that way," the young lady explained with a friendly smile.

I propped the door open so Tetler could get in without waking me, and called the desk to cancel my wake-up call. Our plane was leaving early the next morning and the tour director had arranged a six o'clock wake-up call for everyone. Tetler and I had agreed that we could make the airport bus if we got up at six-thirty, so I set my wristwatch alarm and fell asleep.

Two hours later the phone rang. It was Tetler, calling from the lobby. "I don't have a key," he said.

"I left the door open," I said. "So you wouldn't have to wake me."

I was asleep again by the time he came up. Two hours later an alarm went off. I jumped up, startled, as his arm reached out and shut it off. It was one of those digital travel alarms, and he had set it on the table between our two beds, close by my head. "Have to take my pills," he said, sitting up and doing so.

"Every night?" I asked.

"Every two hours," he said, and was immediately asleep again. Before I could follow him, he began snoring.

I tried to stand it. I thought of the horrors that had befallen all previous explorers to the North Pole, jammed my head under the pillow and tried to smile, but finally I woke him up. He turned over on his side and stopped, and I fell back to sleep until the alarm went off again two hours later.

At six o'clock the fire alarm jangled raucously. I staggered out of bed and called the desk. "What's wrong?" I asked.

"That's just your six o'clock wake-up call," she said.

"I canceled the call!"

"Oh no, sir, I have it written down right here. Six o'clock wake-up call."

I couldn't argue. I just wanted to know how to turn it off. There was a switch behind the headboard, she said. I couldn't find it and the alarm kept ringing. She thought this funny. "We make it hard to find," she said, "because otherwise people turn it off and go back to sleep." I finally found it, turned it off and sat back down on the bed, exhausted. Tetler sat up, stretched and belched.

"Good morning," he smiled brightly, and I thought I'd never last three weeks without killing him.

THE VOYAGE

JULY 27

At 10 P.M., with the sun low on the horizon but still shining brightly, we set sail from Murmansk to the accompaniment of a Soviet navy brass band echoed from the mid-deck by a saxophone played by the one young, single woman on board.

The ship seemed to be moved by a tide or river current, for there was no sound of heavy motors and no vibration; nor did the thick oily smoke normally to be expected come pouring out of the funnel. But within moments we were heading due north at a speed far surpassing any possible tide; the silence, smoothness and good clean air come from sailing on a nuclear-powered vessel.

We headed out of the Kola River at 69° North latitude, and as the sun set at midnight we were in the Kara Sea. Over the horizon to the east was Novaya Zemlya, where polar exploration began in 1553.

It is said (without adequate foundation, it is true) that when Jane Seymour was in danger of losing her child through a breech birth, Henry VIII gave orders that she be ripped open and the child dragged safely forth. A cesarean operation performed without benefit of anesthetic would have been more a butcher's job than a surgeon's, but at any rate the young boy was born and Jane Seymour died. Nine years later the boy became Edward VI of England.

One of his ministers' first acts was to bring home Sebastian Cabot, the less accomplished son of the great sailor John Cabot, from his post as Master Navigator of Spain to the new position of Pilot Major of England and Governour of the Mysterie and Companie of the Merchants Adventurers for the Discoverie of Regions, Dominions, Seignories and Places Unknowen.

The Place Unknowen that Cabot was intended to discover was known well enough: it was China, which the maps of that time showed just to the right of the Siberian coast. It seemed to be a small matter to sail northward, pass over the top of Europe and reach the great treasures of Cathay. And the English, after all, had little choice in the matter. The Spanish ruled the Atlantic Ocean to the southwest and the Portuguese had taken it to the southeast. The only choice left was either to fight a war the British weren't yet ready for, or to head north.

Cabot was canny enough to stay at home enjoying the wealth that came with his new office, journeying only as far as the docks where he saw off Sir Hugh Willoughby, a tall, grandiose army officer with little experience of the sea and none at all of the regions to the north. In an accompanying ship was Richard Chancellor, a naval man whose entire experience of the sea lay in the Mediterranean, serving as second in command.

Sir Hugh may not have known much about the sea, but he did know about right and wrong. All crew members serving under him were warned in writing: "Item, that no blaspheming of God or detestable swearing be used in any ship, nor communication of ribaldrie, filthy tales, or ungodly talks to be suff'red in the company of any ship." Commendable as this might have been, it seems to have done little good. A storm struck off the coast of Norway, the ships were driven apart, and no one ever saw Sir Hugh Willoughby alive again.

Chancellor ended up on the Russian coast near Archangel and made his way with a few of his crew to Muscovy, where he was greeted with great friendliness by Ivan the Terrible, who was fascinated by what was possibly the world's greatest beard: the great czar "took into his hand Master George Killingsworth's beard, which reached over the table, and pleasantlie delivered it to the Metropolitane, who, seeming to blesse it, saide in Russ, 'this is God's gift'; as indeed at that time it was not only thicke, broad, and yellow colored, but in length five foote and two inches of assize."

The Russia Company was formed from this meeting, and though it prospered it did not match the profits expected from the reaching of Cathay. Hence Sebastian Cabot and the board of governors of the Merchants Adventurers for the Discoverie of Regions, Dominions, Seignories and Places Unknowen eagerly awaited word of Sir Hugh Willoughby aboard the *Bona Esperanza*.

The word did not reach them till spring of the next year, and when it came it was in the form of a sea-soaked journal rescued by Russian fishermen from the barren shores of the "New Land," Novaya Zemlya.

Willoughby had sailed on into what was later named the Barents Sea after the storm which had separated him from Chancellor. On the 14th of August, 1553, he sighted land directly across his bow. Mistaking the then-unknown coast of Novaya Zemlya for the northern coast of Russia he heaved to port and began to follow it, hoping to turn the corner into Cathay. But as he passed into higher latitudes, reaching just beyond 72° N, he ran into the usual summer Arctic weather: fog, squalls, wind and ice.

As August ran out and winter showed signs of rushing in, Willoughby decided to put in to land and wait it out until the following spring, anticipating the strategy of every polar explorer who followed him—and with the same result that befell most of them. He found little shelter and firewood, and less food, and one by one he and his men died there on the cold shore. By the time their bodies and Willoughby's diary were found the following spring, their ship had long ago been taken by the winter winds.

By midnight the *Sovetskiy Soyuz* passes the 72nd parallel, where Willoughby met his death, and we are out of sight of land. The ship is not pitching or rolling at all; the seas are calm. The sun is low on the horizon but has not yet set, though it is hidden by thick gray clouds. It is cold with no direct sunlight, and there is nothing to be seen but fog and clouds. You cannot see the sun, or even be sure where it is since its light is reflected by the clouds all around us. The night (or day) consists of an even gray light all around. It is as if the ship is suspended under an inverted translucent bowl, all alone in its own universe.

But though it is cold, there is no ice in the sea, nothing but open water. The world is obviously a much warmer place than it was in the summer of 1553, when these seas were packed with ice and stirred with wind. Nowhere do you see the difference so obviously as here in the northern waters. This is what makes these regions, and especially the polar regions above us, so important in investigating the earth's changing climate and its implications for the future. Unfortunately the *Soyuz* will not be conducting any such experiments: the Russians have refused permission to the dozen American scientists who had planned to join us.

That was one of two surprises I found when I boarded the ship this evening. The other was that my Helsinki roommate, Howard Tetler, is not to be my shipboard room-mate, thus saving his life. I will be sharing quarters with a young Englishman, John Tolson, who is shooting a docu-mentary of the voyage for the BBC. He doesn't take any pills and hasn't even brought an alarm clock with him; we'll get along just fine.

The canceling of the scientists took everyone by surprise. Mike McDowell, the Australian physicist who organized the trip, said it happened just a few days before departure. "The NSF had gone to a lot of trouble and put up a lot of money preparing their science equipment," he said. "They had all the science picked out, though right up till the end there was no actual permission from the Soviets. It was sort of a moot point because the contract was we could take anyone we wanted on board but if we had anyone doing science we had to have permission from the Soviet authorities to do it. The shipping company didn't want to get their head chopped off—"

He is interrupted by the loudspeaker in every cabin: "There are whales dead ahead, and they are blowing! Whales fifty yards off the port bow." In a moment we could hear hundreds of feet running along the passageways to the bow deck to catch their first look.

"So anyhow," Mike went on, "NSF had started the permission application procedure about seven months ago, and they were dealing with fairly high levels, but typical of the Soviet bureaucracy, it just ground on, and toward the end everyone was starting to get a bit panicky. And of course it affected us because they were paying passengers and we had to keep space for them. So we're going on and on and on, and then it was getting close and closer, so there was pressure being put on in Moscow, and the shipping company"—the Murmansk Shipping Company, which owned the *Soyuz* and was chartering it to McDowell—"was trying to help. And it got to a point where it looked as if the answer would be no to science inside the economic zone but yes to science outside the economic zone, because basically outside the economic zone we're in international waters and so the Soviets have no direct control. The only control is that it's a Soviet vessel, but you know when you charter it that it becomes your vessel.

"Anyway, that would be the case anywhere else in the world, but here it's not quite that simple. Then, surprisingly—and the NSF were dumbfounded by it all—word came through that no, they wouldn't give permission for any science at all. It went all the way up to some sort of legal committee at the Soviet Academy of Sciences, from what I understand, and I've heard various versions. One of the things that came out of discussions with the Soviets here is that they felt that some group within the bureaucracy there thought that the Americans were getting science on the cheap—that the Americans should be chartering a whole vessel and a lot more money should be coming to the Soviet Union. As I told the Russkis here, I think that's the most ludicrous bullshit. The sort of stuff that was going to be studied is basically vital science—trying to find out what's happening in the Arctic, the ice melting, climatic effects, pollution effects—all of which will have a terrific effect on the Soviet Union. So to have some committee saying we want more dollars to do this basic science is rubbish. Especially when the Soviet Union and the Americans are signing lots of bilateral accords to cooperate scientifically."

"Did they actually say this?"

"This is scuttlebutt. What they did say was that they did not think it was appropriate to do science on a tourist voyage. Of course the Americans went back and said that was rubbish because the voyage would give the scientists access to areas they couldn't otherwise get to. It would also give them a chance to do science on the ice where they ordinarily couldn't afford it. This was an ideal opportunity to do science within a budget the NSF could afford; you get good value for your science and to call this 'not appropriate' is bullshit. The NSF guy was really pissed off. They had put a lot of money and effort into it, and they felt it was

a great opportunity lost just because of stultifying nonsense. The Soviet scientists were supportive, but some jerk
sitting on a committee in Moscow decided we couldn't do
it."

So the combined science-tourist cruise would be a purely
tourist cruise instead. As events turned out later that summer and fall of 1991, this was probably the last decision
ever made by a Soviet scientific bureaucracy, a fitting end
to a failed sociological experiment.

Mike and I went outside to take a look at the whales, but
they had disappeared. Heading back inside, the other passengers said they had seen a flash or two of tails but nothing else. I stayed out on deck, watching the waters flow by
as we passed Novaya Zemlya, heading due north for the
pole.

It was Frederick Cook, the much-disputed and disbelieved
explorer, who first claimed to have discovered the North
Pole. The controversy over his claim still rages today, but
no one disputes that it was Cook who discovered the polar
luxury tourist cruise—though, like almost everything else
in his charmed and cursed life, he didn't make a success of
it.

Cook graduated from medical school in 1891 and opened
a practice in Brooklyn, but he was never cut out for the
sedentary life. He saw a newspaper advertisement for a
surgeon/scientist to accompany an expedition to find if
there was a northern coast to Greenland, and he signed on.
Afterward he returned to Brooklyn, but the bug was in his
blood. However, he wanted to go back not as a hired hand
but as an expedition leader, and this meant first and foremost raising the money.

So Cook booked passage back to Greenland and picked
up a bunch of Eskimo articles—a kayak and a harpoon,
snowshoes, clothing made of sealskin and polar bear fur,
fishhooks and knives—and a couple of real live Eskimos, a

husband and wife named Mikok and Kalahkatah, and took the whole shebang on a coast-to-coast "lecture" tour. He was more a snake-oil pitchman than a scientific lecturer, but he was good. He was a handsome man—when the television producers put together a movie of his life they cast Richard Chamberlain, and they weren't far wrong—and a charmer, and he played the part of the gentleman explorer to perfection. (The Arctic explorer Peter Freuchen would later say: "Cook is a gentleman and a liar. Peary is neither.")

Cook raised some but not all the money necessary for his proposed expedition, and when the crowds began to thin out he thought of the idea of a tourist cruise to the far north. He chartered a British steamer, the *Miranda*, and advertised a cruise in the summer of 1894, the world's first tourist cruise to Arctic sites. They would voyage far enough north to see the pack ice and would stop at places where noted explorers of the past had made their winter homes while waiting for the snows to melt and the ice to break up. He touted the voyage as fit for tourists, sportsmen—there would be hunting aplenty—scientists or artists.

All the categories but the last were represented, each passenger paying $500, when the *Miranda* sailed out of New York that July. As with the *Sovetskiy Soyuz* a hundred years later, there were problems with the ship. The *Soyuz* would be denied permission to berth in Nome because the American authorities were frightened of nuclear power, and the *Miranda* and its captain had a tendency to hit objects. She had recently had not one but two separate collisions, the last one ending with her actually sinking. But she had been brought back up and dried out; now she went out again—and collided almost immediately with a small ship.

She bounced off unharmed and set her nose for the far north. There were differences and similarities between her voyage and that of the *Soyuz* almost immediately. We would be awakened at all hours of the night whenever a whale, seal or polar bear came into view. "Attention all passengers!" the Klaxon would ring out, shattering sleep. "Attention! Polar bear 500 yards to port!" Or, "Whales sounding to starboard! Whales to starboard . . ." We would stagger out of bed and either peer out our portholes if we were on the right side, or pull on our clothes and rush out on deck with binoculars, cameras and camcorders to see the creatures. It did not matter what time of the night it was, for the sun never set; we would stare at the foreign beasts, take our pictures, marvel at their size and grace and then go back to sleep.

The passengers on the *Miranda* had much the same experience, except that they didn't have camcorders and they did have guns. The thought of shooting these creatures would have horrified us; it never occurred to the Miranderers to do anything but. The world then was still a place where all things existed for our pleasure.

There were other similarities and differences. The crewmen of the *Miranda* mutinied, broke into the liquor hamper and rampaged through the ship until they were finally brought under control. Our Russian crewmen were less savage but just as happy to take whatever liquor became available. On the second night out when I asked at the bar for a St. Pauli dark—all our beer on board was German—I was told that all we had left was Beck's.

"How can we be out of anything so soon?" I asked.

"I goofed," the bartender admitted. "We don't have much refrigerator space, so I stacked all the St. Pauli's out on deck to keep it cold. When I went to get a can fifteen minutes later it was all gone. Sixty cases."

"In fifteen minutes?"

He shrugged. "I guess they don't get much German beer. Have a Beck's on the house."

The main difference between the two ships was that the *Miranda* didn't have radar. Running through a thick fog in the Strait of Belle Isle she ran right into an iceberg. It wasn't as bad an accident as the one which would take down the *Titanic* some twenty years later, but they had to put in for repairs. A bunch of the passengers had begun to get the drift by then, and they suggested an easier cruise. How about just going around the north coast of England and then back home again? Cook put it to a vote, and the result was a determination to continue to the far north.

They set off once again, and soon hit a reef. The *Miranda* didn't sink, but she was hard aground. Dr. Cook told them to hang tight, and went off in the ship's boat for help; this was in the days before not only radar but also radio. He sailed a hundred miles along the treacherous coast of Greenland before he found a fishing ship and hailed it. When he came aboard he explained the situation, but the captain said it would ruin his short fishing season if he upped anchor and headed for the *Miranda*. "Are they sinking?" he asked, for if they were he would have had to go, according to the code of the sea. "Not exactly," was the reply. "Not yet, anyway. At least, not when I left them."

"Well, all right, then, they're okay. We'll get on with our fishing."

But a bargain was struck, and for $4,000 cash the *Rigel* hauled in her nets and headed north. The fishing captain found the *Miranda* floundering helplessly, and took the passengers and crew on board. They attached a tow line to the *Miranda* and headed for home. Two days later the *Miranda* sank.

The *Rigel* took the passengers to Nova Scotia where they were picked up by a sister ship of the *Miranda*, the *Portia*. She turned her bow for New York, and in another fog collided with a smaller ship, the *Dora French*. The *French* sank and her crew drowned in the fog. But the journey had been adventurous. The *Miranda* passengers got together and, instead of suing Cook for a disastrously managed voyage, founded the Arctic Club to celebrate their adventure.

The club grew into the prototype of such organizations as today's Explorers Club, the Circumnavigators Club, the Peary Arctic Club and indeed the National Geographic Society—organizations of rich people, more tourists than explorers, but still passionately involved in the idea of exploration, ready to lend their prestige and, more importantly, their money to those who would unveil the mysteries of the north. With the birth of this first club, the virginity of the North Pole was doomed.

But not quite yet.

JULY 28

‑‑‑‑‑‑‑‑ ·ı|||||ı· ‑‑‑‑‑‑‑‑

By midmorning we are passing latitude 75° N, and I am leaning over the rail searching for mermaids. I'm not entirely without hope, for though the mythology of mermaids places them usually in the warm waters of the South Pacific where their exposed breasts would not be overly chilled, the facts about mermaids place them firmly in northern waters. In absolute fact, the one authorized and witnessed sighting that I know about took place right here at latitude 75° N, and was recorded by no less a person than Henry Hudson, the Navigator. In 1608 he had embarked on his second voyage of northern exploration, setting sail from Saint Catherines Point, England, on April 22. By June 15 he was at 75°07', heading northeast:

"The 15th, all day and night cleere sunshine; the wind at east. . . . This morning, one of our companie looking over boord saw a mermaid, and calling up some of the companie to see her, one more came up, and by that time shee was come close to the ship's side, looking earnestly on the men: a little after, a sea came and overturned her: from the navill upward, her backe and breasts were like a woman's, as they say that saw her; her body as big as one of us; her skin very white; and long haire hanging downe behinde, of colour blacke: in her going downe they saw her tayle, which was like the tayle of a porposse, and speckled like a macrell. Their names that saw her, were Thomas Hilles and Robert Rayner."

The editor of the 1860 edition of Hudson's journal inserted a footnote that the sighting was probably that of a seal. "There is something in the appearance and the movements of this animal strongly akin to those of human beings."

Well, yes, I have known some human beings that look and sound a lot like seals, but I can still tell the difference. Despite the editor, I hang over the ship's rail for hours, searching the empty seas for a glimpse of a vision.

> Great God! I'd rather be
> A Pagan suckled in a creed outworn;
> So might I, standing on this pleasant ship,
> Have glimpses that would make me less forlorn;
> Have sight of Proteus rising from the sea
> Or hear old Triton blow his wreathed horn. . . .

Breakfast is served buffet-style, with people coming and going throughout the allotted two hours, so it is only when we all sit down to lunch that I get my first sight of the assembled guests. My first impression at the Helsinki hotel is now reinforced: we are a group of middle-aged to elderly tourists, and although we come from more than a dozen nations we are all much of a kind. Though elderly, the women on board are on average ten years younger than their husbands and almost uniformly pretty in a Katharine Hepburn sort of way: good bones and slim bodies well taken care of. One can tell they must have been something when they were young. Which no doubt is why they ended up marrying older men who can afford $60,000 for a three-week cruise for two. Obviously they still take care of themselves. Most of them, I later discover, are the second wives of their husbands, who have lost or misplaced their first wives. Hemingway was nearly right: the rich are different from us; they have prettier wives. (Except me. When I was a young assistant professor at Cornell I was approached at a faculty party by Peter Hilton, a brilliant mathematics professor married to the actress Meg Hilton. He introduced himself and said, "I understand we have something in common. We're the only ones in Ithaca with beautiful wives.")

I wonder if the next generation, taking tourist trips to the moon, will include old women who have divorced the husbands who put them through law and medical school and carry with them younger, handsome second husbands.

The seating is open, and I take a table with the Nishtars, Motilal and Kamala, both of them physicians born in India but educated in England and now living in Manchester. He is a short, roly-poly man with small, likable features and almost no hair; what remains is close-cropped and slicked down on his head. He talks loudly and incessantly, with a childish charm, as if always asking, aren't I cute? Don't you like me? But there's not a mean bone in his body, and I *do* like him. Kamala is a large maternal woman, quite attractive, who wears saris and almost never speaks. From the way she listens attentively to everything he says, without quite looking at him and always with a small, proud smile, I would bet that they have no children. Like most of the passengers on this cruise, Motilal is an inveterate traveler to exotic climes; his wife is not so enthusiastic but she comes along to keep him company. Since he first went to the festival in Rio five years ago he has never missed one, he proudly claims, and never intends to. He has also been to Antarctica, Borneo and the Amazon, and next year intends to visit New Jersey. He's a lot of fun, and I tell him if he ever comes to Miami to look me up.

"Oh, no," he replies seriously. "I would never go to Miami. It is much too dangerous."

I try to argue with him, but my heart's not in it. He tells me that he never gets sick, no matter where he goes. His recipe for health is simple: "Never eat breakfast, and have a small glass of Scotch whiskey before lunch and dinner. It doesn't *have* to be small," he adds in his perfect Peter Sellers accent, "but you must drink it every day without fail before lunch and dinner. And of course you must never, never drink any water. That is the problem with you Americans, you know. You put ice in the whiskey, and when it melts . . ." He shrugs. "Water, you see." He leans back in his chair, puffs at his cigarette and takes a long swallow of beer.

For the rest of the voyage I never see him drink anything but beer. Like physicians everywhere, he doesn't follow his own advice.

After a mediocre lunch of consommé, poached snapper and trifle we troop down to the first deck below water level and find seats in the auditorium for a slide lecture by Dennis Puleston on birds of the Arctic. Dennis is the dullest lecturer who has led the most exciting life of anyone I have ever met. At the age of eighteen he left home to sail around the world with a friend. In China, the friend caught typhoid; this was in 1937, when the Japanese were invading. Somehow Dennis got his friend on a boat home, but didn't have money for the trip himself. He is British, but the consul in Peking would have nothing to do with him; he wasn't the right sort, after all. He was a scraggly, bearded kid without a job at home or references from anyone, and they kicked him out into the streets, which were being looted and razed by the Japanese army; this was the time of the Rape of Nanking.

But the previous spring, while sailing through the Borneo archipelago, Dennis and his friend had captured a rare

species of parrot. By chance they had then encountered a
Japanese scientist, and over a few beers they discussed
their achievement. The Japanese scientist told them that he
worked for the emperor of Japan, who was an enthusiastic
biologist, and that he was sure the emperor would be most
grateful if Dennis and his friend would consider donating
him their catch.

So they did, and a month later they received in return a
personal letter of thanks from Hirohito. Now, trapped in
Peking, Dennis encountered a Japanese army officer in one
of the few hotel bars not yet ransacked. The officer was
eager to practice his English—presumably in preparation
for accepting the surrender of Singapore—and they got
into conversation, which led from one thing to another
and finally to the parrot. When the officer expressed polite
disbelief, Dennis pulled out his letter from the emperor.

The army officer read it, looked up at Dennis, read it
again, then jumped up from his chair, bowed low and informed Dennis that he would be honored to do anything in
his power for a personal friend of the emperor. The next
day Dennis found himself on a train heading north toward
Vladivostok, with a letter of reference from the Japanese
army and a paid ticket in his pocket all the way on the
Trans-Siberian Express to Moscow. I never did find out
how he got home from Moscow.

Dennis has many such incredible stories to tell around
the bar. His lecture on Arctic birds, on the other hand, is
stultifyingly boring. Within ten minutes I am asleep.

Afterward, trying to wake up, I walk around the deck.
The sun is still nowhere to be seen and the ship is moving
through a thick fog. Another stroller comes my way, a
short, wiry man with a full gray beard, whom I recognize
as the man two rows in front of me at Puleston's lecture
who actually fell asleep before I did. I introduce myself,
and he turns out to be Wally Herbert, probably the first
man to reach the North Pole and return on his own. In 1968

he set out from Pt. Barrow, Alaska, with a team of three companions, together with dogs and sleds, and led them across the very top of the world to the North Pole and on to Spitsbergen thirteen months later. If neither Cook nor Peary got there—which is still a matter of dispute that will be discussed later—and if you don't count Ralph Plaisted, who got there by snowmobile and was flown home, then Herbert is the first man to reach the pole. For a variety of reasons he never received much credit for this feat and is understandably bitter, though he maintains a philosophic calm and sense of humor about it.

Herbert is also something of a mystic, obsessed with coincidences between his life and Peary's (more of which later). Today, referring to himself and other Arctic explorers such as Peary, he says, "If you accept the concept of the soul, then perhaps we all share the same soul and are each a little part of it."

Well, maybe. After he leaves I stay out on the deck, leaning over the rail. We are passing 76° N, and I wonder what those of us on this voyage share with Sir John Franklin, who disappeared here in 1847 and became the *cause célèbre* of nineteenth-century Arctic exploration.

That century's most suspenseful series of events began without notice some years earlier when Jane Griffin, a London beauty and the daughter of a wealthy merchant, turned down an offer for her hand by one of her many suitors. She regretted spurning the man almost immediately, but it was too late; he turned around and proposed to someone else, who had the good sense to accept him.

Thinking herself now a sadder but wiser woman, Jane determined upon a life of the intellect. She studied and read voraciously on a host of subjects, traveled incessantly, argued vociferously and finally at the age of thirty-six met and married the eminent but superannuated Arctic explorer Sir John Franklin.

Franklin had already sailed twice across the Atlantic to the northern stretches of America in search of the Northwest Passage. Recently widowed, he was now entering his sixth decade and a virtual forced retirement from active service in the Royal Navy. After two years of nothing at all, the Admiralty offered him a year's command of a frigate in the Mediterranean. This was followed by another year without work. Then they found something for him: the governorship of Antigua. Jane Franklin was insulted at the offer; it was beneath their dignity, and he refused it. Some months later another letter from the Admiralty arrived with a marginally better offer. He was invited to become governor of Van Diemen's Land, a penal colony south of Australia. Now called Tasmania, the land was at least an island of a reasonable size, Franklin would head a group larger than he had ever commanded aboard ship, and though the subjects were all criminals, at least they were white. He and his new wife considered the offer during the course of many long conversations; finally Lady Jane nodded her head and Sir John accepted the post.

It turned out to be a disaster. For six years Franklin tried to administer the island according to his principles, and found that the well-entrenched civil service system there was accustomed to running things its own way. Though he had the authority, he lacked the practical knowledge of how things worked locally that was necessary to enforce it, and the Machiavellian intrigues of the place did him in. His wife was no help; she attracted enemies like a magnet attracts iron filings and was not the locals' idea of a gracious lady. In fact she reminds one a good deal of Eleanor Roosevelt: she barged in where she wasn't wanted, acted as if she were entitled to be listened to as a man might be listened to, behaved as if she were not only her husband's equal but the equal of any man on that godforsaken island. Everyone agreed that she was really insufferable.

In the end Franklin was retired from the post amid a series of complaints, and admitted defeat as he returned to England. Such a political post was simply not within his capabilities; he was a naval officer and belonged aboard ship. But where was he to find one?

Finally, in 1843, a slight chink opened in the Admiralty's stubborn refusal to employ him where he belonged. Another expedition was being planned to seek the Northwest Passage, and when a list of possible leaders was drawn up Franklin's name was there—at the bottom, to be sure, but still there. Then one by one the names above him were crossed off, either by the persons themselves or by the enemies it was impossible to avoid accumulating in those days of salon intrigues and political appointments.

The Admiralty understood Franklin's failure in Van Diemen's Land; it was the failure of a simple sailor confronted with the baneful intricacies of life on land, and as such was no disgrace. Indeed, it probably counted in his favor. What argued against his appointment was his age. Lord Haddington, First Lord of the Admiralty, spoke bluntly. "It's unfortunate," he said. "A while back you would certainly have been our choice. But I understand you are sixty years old, and an Arctic voyage is a physically arduous experience—"

"No, no, My Lord," Franklin interrupted. "You have been misinformed as to my age, and an Arctic voyage is not so physically exhausting as all that, you know. It's not like an overland sledging haul, not at all. It needs experience, a calm mind, the authority of command . . ." He went on and on, and when he departed Lord Haddington had been convinced. The subject of his age was not brought up again, and he stepped down the steps of Admiralty House jauntily. Sixty years old, indeed, he snorted! In actual fact, he was only fifty-nine and a bit . . .

In 1845 Franklin left England behind, in command of a two-ship flotilla, the *Erebus* and the *Terror*, 128 men, one dog and one pet monkey. Word came back to England later that summer from a whaler that the two ships had been seen in Greenland, moored to an iceberg in Disko Bay, awaiting the proper winds to send them northward.

Then silence. Silence for the rest of that year, and for the next, and for the year after that. Silence forever. Neither the *Erebus* nor the *Terror* nor Sir John Franklin nor any of his crew ever came home.

The following year Lady Jane pressed for a rescue operation, but the Admiralty tut-tutted her into silence. The two ships carried provisions for three years, she was told. Not to worry.

By the next year, 1847, the Admiralty began to get a bit uneasy, and sent a couple of ships to look for Franklin. These got caught in the ice, and when they returned the following summer they reported not a trace of him. Two more expeditions were sent out in 1848, and when these also returned without a sighting the mystery began to spread beyond Admiralty House to the imaginations and hearts of the people. In 1850 ten different expeditions were sent to look for Franklin, and when Lady Franklin sailed to the United States to plead her cause the Yankees sent out one of their own.

Initially the American response had been lukewarm. President Zachary Taylor responded to Lady Franklin's pleas with assurances that all America would pray for her husband, and when she was not satisfied with this he dismissed her as an insufferable bore. But she spoke publicly, loudly and passionately, and convinced a New York shipping magnate to buy two ships for $30,000 and turn them over to the government for use in searching for Franklin. The government agreed to provide the personnel, but it all came to naught. None of the expeditions sighted any trace of the lost crews.

Within the next half dozen years another three dozen expeditions set out to find Franklin, or whomever of his men might yet remain alive, or, finally, what traces might be left. Lady Jane herself raised the money to finance four of these ships. It turned into the greatest search ever mounted, before or since, and it resulted in a victory of sorts.

No one ever did find Franklin or any of his men alive. But in the process they found out more about the unexplored Arctic regions than all previous expeditions had— indeed, more than Franklin himself could have found had his expedition been successful. And finally they did find out what had happened.

The first clue came entirely by accident in 1854, just four months after the Admiralty officially gave up all hope and pronounced the men dead. It came from an expedition which was not searching for Franklin at all. Dr. John Rae, a civilian employee of the Hudson's Bay Company, was commissioned to explore the Boothia Peninsula, a spit of land stretching far north of Canada between Baffin and Victoria islands. Trekking across the ice, he happened to come across a lone Eskimo. Rae asked him about the Franklin expedition: had he ever seen white men before?

"The man was very communicative and . . . said that a party of 'Kabloonans' (whites) had died of starvation a long distance to the west of where we were then, and beyond a large river. He stated that he did not know the exact place, that he had never been there, and that he could not accompany us that far."

Rae questioned the man further and was taken by him to meet other Eskimos who had more information. "In the spring four winters past," he was told, "forty white men were seen travelling in company southward over the ice, dragging a boat and sledges with them."

None of the Englishmen could speak the Eskimo language very well, Rae later reported, but "by signs the natives were led to believe their ship had been crushed by the ice, and they were going to where they expected to find some deer to shoot." The Eskimos had given the men directions toward the nearest village and some meat, but had been unable to feed so many starving men and had abandoned them to their fate.

This seemed callous at first, but on a moment's reflection is reasonable. The Arctic is a dismal, unforgiving place in which to live. The inhabitants help each other as best they can, but not to the extent of endangering their own lives. A hunting party of Eskimos, finding a lone man, will care for him, feed him, nurse him back to health, and take him home with them. But they couldn't possibly do that for more than a hundred men. They barely carve out an existence for themselves and, according to their code, they abandon on the ice those of their tribe too sick or too old to care for themselves. They did the best they could for the white strangers, and then they left.

"At a later date the same season," Rae continued, "the corpses of some thirty persons and some graves were discovered on the continent, and five bodies on an island near it, about a long day's journey to the . . . Great Fish River. . . . Some of the bodies were in a tent or tents, others were under the boats which had been turned over to make a shelter, and some lay scattered about in different directions. . . . There appears to have been an abundant store of ammunition . . . a number of telescopes, guns, watches, compasses, etc., all of which seem to have been broken up, as I saw pieces of these different articles with the natives, and I purchased as many as possible, together with some silver spoons and forks, an Order of Merit in the form of a star, and a small plate engraved 'Sir John Franklin, K.C.B.' "

Gruesome news. But it was to be even worse. "Subsequently," Rae reported, "further particulars were received, and a number of articles purchased, which place the fate of . . . Sir John Franklin's long-lost party beyond a doubt—a fate terrible as the imagination can conceive. . . . From the mutilated state of many of the corpses and the contents of the kettles, it is evident that our wretched countrymen had been driven to the last resource—cannibalism—as a means of prolonging existence."

The Admiralty was not pleased to hear this last comment, and so simply pretended that it hadn't. On the other hand, it was quite glad to hear that its decision to declare the members of the Franklin Expedition dead had been justified. They ruled the matter closed. Lady Franklin was not so sanguine. She was willing to accept her husband's death, but not his total annihilation. She asked that a "careful search be made for any possible survivor, that the bones of the dead be sought for . . . that their buried records be unearthed . . . and their last written words . . . be saved from destruction. . . . This final and exhausting search is all I seek."

The Admiralty refused. "The matter, Madame, is closed."

By now Lady Jane had spent her entire considerable fortune outfitting rescue expeditions. Still she didn't give up; she devoted herself to raising money from the public for one final expedition—not to rescue any survivors, for she accepted that there were none, but to find a record, a body, some tangible icon that she could enshrine or bury.

She raised enough money to buy a steam yacht, the *Fox*, which was manned entirely by volunteers. The captain was Leopold M'Clintock, who had served on previous rescue expeditions and during these had mastered the art of ice sledging. He left in 1857 and was soon caught in the ice, held captive all winter, nearly smashed to bits but finally set free in the summer of 1858. He sailed as far north as he could, and then again settled in for the winter.

The following spring, sledging across the ice of the Boothia Peninsula, M'Clintock came across the final pieces of the puzzle. He met some Eskimos who told him that they had met a group of sick and starving white men in 1848, survivors of a wrecked ship, who were dragging their small boats and scanty provisions toward the south. M'Clintock continued along the direction they pointed him. One of the Eskimo women told him that the survivors had been in terrible condition, falling down and dying as they walked. M'Clintock soon found evidence of this death march: a boat containing two skeletons and a store of chocolate and tea—good stuff for a party, but not high enough in vitamins or protein to keep the men alive. Searching further, he found a bleached human skeleton prone on its face, as though indeed the man had simply fallen as he walked.

Finally, late in May of 1859, the M'Clintock party reached a promontory named Point Victory, and there discovered a cairn. Cairns were mail drop-offs used by every expedition in those times: as one progressed, one would leave notes behind to tell others who might follow where one had gone and where one was heading. The cairns usually consisted of a pile of rocks, erected pyramid-style on a high point near the sea, tall enough to be seen by a passing ship and surrounding a cavity within which the message would be left.

The note at Point Victory consisted of three parts. The first was the standard printed notice, in the six languages of the nations most devoted to exploration: "Whoever finds this paper is requested to forward it to the Secretary of the Admiralty, London, with a note of the time and place at which it was found; or, if more convenient, to deliver it for that purpose to the British Consulate at the nearest Port.''

The second part was a handwritten note:

28 of May, 1847   H.M. ships *Erebus* and *Terror* wintered in the ice in lat. 70°05' N; long. 98°23' W

Having wintered in 1846–7 at Beechey Island, in lat. 74°43'28" N. long., 91°39'15" W., after having ascended Wellington Channel to lat. 77°, and returned by the west side of Cornwallis Island. Sir John Franklin commanding the expedition. All well. Party consisting of 2 officers and 6 men left the ships on Monday 24th May, 1847.

Gm. Gore, Lieut.
Chas. F. Des Voeux, Mate

This part of the note was reasonable enough, but the third part testified to the fact that despite the definite statement, all was *not* well. It was a scribbled note around the borders of the original, and read:

April 25, 1848. H.M. Ships 'Terror' and 'Erebus' were deserted on the 22nd April, 5 leagues NNW of this, having been beset since 12 Sept. 1846. The officers and crews consisting of 105 souls under the command of Captain F.R.M. Crozier, landed here in Lat. 69°37'42" N. and Long. 98°41' W. This paper was found by Lieut. Irving under the cairn supposed to have been built by Sir James Ross in 1831 4 miles to the northward where it had been deposited by the late Commander Gore in June, 1847. Sir James Ross's pillar has not however been found, and the paper has been transferred to this position, which is that in which Sir J. Ross's pillar was erected—Sir John Franklin died on the 11th June 1847, and the total loss by

deaths in the Expedition has been to this date 9 officers
and 15 men.

James Fitzjames, Captain, HMS *Erebus*

F.R.M. Crozier, Captain and Senior Officer and start on
tomorrow 26th for Back's Fish River.

This was the last word left by the men of the Franklin
expedition. It was a dismal picture, but one not unexpected. Starvation was the omnipresent specter of Arctic
exploration, and was no stranger to Franklin. Writing on
his return from an earlier expedition, he had told of his
men growing weaker and weaker as their food gave out,
until, on the verge of starvation, they happened on a herd
of musk-oxen. Their lives lay pinned on the hope of killing
one. "The best hunters were sent out; they approached the
animals with the utmost caution, no less than two hours
being consumed before they got within gunshot. In the
meantime we beheld their proceedings with extreme anxiety, and many secret prayers were, doubtless, offered up
for their success. At length they opened their fire, and we
had the satisfaction of seeing one of the largest cows fall
. . . To skin and cut up the animal was the work of a few
minutes. The contents of its stomach were devoured upon
the spot, and the raw intestines, which were next attacked,
were pronounced by the most delicate amongst us to be
excellent."

This time they were not so lucky; they found no herd of
musk-oxen. One pictures them struggling south, straggling
one behind the other, dragging their boats in the hope of
open water which never appeared, eating the last of their
provisions, dropping one by one as weariness, hunger and
cold overcame them, leaving their skeletons to be found,
years too late.

JULY 29

I woke up during the night to the sound and feel of heavy thuds, as if we were banging against something. When I opened my eyes I was confused; the sky outside the porthole was a light gray, and I thought I must have slept through the night, but the clock on the wall said it was three o'clock. Then I realized it was 3:00 A.M.; we were passing the 80th parallel, and the night had lasted only a few hours. I lay in bed feeling and hearing the thumps. Looking out the porthole I saw occasional chunks of ice, then went back to sleep.

After breakfast I walked around the deck. The ship was surrounded by fog and clouds, with perhaps a mile visibility. The sky was totally gray, giving no hint of where the sun might be.

At ten o'clock we were treated to a lecture on the geology of Franz Josef Land. I slept through it, and as soon as it was over (I have never seen an audience leave so quickly as when the speaker said "In conclusion . . .") I went right back to the room and continued my sleep. Something about the cold and the motion of the boat combined to bring on an incredible lethargy.

At lunch we heard the first jokes about being on a nuclear ship: we'll be able to save on our electric bills when we get home since we'll all be glowing in the dark; and we'd better have no more grandchildren—a joke bearing not only on the effects of radiation but on the fact that the mean age of the passengers was about seventy. While we were telling each other these hilarious jokes, an announcement came over the speakers: land had been sighted dead ahead.

Franz Josef Land. We all stream outside and line the deck; there in the distance is a low black hump, its top lost in a bank of clouds. Amazingly, it is surrounded by water with only occasional chunks of ice. In the summer of 1872 the first men to sight this island walked across a frozen sea to it, blessing God for it and for their lives.

A hundred and twenty years ago a German geographer named Petermann suggested that an open sea route to the North Pole might be found by following the last vestiges of the Gulf Stream, which seemed to disappear in a northward direction after passing the North Cape. In the summer of 1872 two Austrian military men, naval lieutenant Karl Weyprecht and army lieutenant Julius von Payer, set off to test this theory, sailing in the *Tegetthoff* with a German, Italian, and Hungarian crew of two dozen sailors and mountaineers. As they passed the northern coast of Novaya Zemlya—far to the south of where we were last night—they began to encounter not the occasional floes we bumped into, but serious packs of ice. As they left the coast of Zemlya behind they had to begin picking a careful route along narrow channels of water between ice floes, and a few hours later they came to a crunching stop. "No water was to be seen around us," von Payer later wrote, "and never again were we destined to see our vessel in water. From day to day we hoped for the hour of our deliverance. At first we expected it hourly, then daily, then from week to week; then at the seasons of the year and changes of the weather, then in the changes of the new year. But that hour never came . . ."

They were stuck in the ice, and stuck they remained, drifting northward until the coast of Novaya Zemlya faded behind them into the fog and mists, and they were alone in the midst of nothing but ice and snow. Day after day they sat in their cabins or bundled up and walked for a few moments on deck, waiting for something to happen. Something, anything . . .

Then one day, "as we sat at our breakfast, our floe burst across immediately under our ship. Rushing on deck we discovered that we were surrounded and squeezed by the ice; the after part of the ship was already nipped and pressed, and the rudder, which was the first to encounter its assault, shook and groaned. . . . We next sprang on the ice. . . . But just as in the risings of a people, the wave of revolt spreads on every side, so now the ice rose up against us. . . . Noise and confusion reigned supreme, and step by step destruction drew nigh in the crushing together of the fields of ice. Our floe was now crushed, and its blocks, piled up into mountains, drove hither and thither. Here, they towered fathoms high above the ship and forced the protesting timbers of the massive oak, as if in mockery of their purpose, against the hull of the vessel; there masses of ice fell down as into an abyss under the ship, to be engulfed in the rushing waters, so that the quantity of ice beneath the ship was constantly increased, and at last began to raise her quite above the level of the sea. . . . The pressure reached a frightful height . . . the *Tegetthoff* heeled over on her side, and huge piles of ice threatened to precipitate themselves on her."

Quickly the crew gathered what articles of survival were closest to hand and prepared to abandon ship—but where could they jump to? They would freeze in minutes in the icy waters, and the crashing floes of ice provided no firmer refuge: "Not a fragment of the ice remained whole. A

sledge would have been swallowed up, and in this circum-
stance lay the horror of our situation. For if the ship should
sink, whither should we go amid this confusion, how reach
the land?''

But the ship didn't sink. The storming ice surges less-
ened, and the ship, still firmly trapped, continued its slow
drift while the crew worked to free her. "All spring, all
summer we dug and sawed to get the *Tegetthoff* free, but to
no avail. We bored through the ice to see how deeply we
were caught, but after going to a depth of 27 feet we still
struck ice.''

The second summer came and went, and the ice hadn't
melted or loosened, but still held them fast. As winter approached again they gave up hope. How long could they
last like this? They didn't have supplies enough to feed
themselves until the next summer, and even if they should
last until then, that season no longer held any hope. Nothing could save them, they realized now, except a miracle.
So they stopped their exertions and simply waited,
wrapped as warmly as they could manage, for the end.

Instead, they got the miracle. One day, which began no
differently from any other day of their imprisonment, "as
we were leaning on the bulwarks of the ship and scanning
the gliding mists through which the rays of the sun broke
ever and anon, a wall of the mist, lifting itself up suddenly,
revealed to us afar off in the north-west the outlines of bold
rocks, which in a few moments seemed to grow into a
radiant Alpine land! At first we all stood transfixed, and
hardly believing what we saw. Then, carried away by the
reality of our good fortune, we burst into shouts of joy:
'Land, Land, Land at last!' ''

It was the 28th of October, 1873, and they had drifted
northward to the southern tip of the archipelago they
would name Franz Josef Land. "There before us lay the
prize that could not be snatched from us. Yet not by our
action, but through the happy caprice of the floe, and as in

a dream we had won it. . . . We beheld from a ridge of ice the mountains and glaciers of the mysterious land. Its valleys seemed to our fond imagination clothed with green pastures over which herds of reindeer roamed in undisturbed enjoyment of their liberty, and far from all foes. For thousands of years this land had lain buried from the knowledge of man, and now its discovery had fallen into the lap of a small band, themselves almost lost to the world."

It looked to them like the promised land, and like Moses they were allowed by God to see it but not to reach it. The shifting pack ice twisted and began to drift south again, pulling them away from the "green pastures" and back out into the frozen inferno of the polar sea. The land disappeared, and once again all was fog. Then, indiscernibly, the ice changed course once again; on the following day the land appeared once more and grew larger every hour until with a shuddering crash their ice floe rammed right into it and they clambered down from the trapped ship and climbed ashore.

But the "green pastures" had been a vision born of hope and desperation, not of reality. "Snow and rock and broken ice surrounded us on every side. A land more desolate could not have been found on earth than the island we walked on. But all this we saw not. To us it was a paradise. . . . The vegetation was indescribably meager and miserable, consisting of a few lichens. The drift-wood we expected to find was nowhere to be seen. We looked for traces of the reindeer and fox, but our search was utterly fruitless. The land appeared to be without a single living creature."

They spent the winter there, their second winter since leaving home. Temperatures dropped to 59 degrees below zero. Their eyelids froze shut and had to be carefully warmed in order to open their eyes; panic and haste meant eyelids torn loose from their faces. They discovered that intense cold somehow generated an overwhelming thirst, and despite the presence of snow and ice everywhere there was a great scarcity of water, for the snow and ice were of such a low temperature that it couldn't be put into their mouths; to do so felt "like hot iron in the mouth, and does not quench but increases the thirst. Snow-eaters were regarded in much the same way as opium-eaters are."

When spring came once again von Payer took a party of ten men and three dogs, and left the *Tegetthoff*—not heading south in hope of rescue, but north to complete his mission of finding a route to the pole. They left in early spring while the blizzards still raged, for the plan was to explore as much as they could and still return to the ship in time to make one last effort to free her and sail south before the summer ended.

They encountered violent blizzards, mountains of rough ice, unbelievable cold. The men could go no further, so von Payer struck camp, then went on himself with one sledge and a driver. As they crossed the Middendorf glacier the ice collapsed beneath them, splitting open into a dark hole into which the sled fell. The dogs and driver tumbled down into the black abyss. Von Payer was jerked backward toward it, when suddenly the fall stopped. He was caught on the brink of the shattered ice, staring down into what at first appeared to be a bottomless pit. But as he shielded his eyes from the glare of the snow he saw the dogs dangling below, still in their harness, while the driver lay unconscious on an ice shelf.

He couldn't do anything. The camp with the other men was six miles behind. He called to the man on the ledge that he was going for help, but there was no answer. He took off his outer clothing, divesting as much weight as he dared in the cold, and ran back through the snow. He made the six miles back to camp in just over two hours, and in another two hours was back at the crevasse with help. The man on the ledge was sitting up now, and they lowered ropes and brought up not only him but also the sled and dogs.

Despite this near calamity, von Payer headed north once again and eventually reached the northernmost edge of this new world they had discovered. Looking out from the cliffs he saw an ice-covered stretch of water, beyond which rose the craggy outlines of distant mountains. He named these far northern lands King Oscar Land and Petermann Land, and turned back toward the ship: the distance to them was filled with stretches of black open water roiling with shifting, dangerous mountains of ice. Petermann had been wrong, von Payer realized; no ship would ever sail over that frozen, treacherous sea to the pole.

The same treacherous ice now lay between him and his ship 165 miles to the south. As they trekked back, zigging and zagging to follow the most solid ice, they heard a hollow thunder ahead of them, sounding like the familiar sound of booming surf. As they came closer they saw that this was exactly what it was: the solid ice over which they had passed on their way north had broken up and was now nothing but individual floes floating and bounding in an open sea. "The spray of its surf dashed for a distance of thirty yards over the icy shore. . . . The icebergs, under which we had passed a month before, were now floating. That on which lay our depot of provisions was floating in the midst of them; and here we were, without a boat, almost without provisions, fifty-five miles from the ship. What were we to do, what direction were we to follow? . . . In what direction did the ice still lie unbroken?"

Step by step von Payer forged a path forward, sideways, backward, and ever again a little forward. He found a small pack of provisions floating on a floe close enough to capture. He fed his men one last time, and again began to inch his way across the ice. The important thing was to keep moving, in any direction, just to keep from being isolated and trapped on a floe that might float loose and be isolated in the foaming sea. Proceeding in this manner, his eyes locked more on the few inches in front of his feet than on the horizon, he finally looked up and saw the masts of his ship less than a mile away, with nothing but solid ice separating them. Quickly he dashed across the expanse before it could break up, and reached the relative sanctuary of the *Tegetthoff.*

But it *was* only relative. They were still stuck in the ice hundreds of miles from civilization. With no sign of the ship being freed, they decided to abandon it and head south in the ship's lifeboats. But first they had to drag the boats to the open sea, over piled-up ice and through waist-deep snow, mile after mile.

As summer came on, the ice began to melt, but tantalizingly slowly. A lead here, and they would sail down it for a few miles—then a dead-end wall of ice. They would camp again and wait while their provisions dwindled steadily. Then again a small lead, a short sail and again a blockage.

June went, July came and went, and they had managed to cover only nine miles. With the end of August would come the end of summer, and the ice would begin to freeze instead of melting. "Dreadful indeed was the solemn lapse of time," von Payer wrote. Then another ice hole opened; they launched the boats once more and saw open water ahead: "The last line of ice lay ahead of us, and beyond it the boundless sea!"

They reached Novaya Zemlya on August 24, found a Russian fishing trawler and clambered safely aboard. They returned, as von Payer wrote, with honor. They had not found Petermann's route to the pole, but they had shown that it was an illusion, and they had discovered new lands: Franz Josef Land, King Oscar Land and Petermann Land.

Unfortunately, the last two did not exist. They were mirages, born of inversions of cold air common in the Arctic regions. Chasing these mirages would nearly cost the life of the next man to try for the pole.

* * *

It was twenty years after von Payer and Weyprecht returned that a blond, blue-eyed, six-foot Norwegian, built
like an athlete yet holding a doctorate in science, later to
win the Nobel Peace Prize for his work aiding refugees and
prisoners in World War I, Fridtjof Nansen, took a different
tack for reaching the pole. For several years explorers of the
southwest coast of Greenland had found driftwood which
looked suspiciously similar to trees growing on the northern coast of Siberia, and then in 1884 articles were brought
back from Greenland which were positively identified as
fragments of the *Jeannette.*

Several years earlier the *Jeannette* had taken one of the
shortest voyages on record in an effort to reach the pole.
George Washington De Long, a lieutenant in the United
States Navy, had worked out a new path to the pole. He
would take advantage of the Japanese Current, riding it
north through the Bering Strait and along the coast of the
polar continent known as Wrangel Land. When eventually
they were stopped by ice, De Long would proceed on
sledge across the Wrangel continent to the pole. Financed
by James Gordon Bennett, publisher of the *New York Herald*
—the man who had sent Stanley to look for Livingstone—
De Long set off from San Francisco in the *Jeannette* with a
crew of two dozen in July 1879. On September 4 they lay to
beside a passing whaler to send home their last messages,
and on the sixth they entered a lane between two ice packs,
prepared to follow it to the pole. But by four o'clock that
same afternoon the *Jeannette* was caught fast in the ice, and
its sailing voyage was over. De Long thought this a bit
premature; daily he expected the grip of the ice to loosen
and free the ship, but it never did.

Never. They drifted northwest with the pack ice, past
Wrangel Land (which turned out to be Wrangel Island, not
a continent at all) and into the polar wastes. Each day they
hoped the ice might melt and free them; each day they

feared it might tighten and crush them, and there was nothing they could do about it except sit and wait. "Occasionally," De Long noted in his diary, "I go out on the ice on these beautiful evenings, and try to make words express my feelings suitably; but a lot of dogs wrangling over an empty meat can, trying to find a meal in it, surround me and drag me down to plain matter-of-fact. So I take my half frozen nose tenderly in my hand, and lead myself back to the ship."

The ice carried them all that winter, and when the summer of 1880 came and the sun came out again they found they had drifted so far north that the ice would not melt even in the sunshine. They stood on the deck and watched the sun, then looked at the ice, but nothing changed. Soon the sun went down again, and the dark winter held them once more.

They drifted throughout that second winter. "People beset in the pack before always drifted somewhere to some land; but we are drifting about like a modern Flying Dutchman, never getting anywhere, but always restless and on the move. Coals are burning up, food is being consumed, the pumps are still going, and thirty-three people are wearing out their lives and souls like men doomed to imprisonment for life."

In the spring of their second year of prison, on May 17, 1881, through the creeping mists they sighted land ahead of them. It was only a tiny bit of land which they named for their ship, Jeannette Island, but they yearned for it: "It appears to be an island. . . . a poor, desolate island among icy wastes . . . but it is solid land, at least, and will stand still long enough to let a man realize where he is." It was the first land they had seen for more than a year, but the ice carried them past it, and De Long wisely decided not to abandon the ship and try to reach it over the ice, for the island was unoccupied and barren.

Things got worse. The ship was slowly being crushed by

the ice as she was carried along, and though the crew worked frantically to repair each bit of damage as it occurred, it was a losing fight. On May 25 they drifted close by another island that they named Henrietta, but it too was barren and offered no safe refuge; it passed out of sight as they drifted on. Two weeks later the *Jeannette* was shaken by a series of reverberations as the ice pack shifted, and finally she crumpled and began to fall apart. All that day and night the crew labored to bring food, clothing, fuel and lifeboats off the ship and onto the ice, until at four o'clock A.M. the water rising from below into the hold reached a weight too great to be borne by the ice; then the *Jeannette* shivered, settled and disappeared beneath the ice into the waters below.

Six weeks later the crew reached an island of the New Siberian group, which they named Bennett in honor of the man who had given them the privilege of dying there. They rested for ten days while a "westerly gale, fog, sleet, and snow" blew over them, and then set out for the Siberian coast in their three small boats.

They rowed and sailed for a month. The coast was only a few miles distant; they could see it through the foggy mists but they couldn't reach it; each time they thought they had a chance they were blocked by the shifting pack ice. They began to pray for a mighty gale that might disperse the ice, and in early September they got it. But it dispersed their boats, too. One of them was blown away and never seen again. A second made it to the Siberian mainland, where the crew headed inland and found a native village.

The third boat, carrying De Long, reached the Lena Delta, where the river empties into the Arctic Ocean. They unloaded their supplies and waded through the knee-deep icy waters of the delta toward solid land a mile and a half away, through snow, hail, sleet and a strong wind. The only map they had showed a land uninhabited except for a village nearly a hundred miles away. They had less than ten days' food supply, and were lost with winter approaching in the coldest place on earth, where temperatures of 93 degrees below zero have been recorded, where milk is traded—when one can find people to trade with—by the piece rather than the quart. The land they finally reached consisted of spongy, slick tundra which sank and slipped under their feet with every step. With the coming of winter it froze solid, but was soon covered with snow and ice.

"My chart is simply useless. I must go on plodding to the southward, trusting in God to guide me to some settlement," De Long wrote, but he was so lost not even God could find him. The first man died the day before they finished the last of their food. "One does not like to feel he is caught in a trap," De Long confided to his diary, but he was. He made camp as best he could, sent the two healthiest men to find help, and settled down to die with the rest of his men.

The two who left were found by a native hunter who took them to his village. More dead than alive, unable to speak their language, the two men tried to indicate that they had companions who needed help. Misunderstanding the men's pleadings, the villagers took them south to some of their own kind: the crew of the second boat, who had made it to shore and were now resting in a nearby village. They mounted a dog-sled expedition to rescue De Long, but winter was already closing in by the time they reached the northern coast, and they had to wait till spring.

De Long and his men, alone and without food or shelter, couldn't wait that long. "Tonight for supper nothing remains but the dog," he wrote on October 3rd. Three weeks later he wrote simply, "A hard night." It was just a few days before his last entry, on October 30, 1881, that the rescue expedition gave up.

Four years after De Long died, artifacts from the *Jeannette* were found on the southwestern coast of Greenland, explaining the earlier finds of driftwood on that coast which looked so like the trees growing on the northern Siberian coastline. The explanation had to be that the Arctic ice drifted from Siberia across the polar sea toward Greenland, and the Siberian trees and pieces of the *Jeannette*, caught in the ice, drifted with it. All of which gave Fridtjof Nansen his idea of emulating the fallen trees and wreckage and drifting across the North Pole in the grip of the wandering pack ice.

He calculated that in drifting from Siberia to Greenland the trees and *Jeannette* artifacts must have passed close to the pole, so he decided to become, in effect, a Siberian tree. He designed a wooden ship, the *Fram*, which instead of being built to resist the crushing ice would cooperate with it; instead of trying to break through the ice it would ride up on it, settle there and be carried along with the drifting pack up to the pole and down again to civilization.

Well, that was the idea. The *Fram* was built more like an eggshell than a seagoing ship, and when in the summer of 1893 it sailed out of Christiania it behaved like one. In its first North Sea storm it "rolled like a log," and most of the thirteen-member crew—including Nansen—were horribly seasick. The ship dove into the waves instead of sailing over them, barely bringing its nose back up above water after each dunking. It had been provisioned for six years— the ice pack drifts very slowly across the Arctic Ocean, and no one knew how long the journey would take—and its deck was loaded with corded piles of provisions. One by one they broke loose under the force of the battering waves, and one by one they sailed overboard.

But when finally the storm was over, the *Fram* was still afloat. She continued northward, rounding Cape Chelyus-kin, the northernmost tip of Asia, and sailing eastward along the Siberian coast. Nansen took her nearly as far as the New Siberian Islands—where the *Jeannette* sank, and where the *Soyuz* would finish its journey nearly a hundred years later—and at 135° East he turned north to begin the real part of his journey, riding a warm current from the Lena River to get as far as he could before the pack ice caught him.

Suddenly it did: "All at once in the afternoon, as we were sitting idly chattering, a deafening noise began and the whole ship shook. This was the first ice-pressure. Everyone rushed on deck to look. The *Fram* behaved beautifully. On pushed the ice, but down under us it had to go, and we were slowly lifted up."

The *Fram* had behaved exactly as designed: as the ice squeezed her hull, the canted sides of the egg-shaped hull allowed her to ride higher and higher instead of being crushed, until finally she was caught firmly but safely, riding high and stuck fast. On September 25, 1893, Nansen lifted his rudder free from its perch and brought it up on deck; he would have no further use for it for several years, because you can't steer a pack of ice as thick as a mountain. The ship's engine was taken apart and put into storage. A windmill-powered electric generator was set up on deck, since without the engine running there was no power. The *Fram* had changed from a skittish, lumbering ship into a firm, snug ice station.

Boredom was now the enemy, as it is with most human adventures, from war to flying to the moon to performing neurosurgery: hours, days, months of boredom, then suddenly moments of terror. But always first, came the boredom.

They printed a ship's paper, the *Framsjaa;* they celebrated every imaginable occasion from birthdays to national holidays. They took astronomical and oceanographic observations, measuring the height of the stars, the depth of the ocean and the variation of the compass, not only to find out where they were drifting but someday to prove to others where they had been. They hunted for food, and were hunted in return by wandering polar bears.

And they were bored: "If I am to be perfectly honest, I think this is a wretched state of matters. We are now in about 80° N lat, in September we were in 79°; that is, let us say, one degree for five months. If we go on at this rate we shall be at the Pole in forty-five or say fifty months, and in ninety or one hundred months at 80° N latitude on the other side, with probably some prospect of getting out of the ice and home in a month or two more. At best, if things go on as they are doing now, we shall be home in eight years. . . .

"Oh, at times this inactivity crushes one's very soul: one's life seems as dark as the winter night outside; there is sunlight upon no part of it except the past and the far, far distant future. I feel as if I must break through this deadness, this inertia, and find some outlet for my energies. Can't something happen? Could not a hurricane come and tear up this ice, and set it rolling in high waves like the open sea? Welcome danger, if it only brings us the chance of fighting for our lives—only lets us move onwards!

"It wants ten times more strength of mind to sit still and trust in your theories and let nature work them out without your being able so much as to lay one stick across another to help, than it does to trust in working them out by your own energy. . . . Here I sit, whining like an old woman. . . ."

Finally the boredom won. In the spring of 1895, after "only" a year and a half of drifting with the ice, Nansen decided to leave the *Fram* and strike out for the pole on his own. His daily observations had indicated that they had, in effect, taken the wrong train: the ice drifting from where they had caught it would not pass close to the pole, but was sliding along to the south and west. Nansen left the ship to drift southward until the ice freed her, from which point she would return home. He would take to the ice and head north.

He took with him one companion—Frederik Hjalmar Johansen, a Danish naval lieutenant who had signed on as ordinary stoker when no other position could be found for him—three sleds pulled by twenty-eight dogs, provisions for three months and two portable kayaks.

At first they moved smoothly and easily: "We found large expanses of flat ice, and covered the ground quickly, farther and farther away from our comrades, into the unknown, where we two alone and the dogs were to wander for months," Nansen wrote in his book *Farthest North*. But then the ice began to pile up in high pressure ridges. These are one of the three banes of polar travelers, consisting of huge piled-up blocks of ice caused by the collision of ice packs, in which the ice crumples and forms hummocks and hills that can reach heights of thirty to fifty feet, are so steeply angled as to be nearly impossible to climb with loaded dogsleds, and can extend for miles without a break.

The second bane of the Arctic, open water, also assailed them. Between climbing the smaller ridges and detouring around the larger ones, between waiting for open water to freeze over and detouring around it when it didn't, the miles and the days began to pile up as the store of provisions grew smaller.

The third bane was the worst. Though they were traveling over seemingly solid ground, it was moving beneath them. For it was not solid ground; it was ice—fifteen feet thick, to be sure, but nevertheless only ice floating on the water below. And the water below, like all ocean waters, was moving. Unfortunately, it turned out to be moving south as they marched north. It was like walking on a treadmill: "In its capricious drift, at the mercy of wind and current, we had our worst enemy to combat."

Despite the subfreezing temperatures their exertions led to sweating, which was a curse in itself: The sweat "condensed in our outer garments, which were now a mass of ice and transformed into complete suits of ice-armor. They were so hard and stiff . . . that the arm of my coat actually rubbed deep sores in my wrists during our marches. . . . When we got into our sleeping-bags in the evening our clothes began to thaw slowly. . . . At last [they] became wet and pliant, only to freeze again a few minutes after we had turned out of our bag in the morning."

Finally, it was all too much. The dwindling provisions, combined with the southward drift of the ice and their consequently slow progress toward the pole, convinced Nansen that they simply could not make it. Ahead lay nothing else but more of the same: "Ridge after ridge, and nothing but rubble to travel over. . . . I went on a good way ahead on snow-shoes, and from the highest hummock only the same kind of ice was to be seen. It was a veritable chaos of ice-blocks, stretching as far as the horizon. . . . It brought me to the verge of despair."

On April 8, nearly a month after leaving the *Fram*, Nansen turned back from the pole and set his course for civilization—or its nearest equivalent, Franz Josef Land. That is, he set his course as best he could. But he had two problems. The first was that the going was too easy at first. Eager to take advantage of the sudden calm in the weather—what little wind there was blew at their backs instead of in their faces—and anxious to make as much mileage as possible over the ice which now turned flat and steady in front of them, Nansen led Johansen in a nonstop march of thirty-six hours before pausing for rest. This gave them another problem: during this long march they forgot to wind their chronometers.

Not knowing what time it is doesn't seem to be a terrible thing, but on the open seas, or the open ice, time translates into position. To measure latitude you need measure only the sun's greatest height above the horizon, but to measure longitude you must also know the *time* of that greatest height (local noon) and compare it to Greenwich time. Without a working chronometer, Nansen and Johansen didn't know where they were.

Their second problem was that the first stop they were heading for on their way to Franz Josef Land was Petermann Land, discovered by von Payer and Weyprecht twenty-two years before. But Petermann Land didn't exist; the distant hills seen by the two Austrians had been only a mirage. The "land" Nansen now headed for was nothing but ice, snow and water.

After that first thirty-six hours, the weather reverted to normal: fog, hail, sleet and snow, unchanging for the next three months. Every few days they would pick out the weakest of their dogs and kill it to feed the others, until finally they were down to the last two dogs, one for each of their sleds.

And always there was the hidden threat of sudden attack by a polar bear. When it finally happened, it came without warning. They had just reached a lane of open water and Nansen was preparing to lower his kayak when he heard Johansen's voice behind him calling, "Take the gun!" Holding on to the kayak with one hand, he turned around to see a gigantic white polar bear throwing itself on Johansen, who was lying on the ground. Without thinking, Nansen reached for his rifle—and in doing so let go of the kayak, which lurched and slipped off the ice into the water. If it went, every chance of survival went with it.

He lunged after it and managed to catch it just before it slipped out to sea. Its weight was too much for one man to haul back up onto the ice, but its loss was too much to bear. Slowly, second by second, the young giant somehow managed to pull it back up. Behind him he heard nothing, and then Johansen spoke calmly, without panic: "You must look sharp if you want to be in time!"

"Look sharp? I should think so. At last I got hold of the butt-end, dragged the gun out, turned round in a sitting position and gave [the bear] a charge of shot behind the ear, and it fell down dead between us. The bear must have followed our track like a cat, and, covered by the ice-blocks, have slunk up while we were clearing the ice from the lane and had our backs to him. . . . It was just as the bear was about to bite Johansen in the head that he uttered the memorable words, 'Look sharp!' . . ."

Finally they reached open water, and celebrated by having a piece of chocolate. They lashed their kayaks together and tied the sledges on top, then set off for the south. Suddenly life was lovely again. "It was a real pleasure to let the kayaks dance over the water and hear the little waves splashing against the sides . . . we found that the wind was so good that we ought to make use of it, and so we rigged up a sail on our fleet. We glided easily before the wind in towards the land we had so longed for all these many months. What a change, after having forced one's way inch by inch by foot on ice."

They never found Petermann Land, of course, but on the 28th of August by nothing but good luck they arrived at one of the southern islands of Franz Josef Land, though without accurate timekeeping from their chronometers and with the errors in the maps they had they didn't really know *where* they were. But it was land, solid and unmoving, and they settled in for the winter. They killed a walrus, and from its shoulder blade fashioned a sort of shovel. With this they dug a hole in the rocky ground. They pushed stones around the hole, then piled them up plastered with a mixture of moss and dirt. On one of their hunting expeditions they found a gigantic drift log lying on the beach, and somehow managed to drag it back and use it as a central beam, holding up a roof of walrus hide over the hole which now became their winter home. "Using lamps fueled with walrus blubber we managed to keep the temperature in the middle of the hut at about the freezing point. It was, of course, much colder nearer the walls."

So the long night of winter came. There was melted snow to drink, and game enough to eat. Polar bears visited them frequently, and they never went outside without their rifles. Heat was their main problem. They couldn't wash, of course, except on Christmas Eve when they squandered enough fuel to heat a quarter cup of water with which they scrubbed down their bodies and then turned their shirts inside out to maintain a figment of hygiene. "I have never before realized what a magnificent invention soap really is," Nansen wrote.

In May of 1896 they broke camp and headed south again. "In the evening we put in to the edge of the ice, so as to stretch our legs a little; they were stiff with sitting in the kayak all day, and we wanted to get a little view over the water to the west by ascending a hummock. As we went ashore the question arose how we should moor our precious vessel. 'Oh, well, it doesn't require much to hold these light kayaks,' said I. . . . We went up on a hummock. . . . As we stood there, Johansen suddenly cried, 'I say! The kayaks are adrift!' We ran down as hard as we could. They were already a little way out and were drifting quickly off; the painter had given way. 'Here, take my watch,' I said to Johansen, giving it to him; and as quickly as possible I threw off some clothing, so as to be able to swim more easily. I did not dare to take everything off, as I might so easily get a cramp. I sprang into the water but the wind was off the ice, and the light kayaks, with their high rigging, gave it good hold. They were already well out, and were drifting rapidly. The water was icy cold; it was hard work swimming with clothes on; and the kayaks drifted farther and farther, often quicker than I could swim. It seemed more than doubtful whether I could manage it. But all our hope was drifting there; all we possessed was on board—we had not even a knife with us; and whether I got cramp and sank here, or turned back without the kayaks, it would come to pretty much the same thing; so I exerted myself to the utmost.

"When I got tired, I turned over and swam on my back and then I could see Johansen walking restlessly up and down on the ice. Poor lad! He couldn't stand still, and thought it dreadful not to be able to do anything. . . . He said afterwards that these were the worst moments he had ever lived through. But when I turned over again and saw that I was nearer the kayaks my courage rose, and I redoubled my exertions. I felt, however, that my limbs were gradually stiffening and losing all feeling, and I knew that in a short time I should not be able to move them. But there was not far to go now; if I could only hold out a little longer we should all be saved—and I went on.

"The strikes became more and more feeble, but the distance became shorter and shorter, and I began to think I should reach the kayaks. At last I was able to stretch out my hand to the snow-shoe which lay across the sterns. I grasped it, pulled myself in to the edge of the kayak—and we were saved! I tried to pull myself up, but the whole of my body was so stiff with cold that this was an impossibility. For a moment I thought that, after all, it was too late; I was to get so far, but not be able to get in. After a few moments, however, I managed to swing one leg up on to the edge of the sledge which lay on the deck, and in this way managed to tumble up. There I sat, but so stiff with cold that I had difficulty in paddling. Nor was it easy to paddle in the double vessel. . . . I shivered, my teeth chattered, and I was numb all over."

He turned the kayaks and headed back to shore, reaching it too exhausted and cold to move. Johansen waded out to the boat and pulled the kayaks ashore, then carried him off and laid him down. He stripped the soaking clothes off the exhausted Nansen and put him in a sleeping bag, where he immediately fell asleep while Johansen put together their camp, started a fire, and cooked supper. "Auk and hot soup soon effaced the last traces of my swim. During the night my clothes were hung out to dry, and the next day were all nearly dry again."

The next day they set sail again, and a few days later landed once more on solid ground and set up a temporary camp. It was a land "which I believed to be unseen by any human eye and untrodden by any human foot, reposing in Arctic majesty behind its mantle of mist." But Nansen was wrong. "A sound suddenly reached my ear so like the barking of a dog that I started. It was only a couple of barks, but it could not be anything else. I strained my ears, but heard no more, only the same bubbling noise of thousands of birds. I must have been mistaken after all. . . . Then the barking came again . . . there was no longer any room for doubt. . . . I now shouted to Johansen that I heard dogs farther inland. He started up from the bag where he lay sleeping and tumbled out of the tent. . . . Was all our toil, were all our troubles, privations, and sufferings to end here? It seemed incredible, and yet—"

Nansen ran, stumbling, a filthy giant of a man, over the hilly, rocky terrain. He came around a boulder, stepped over a hummock, and . . .

During these past few years when Nansen was wandering lost in the Arctic, a British expedition had been sent out to find a path to the North Pole. Financed by the newspaper magnate Lord Northcliffe—polar exploration vied with African exploration in the Victorian era as the best way to sell newspapers—it set off in 1894 under the direction of Frederick Jackson, a typically Victorian sporting gentleman. He had wintered two years on Cape Flora, one of the southernmost islands of the Franz Josef archipelago (the island which the *Sovetskiy Soyuz* was now approaching), and as June broke out in 1896 was leading a hunting party along the beach. Taking a break, he led his dog inland for a stroll.

He was carefully washed and shaved, and dressed in a casual cap and tweeds. He came over a hill and saw what must have looked like an apparition: a huge, dirty, bearded man.

Cautiously, each of them not quite able to believe their eyes, the two men approached each other. "On one side the civilized European in an English check suit and high rubber boots, well shaved, well groomed, bringing with him a perfume of scented soap, perceptible to the wild man's sharpened senses; on the other side the wild man clad in dirty rags, black with oil and soot, with long uncombed hair and shaggy beard, black with smoke, with a face in which the natural fair complexion could not possibly be discerned through the thick layer of fat and soot which a winter's endeavors with warm water, moss, rags, and at last a knife had sought in vain to remove. No one suspected who he was or whence he came."

"Hello," the Englishman said politely, lifting his cap.

The giant answered, and they approached and shook hands. "I'm immensely glad to see you," Jackson went on.

"Thank you," the giant replied. "I also," he added.

They turned and headed back toward the hunting party. As they strolled along Jackson made conventional polite conversation. "Have you a ship here?" he asked.

"No, my ship is not here," the giant answered. Which was odd, Jackson thought. After all, one doesn't wander around the Arctic without a ship . . .

Then he thought, Oh my God! "Are you Nansen?" he asked.

"Yes, I am."

"By Jove! I *am* glad to see you."

The meeting was as astonishing to both men as it was fortuitous. Nansen had not been looking for Jackson, nor had Jackson come looking for Nansen; he knew only that the man had disappeared three years ago and had never been heard from since.

Nor, but for this strange meeting, would Nansen ever have been heard from again, for he and Johansen were in the last extremities. From Jackson's diary we know that "they had a lump or two of evil-looking walrus meat and two or three draggled-looking loons in their kayaks, which was all the food they had with them, poor chaps. On the night of their arrival we sat up talking till 8 A.M. of the following day, and then turned into our blankets, but we soon turned out again and renewed our conversations for hours. . . .

"A more remarkable meeting than ours was never heard of. Nansen did not know that I was in Franz Josef Land, as I did not leave England until a year after he had started, and I had not the slightest idea he was within hundreds of miles of me; in addition to that, Nansen was very uncertain as to what part of the world he was in. . . . Had he missed meeting with us, he could not have left Franz Josef Land, for there is nothing but a stretch of open sea more than 160 miles in extent between [Cape Flora] and the nearest known land, which cannot be crossed in leaky canvas canoes. . . . Nansen repeatedly remarks that nothing will ever induce him to undertake such a trip again."

Today, July 29, 1991, the *Sovetskiy Soyuz* was approaching Cape Flora. We dropped anchor after lunch and I killed an hour in my cabin, hoping to avoid the rush to get into the small rubber Zodiacs, but when I came out on deck I found everyone still standing in line; the crew was having trouble getting the boats launched. They take twelve people at a time, and since there were fifty people ahead of me, and it soon became apparent that it was taking twenty minutes for a round trip, it looked like a long wait.

I wandered around the boat, ending up at the helicopter pad, and found they were preparing to augment the Zodiacs with a heli-shuttle. I was first in line.

It was a lovely, smooth ten-minute flight, and we set

down on a type of land I had never touched before: the Arctic tundra. A foot or two under the surface of the ground is a layer of permafrost, subsoil which is permanently frozen, acting as a barrier against water drainage. Hence, in summer the melting ice has no place to go; it seeps down to the permafrost layer, and then stops. The result is that the topsoil—the tundra—is soft and giving underfoot, almost as if it were alive. As we walked away from the chopper it sank beneath our feet a few inches with every step; it was rather like walking on a gigantic sponge. But these were the firm parts; the unfirm were worse. One of the men stepped into a narrow mud-hole and sank in up to his thighs. He began to scream, thinking he was caught in quicksand and would sink under the scum, but he reached a solid bottom just as his own bottom began to get wet. He stopped screaming, but couldn't get out without the rest of us grabbing his arms and heaving.

There are no trees anywhere on the island, nor anywhere within hundreds of miles; the cold climate won't support any large vegetation. Instead the tundra is speckled with sparse clumps of small yellow and red flowers and tiny bushes rising only a few inches above the ground.

The tundra here extended in a long meadow, then abruptly shifted gears and sloped upward, its top lost in cloud. Though there were the sounds of millions of birds up there in that cloud, not many of them came down. But one swooped right up to me, a large white gull that looked at me curiously, then sailed away, back up into the white mist.

The natural harbor was nearly ice-free, with only a few floating floes, each with a lovely surreal powder-blue color inside its cover of dirty white ice. A hundred years ago, when Jackson met Nansen on this shore, the sea was white with ice, only speckled with occasional streaks of black water. We tramped along the beach and found Jackson's shack and abandoned campfires: a few holes in the ground, a few logs covering them, scattered firewood lying on the ground. That's all that's left of Jackson and Nansen. Nearly everyone leaned over them, yearning to take home a souvenir, but we were determined to leave the Arctic as we found it, and no one took anything. It is all still there.

The *Soyuz* is nuclear-powered, which means there is no shortage of energy. Consequently the rooms are too hot. The brochure for the trip promised that "all cabins are heated, and the flow of hot air is individually controlled." This is true in a sense: there is indeed a control switch in each room which can be turned from off to full heat. More importantly, however, and not mentioned in the brochure, is that the lever is not connected to anything; you can shove it all the way one direction or the other and it has not the slightest effect on the interminable flow of heat. This is not merely my cabin: the suffocating heat was the major topic of conversation the first few days, until we realized by walking along the decks and peering in through open portholes that each member of the crew keeps his porthole open and has a small fan next to it to blow in cold air. So everyone has realized that the heating system, like our views of the Communist system in the good old days, is a monstrous monolith that cannot be deviated from its factory-set course. Of course there is no concern about conserving energy on board; the nuclear reactors provide essentially unlimited energy. No one here urges you to turn off lights when you leave a room, or not to waste water (which is generated by distilling sea water and, with our infinite energy source, is plentiful).

Given the energy supply, the mentality of the Soviet builders of the ship obviously followed a simple line of reasoning: an icebreaker is made to live in the Arctic; the problem with living in the Arctic is that it is cold; it would be good to be warm; too much of a good thing must be a better thing. One can understand this; there are probably few people living in Russia today who can remember ever having had too much—or even enough—of a good thing.

But last night I nearly suffocated in the heat. This afternoon as we sailed away from Cape Flora I opened the porthole, and by 6 P.M. it was getting comfortably cold inside even without a fan. At about the same time we began plowing through serious pack ice, perhaps six inches thick.

The way the *Sovetskiy Soyuz* does this is interesting. I had expected it to attack the ice head-on, shearing it with a razor-sharp edge to its hull. Not at all. The ship is constructed so that as it encounters an ice shelf its bow rises up over it, much in the manner of the *Fram.* Its two nuclear reactors provide 75,000 horsepower, enough to shove the 20,000 ton monster up over the ice. As it slides forward over it, its weight becomes too much for the ice to bear and it crashes through. For the next two weeks this motion and its accompanying sounds will be continuous: a grinding noise as we are shoved up over the ice, then a sudden crashing, jarring thunder as the ice breaks and we plow forward. Below decks—in the lecture room, for example— the noise is impossibly loud. It will surely drown out the lecturers, so perhaps what my mother told me about clouds and silver linings is true.

The menu tonight is typically impressive: rock lobster with celery and apple nut stuffing for appetizer, cream of onion soup with croutons, a choice of Dover sole or rack of lamb with a sauce of fresh herbs, cauliflower and Parisienne carrots. For dessert a cassata ice with strawberry sauce and whipped cream. The suggested wines are a 1988 Mâcon Lugny-Les Genièvres, Louis Latour, or a 1990 Bernkasteler Schlossberg. A 1987 Château Beau-Site will be provided if anyone insists on a red.

But though the menu is impressive, the food is awful. I eat with Liz Harper and Ken Morgan—the only two young, single people on board, who seem to have found each other after two days of careful eye contact—and Jacqueline Smith of Palm Beach, Florida, who looks like the menu and talks like the food. She has something of the manner of Mrs. Onassis about her, and this, together with her coming from Kennedy country, has quickly led to her becoming known around the ship as Jackie S. She is so thankful that she was able to raise her two girls after her doctor husband died, and now the girls are so ungrateful. They keep asking how she spends her money; they worry that she's spending it all.

"It's hard to know what else you can do with money," I say.

"Why, leave it to them. That's what they want. My youngest called to ask if I'd put her through law school. I said no way. She said I'd once promised to if she wanted to go. I said, well you didn't want to then, did you? If I promised you, I meant it when I said it but I sure as hell don't mean it now."

She is angry that they should expect so much from her, which seems reasonable until you realize that she is spending nearly as much on this three-week vacation (vacation from what? She doesn't work. She's married again to a man who "owns real estate") as it would cost for the three years of law school. It's true that this is a unique experience, but so is the experience of educating your daughter, I always thought. But I don't say this. It's easy to be generous with other people's money. Also, she is not a whiner, she makes a joke of everything and she's charming—like the menu. I enjoy talking to her because then it is possible not to take her seriously. Still, in the end it is depressing.

After dinner we approach another island of the Franz Josef group. This one shows a sheer cliff with birds clinging to its side, flying up and down it, having a wonderful time. When I was a kid I used to lie on the sand at Atlantic City and watch the gulls, thinking what fun they had floating around up there. Those Jersey gulls didn't know a thing

about fun; these Arctic murres and kittiwakes could teach
them how to live.

At midnight we reach another island and the loudspeaker
informs us that the Zodiacs will be running if anyone
wants to go ashore. The sky outside is gray, but still as light
as it was at noon, and I climb into the rubber boat. We
maneuver through the thick pack ice clogging the shore,
and finally find a narrow lead into land. We hop out and
splash through a few feet of icy slush to reach another,
nearly identical, island: Ostrov Gukera if you're Russian,
Hooker Island if you're Anglo.

This island was the site of a Russian meteorological station, inhabited continuously from 1912 till 1964. Among the
deserted shacks is a simple wooden cross: "1913–14. Expedition Lieut. Sedov'a. Lost at the North Pole." Nothing is
known about Lieutenant Sedov'a or his expedition; it is not
mentioned in any book. Evidently he led a group northward from here in 1913 and was never heard from again.
His only memorial is this rough wooden post and a barely
decipherable Russian inscription on a barren island visited
by nobody.

JULY 30

‖|‖|‖

The world of the Arctic is fascinating because it is so different from the temperate world we live in. Hence the most routine events of our daily lives take on a new significance up here. One of the most routine, however, is never discussed. You may have noticed that when the old explorers write their memoirs they tell of all sorts of exciting, dangerous crises and of sudden, frightening events. They fall into cracks in the ice and are attacked by polar bears, they freeze and starve, and they suffer long winters of stupefying boredom waiting for the spring sun to rise and soak up the black night of winter. But there is one discomfiting aspect of life in the Arctic they seem never to mention: defecation.

It's bad enough when you have to get up in the middle of a cold winter's night to use the toilet; the thought of doing so at 50 below is unnerving. Yet the Third Law of Thermodynamics insists that for every physical process waste must necessarily be produced, and so we know that while these men were trapped in the ice, stalking back and forth in their frozen prisons, they must have been producing waste products in their bodies. How did they get rid of them? There were no flush toilets, there was no running water to carry off their wastes, and they couldn't even dig holes in the ground. Or could they? Perhaps holes in the ice? The whole problem sounds like a daunting engineering prospect necessitating a good deal of ingenuity, and one would think that the engineers who solved it would be proud to tell us of their exploits. Sadly they remain largely silent.

Except for one. Wandering around this morning before breakfast I happened upon the ship's library lounge. It was deserted so early in the day except for Liz Harper and Ken Morgan, who were playing a quiet game of Scrabble. The library consisted of a couple of dozen books: one of Arctic poetry, letters by W. H. Auden and Louis MacNeice, a Harold Robbins novel; and the remainder books dealing with Arctic and Antarctic exploration. Browsing through them I found one by Dean Smith, who flew to the South Pole with Richard Byrd in the 1920s, and who explains how polar privies are built and maintained.

"The cold had certain effects on our sanitary arrangement," he writes in *By the Seat of My Pants*. "We had dug a great pit, thirty feet deep and flared out until it measured twelve by fifteen at the bottom. Our calculations indicated this should suffice to meet the needs of our entire group for several years, and we thought we had reason to look forward to comparative comfort throughout the winter night.

"Things worked out much differently than in the Chic Sale designs of our country back-yards. Each deposit solidified almost instantly in the sub-zero temperature that was constant in the deep hole, and stalagmites rose rapidly from the depths. In a few weeks a frozen pillar reached all the way to each hole. Instead of moving the seats we made the mistake of breaking the stalagmites with a crowbar. After this was repeated a few times the crisscrossed lengths piled like jackstraws and soon the once huge cavern was completely filled. Each week a two-man detail to clean out a usable space was selected by means of a freeze-out poker

game. You never saw closer-to-the-vest poker played anywhere.''

After breakfast I climb up to the bridge and find we have
passed the 80th parallel. This is where Andrée left his
mark.

In 1895, while Nansen was still lost somewhere in the
polar sea, a Swedish scientist with a walrus mustache as
impressive as his name, Salomon August Andrée, stood up
in front of the Sixth International Geographical Congress
meeting in London and announced that he was going to go
Nansen one better. Whereas Nansen had set off to drift
across the North Pole on floating ice, Andrée decided to
drift across it on the wings of the wind, in a balloon.

Of course they laughed. Ballooning was a great sport at
that time in Europe, but leaving the civilized world behind
and going to the North Pole was not a game. Exploring was
serious business, and reaching the most inaccessible spot
on earth was the most serious venture of all. It was not for
amateurs, the eminent geographers and explorers of the
Sixth IGC felt. So, one by one, they stood up and offered
their questions and objections.

An admiral pointed out that navigation on a featureless
sea was difficult at best, and that as one got closer to the
pole it became even more so (a presage of Peary's future
difficulties). How could it possibly be done in a balloon?
First of all, the ascension of the sun over the horizon would
be measured by an observer who was himself much higher
than the horizon. Presumably a correction for this effect
could be made by a skilled mathematician, but the admiral
himself wasn't quite sure how to do it, since no one had
ever before been in a position where such a factor was
important. In effect, he said: ''If you should by chance drift
over the pole, and if there should be a red and white pole
sticking up there with a large sign on it, then you can come
back and tell us you've been to the pole. But if you should

just drift over featureless snow and ice, as assuredly you shall, and you should then return safely—which most probably you shall not—how can you possibly tell anyone where you have been? And if you cannot do that, what is the point of going there at all?"

As Andrée struggled to answer this, another man stood up, shaking his head pityingly. Balloons went up in the air and drifted with the wind, to be sure, he pointed out; the trouble was that they tended to come down helter-skelter, anywhere at all, wherever the winds took them and whenever the temperature dropped so that the inflating gas shrank, when condensing moisture built up a layer of heavy water on them, or when they sprang a leak, or . . . "What will you do," he asked Andrée, "if you come down on open water?"

"We will carry a boat with us."

His interrogator shook his head. "There isn't room in a balloon's gondola for a boat."

"We will have a disassembled boat, stored in pieces easily put together."

"Ah, but one often comes down quite suddenly, without warning. What will you do if you find yourself all at once in the water, with no time to assemble your boat?"

Andrée stared at him a moment. "We will drown," he said succinctly. When they laughed at this he reminded them that Sir John Franklin had lost 129 lives on his attempt, and since then scores more had been lost in the traditional attempts by ship. He would take with him two companions. Even if they failed, the loss of life would be minimal. "Dangerous?" he asked himself later, in his diary. "Perhaps. But what am I worth?"

Not much in one sense; quite a bit in another. Not much in the sense that the loss of his life would not give personal grief to anyone else. Andrée abhorred and abjured personal relationships, particularly romantic entanglements, because "they involve factors which cannot be arranged according to plan. If a few heart leaves begin sprouting, I resolutely pull them up by the roots," he wrote. "I know that if I once let such a feeling live, it would become too strong for me. And so I dare not give in to it."

But Andrée was worth something in his own right. He was the kind of man whose life propels all mankind forward one small step. He was a man of intellect, of reason, of science. He explored the world around him in the fullest sense, trying not only to discover the geographical limits of new lands but to discover the limits of our own lives, in matters both great and small. Today his ballooning scheme strikes us as unbearably romantic and unrealistic, but he himself was nothing if not a hardheaded realist. He was almost a caricature of a scientist, living for nothing but the exercise of rational thought and experimentation. He had graduated from Stockholm's premier school of science, the Royal Institute, and worked as a physicist at Sweden's outpost in Spitsbergen, studying Arctic weather conditions and related phenomena. But he carried rationality to irrational extremes. For him, to wonder was to investigate. How many eggs, for example, could a man eat at one sitting, and what would be the result? A useless question, no doubt, but for Andrée the importance of a question was not in its utility but in the fact that he had asked it—in its existence rather than in its essence, as Sartre would later make the distinction. Or as Sir Edmund Hillary might have put it, one answers a question because it's there.

So Andrée went to a restaurant, ordered bread, butter, milk and two dozen eggs. He was prepared to order another two dozen had they proven necessary to answer the question, but they didn't.

Now he was prepared to float to the North Pole, both because it was there and to prove that one could fly anywhere on earth. This was a decade before the Wright brothers demonstrated powered flight; the airplane was still a romantic dream. But the balloon was reality, a simple application of the laws of physics to man's oldest dream. It was possible to generate a gas (hydrogen) from the action of acids on metals. This gas consisted of atoms lighter than those of normal air. Though the actual existence of atoms would not be demonstrated until the upcoming century, when Einstein would explain the Brownian motion of colloids as due to the collision between atoms, a scientist of Andrée's stature nevertheless understood that the atomic concept was the most reasonable one to explain the behavior of the universe.

Granted the existence of atoms, then, the significance of a balloon filled with gaseous atoms lighter than those of the surrounding air was that the balloon must rise due to the differential effects of gravity. It was all very simple. In fact, the first manned balloon ascent in Sweden had been made a hundred years before, and even before then the French had been doing it. By the end of the nineteenth century ballooning had become a popular sport and was on the verge of becoming a business. At the time there was a renewed gold rush to the Klondike, following the discovery of new deposits there, and several people had announced the inauguration of regularly scheduled balloon flights to get people to Alaska quicker than those going overland or by ship.

These Klondike adventures all failed because of one overwhelming difficulty with balloons: they could not be steered. They blew with the wind, and at the pleasure of the wind. This was the problem Andrée attacked with all the rationality of his mind. Sailboats, he reasoned, can steer even though they too are driven by the wind. The reason is that they have a keel, which, embedded in the water, slows the boat enough for the wind to sweep over it and at the same time gives it something to push against. A balloon floating freely in the air moves *with* the wind; in fact one of the great pleasures of balloon travel is the well-known sensation of the lack of any movement, precisely because moving with the wind means no differential movement and thus no breeze in one's face, no sound of air rushing past one's ears. Instead one floats silently in the void while the earth below rushes past.

The trick, then, was to slow the balloon relative to the wind, and to give the wind something to push against. Andrée conceived the idea of drag ropes; he would dangle thick ropes from the gondola. These, dragging across the surface of the earth, would slow the balloon below the pace of the wind and provide a fulcrum against which they could tack by means of sails and thus gain some limited measure of steerability.

Ropes and sails, then, and the balloon would not float freely with random gusts of wind but would instead become a sailboat in the sky, controlled and guided to some small extent by the skill of its occupants, who would use the wind as an instrument of their pleasure. Testing his apparatus, Andrée found that he could tack nearly 30 degrees across the wind. When he managed to procure funding from the Swedish dynamite scientist Alfred Nobel, he decided to recruit a crew and go for it.

Andrée's two companions would be two other bachelors: Dr. Nils Ekholm, another scientist, and Knut Fraenkel, a civil engineer. The attempt, he told the Geological Congress, was the only reasonable way to reach the pole. Petermann's concept of an open polar sea accessible to sailing ships had been proven wrong; nor was the ice solid or smooth enough to employ sledges or people on foot. The path to the pole was one of constantly shifting pack ice building up into impassable ridges, separated by leads of open water; it was impossible either to sail there or to walk, ski or sledge there. The only possible route lay through the air.

In July of 1896 the balloon was assembled at the northern tip of Spitsbergen. In a giant cauldron forty tons of iron were tipped into an equal amount of sulfuric acid. As the iron began to fizzle and dissolve, bubbles of hydrogen gas appeared. These rose from the sulfuric acid and were fed into the sagging silk of the balloon, which slowly began to swell and rise. Soon it was straining at the rigging, eager to be gone.

But the winds did not cooperate. They gusted, swirled or died, never resolving themselves into the steady southerly breeze which might carry the explorers northward. July turned into August, the days of August ran out, and with it their time. The balloon was tipped, the hydrogen evacuated, and they packed up and went home.

Next summer Andrée was back, with Fraenkel but not Ekholm. The latter explained to the press that the previous summer he had become disenchanted with the scheme; the balloon had leaked hydrogen at a rate which made it unlikely to last to the pole. This was a serious problem with balloons: hydrogen, the lightest of atoms, is also the smallest—so small that it slips past the tightest bonds. Indeed, it diffuses even through solid metal, so how can the silk of a balloon hold it?

Not very well, was the answer, though the surface had been shellacked over and over again. Still, Andrée's calculations convinced him, if not Ekholm, that it would last long enough to get them to the pole and back, though perhaps with a smaller margin of error than a scientist like Ekholm would have liked. Or perhaps it was just that the man had married during the past year, and something like that gives a different perspective to life, and to its possible loss.

Ekholm's place was taken by Nils Strindberg, a lecturer at Stockholm's Technical College and nephew of the playwright, recently affianced to a young lady, who tried desperately to talk him out of the voyage. To no avail; on Sunday, July 11, 1897, the winds over Spitsbergen turned northward and "Andrée gave the orders. Everyone was willing and helpful, and everything went well. . . . The balloon rose and tugged against the lines. . . . The moment had come to attach the car. This was done, the bags of ballast were taken on board, and then it was time to say good-bye. This was done heartily and touchingly but without any signs of weakness. . . .

"And now the three of them stand there, on top of the car. There is a moment's solemn silence. . . . The right instant has come. 'Cut away everywhere!' cried Andrée. Three knives cut the three lines holding fast the bearing-ring, and the balloon rises amid the hurrahs of those below."

The *Eagle* was in the air. Barely. It traveled perhaps a hundred yards, rising slightly; then a downdraft apparently caught it, for it dipped toward the sea. The watchers on land saw Andrée and his companions furiously cutting at the ballast lines; at the last moment several large sacks dropped loose, and the *Eagle* rose again. Again it dropped, this time actually banging against the surface of the water, but quickly bounced up again. Then it soared like an elevator, high into the sky toward the clouds, toward the horizon, and soon disappeared, sailing north for the pole.

Those watching breathed a sigh of relief when it bounced from the water back into the air, but it would have been better for all aboard if the balloon had sunk at that moment. Its crew would have been forlorn, their hopes dashed, their dreams ruined, but they would have been alive. As it was, the *Eagle* sailed off majestically, leaving behind in the swirling waters only the lower portion of her drag ropes. Andrée had designed them with twist locks so that if they should catch on a jutting rock as they dragged over the land they could be jettisoned in pieces rather than yanking the balloon down to crash. Unfortunately, when the gondola of the balloon hit the water and the ropes dragged through the waves they somehow twisted and unlocked, and when the *Eagle* rose again the drag ropes remained behind in the water.

This meant that the balloon could not be steered, for the sails were useless without the drag ropes to slow them below the velocity of the wind. Still, the wind was heading north, and willy-nilly and helter-skelter along with it the *Eagle* sailed out of sight, never to be seen again.

The refrain of the Arctic: *never to be seen again* . . .

After lunch I wander up to the flight deck, the top deck in the stern, or whatever they call it, where the two helicopters are kept. As we sail north one of them is flying at all times, scouting the seas ahead of us, looking for large icebergs to avoid or whales we might chase. Just as I reach the deck one of the choppers is landing, and I stand battling the hurricane winds it beats up, watching as it settles down onto the deck like a half-drunk loony-bird, leaning first to one side and then the other in the wind, finally touching down, sighing and going quiet. The rotors slow, then stop, and the two pilots get out for a smoke while the bird is gassed up again.

They offer me a smoke. I shake my head. They think I am rebuffing their Soviet cigarettes, and their feelings are hurt. I manage to make them understand that I don't smoke anything, even American cigarettes, and they smile again. They turn to get back into the chopper; then one says something to the other and they both turn back to me. They say something I don't understand, but by gestures, smiles and nods, and by pulling at my arm and pointing, they make me understand that they're offering me a lift in the chopper.

I love to fly—I have a private license—but aside from yesterday's ten-minute flight to Cape Flora, I've never been in a helicopter, so I climb aboard and strap myself in. There are two seats up front for the pilot and copilot, and a three-man seat behind them. They each stick their heads out the side windows and look around, shout the equivalent of "Contact!" and with a screaming whine the blades begin to spin. The chopper shakes and bounces a bit, sways in the wind and looks as if it is being blown off the stern of the ship, and then suddenly rises straight up. It feels like taking one of those glass elevators on the outsides of fancy department stores in San Francisco or Chicago.

Straight up we go, with the *Soyuz* down beneath us, and then we tilt to head sideways away from her and higher still—until suddenly we're in fog. It doesn't seem to bother the pilots, so it doesn't bother me. I sit there looking out the window, staring in fascination as the whiplets of fog streak the window, turning into drops of water before my eyes.

Eventually I look at my watch. We've been gone thirty minutes. I remember hearing something about these helicopters carrying fuel for an hour and a half. I wonder what the hell we're doing up here in the fog for so long. Now the copilot says something to the pilot, who waves him off, and though I don't understand the words I realize the copilot is wondering the same thing. Do these guys know what the hell they're doing? Suddenly it's very cold in the helicopter.

The copilot speaks again, and again is waved off. He is getting upset, and so is the pilot. He begins to yell, insisting on his point, and it becomes clear to me that he thinks he has seen something but that the pilot doesn't believe him. It looks as if they're having trouble with the radio—the choppers don't carry radar—and I think the copilot believes he saw the ship through the fog over there to the left, but that the captain is sure it has to be somewhere to the right.

They start going down, and I look over their shoulders. The instruments are labeled in Russian, but I know enough to figure out which is the altimeter, even if it hadn't been obvious because it is the one instrument both men are staring at as we drop down toward the water. The needle practically bounces off zero but we are still in the fog; finally the pilot guns the engine and we roar up higher again. Evidently the fog has swept in unexpectedly low and thick, reaching the waves now; we are solidly in it, blind as bats and lost.

I look at my watch. We have been airborne nearly an hour now. The chopper doesn't have floats, so if it runs out of gas and goes down we will all be in the water. We have life vests but I remember how, in World War II, Spitfire pilots were afraid of their engines dying over the North Sea because a person could last only a few minutes in that cold water before freezing to death. Here the water temperature is actually below zero. I begin to panic and try to tell the pilot to listen to the copilot—maybe he *has* seen the ship—but they aren't listening to me, and couldn't understand me anyhow.

Suddenly there is a break in the fog; it lifts as if someone has picked up a blanket, and there is the ship. Over there to the left.

Thirty-three years after Andrée disappeared. The summer of 1930. The Norwegian whaler *Bratvaag* is skirting White Island just above the 80th parallel, one of the most inhospitable pieces of real estate on the surface of the earth. Covered in ice almost permanently, it reveals its surface of stony rocks only at the height of unusually warm summers. This was one of those days, and as the *Bratvaag* rounded the southwestern tip of the island they spotted walrus, dropped anchor and prepared a hunting party.

Once ashore two men went inland to search for fresh water. They found a running stream and, heading up it toward its source, soon ran into deep snowbanks. Pushing their way around them but keeping to the widening stream, they turned past a crook of the water and came on a small boat half buried in the snow. On its prow they could read the name: *Andrees polarexp. 1896.*

They fetched the rest of the crew, who approached the boat reverently and explored the site. "It was with very strange emotions that we stood upon the shore where, thirty years ago, the brave Andrée and his companions had reached the end of their last journey. In deep silence we approached the spot where they had camped. There lay their boat, half buried in snow, its stern pointing inland. Beside it lay a sledge—and beyond it, under a wall of rock, Andrée himself. The Lapp moccasins on his feet were much worn, but otherwise his clothing was in good condition. Beside him lay a gun and a primus stove. There was still paraffin in the tank, and when we pumped, a fine jet spouted from the burner."

What had happened? Everything up till the end was clear, for Andrée had not only kept a comprehensive diary, but had also taken pictures; his was the first polar exploration to include a camera with its equipment.

Without the drag ropes steering had been impossible, and they had sailed at the mercy of the wind. They were carried into fog, and within twenty-four hours the *Eagle* had become overladen with moisture condensing on its surface. The balloon bounced against the ice, rose again, bounced again as they threw overboard all their ballast, finally rose and headed not north but west with the changing wind.

"Is it not strange to be floating here above the Polar Sea," Andrée wrote in his diary. "To be the first to have floated here in a balloon? Shall we be thought mad? . . ."

Once again the balloon sank to the ice, and this time it stayed there for thirteen hours. Finally a strong wind lifted it off again for a short while, then it sank again and began a furious sequence of hard knocks against the ice, rising into the air for a hundred yards or so and then banging down again. Finally, three days after they left Spitsbergen, they came down for good.

They were nearly at the 83rd parallel, lost in the snow and fog, drenched with freezing rain, stumbling through rotten ice which broke beneath their feet. They endured every privation except hunger, for bears were everywhere and they had powerful rifles. "We have wandering butcher shops all around us," Andrée wrote in his diary.

Ironically, it was the butcher shops that killed him. But not with their teeth and claws; it was a more insidious death. When the bodies of Andrée and his companions were found on White Island they were well-fed, so they hadn't starved to death. Nor had they frozen: their tent was in reasonably good condition, and their stove still had fuel. They had simply lain down and died.

Why? The thirty-year mystery of their disappearance was now replaced by a greater mystery. What had killed them? The first suggestion was carbon monoxide poisoning from their primus stove, but I don't think this is reasonable. A scientist like Andrée, who had filled his balloon by generating hydrogen gas from the chemical reaction of iron with sulfuric acid, would surely have known about the dangers of incomplete combustion and carbon monoxide. Moreover, his two companions were another scientist and an engineer; it doesn't seem possible that not one of the three of them would have thought about the dangers of carbon monoxide.

Furthermore, that scenario would necessitate all three dying simultaneously; yet Nils Strindberg's body was buried, so he had died first. Finally, the stove would have had to be in operation when the other two died; yet when the bodies were discovered the stove was still full of paraffin, which meant it had been turned off rather than being allowed to burn till it was empty.

So they didn't freeze, they didn't starve and they weren't killed by polar bears. They were killed, it turned out, by a creature much smaller than a bear.

Some twenty years later a Danish doctor named Tryde, reading the Andrée diary, noted a growing litany of complaints: "fever, cramps, swollen arms and legs, exhausting diarrhea, swelling of the eyelids leading nearly to blindness, gastrointestinal pain, and unaccountable sweating." Tryde diagnosed trichinosis.

A man dedicated to science almost to the point of mania, Andrée must have been familiar with the chemistry of carbon monoxide, but the biology of trichinosis may have been another matter. At the time it was not known or even suspected that polar bears might harbor the parasite; indeed, Andrée must have known that others before him had eaten polar bears and lived to tell of it. The American explorer whose adventures opened this book, Dr. Elisha Kent Kane, had written in 1855: "When I was out in the *Advance,* with Captain De Haven, I satisfied myself that it was a vulgar prejudice to regard the liver of the bear as poisonous. I ate of it freely myself, and succeeded in making it a favorite dish with the mess."

Not all bears are infected, but Dr. Tryde showed that Andrée's bears were. He went to the Andrée Museum in Sweden, was allowed to examine in microscopic thinsection specimens from two polar bears whose meat was found in Andrée's last camp, and found the unmistakable signs of trichinosis infection.

From the *Encyclopaedia Britannica:* "Trichinosis, a disease in man and other animals, is caused by infection by the parasite *Trichina,* obtained from the eating of incompletely cooked animal flesh. The symptoms are occasioned by the presence of the free parasites in the intestine, by the development of young trichinae from the eggs, and most of all by the migration of the parasites from the intestinal canal to the muscles. This cycle occupies from four to six weeks. The final cycles, occupying three to six months, may end fatally, the symptoms being nausea, failure of appetite, diarrhoea and fever; when the migration to the muscles begins there is more fever, stiffness, pain and swelling in the limbs, swelling of the eyelids, continued exhausting diarrhoea, perspiration, and finally delirium and death."

Andrée died three months after shooting his first bear.

* * *

This afternoon we land at Cape Norway on Jackson Island. This is the place Nansen and Johansen wintered before heading south to Cape Flora and running into Jackson. As far as I know, no one has been here since then.

We land by helicopter, since once again the shore is totally blocked by pack ice. The site of Nansen's camp is on a gently sloping rise from the sea, changing into a steep cliff not many yards back. It would be a magnificent place for a summer home: standing here one looks out onto a gentle harbor lined with snow, beyond it a clear sea. The island curls around in a U-shape, shielding the spot from the rest of the world. The cliffs behind are full of thick-billed murres at this time of year, and among the tumbled rocks are colonies of dovekies. Every once in a while a great mass of dovekies rises at once, as if on command from an unseen conductor; the birds whirl around and around in a great circle, singing at the top of their lungs. Then, without warning, the great mass collapses into hundreds of individual birds diving toward the ground, pulling up at the last moment and fluttering back to their nests hidden in the rocks. All that the site needs is a supermarket around the bend of the cliffs. But of course the nearest supermarket is a thousand miles away in Murmansk, and its shelves are empty.

Nansen's hut is remarkably well preserved. From reading about his adventure one is not prepared for the extremely small size of the living quarters. It is a hole less than ten feet long, five or six feet wide, dug a couple of feet into the ground. Most of the walls have crumbled—they were simply stacked-up stones, with dirt and grass to keep out the wind—but the walrus skin roof is still there, torn and partly shredded. It is lying on the ground, since the main beam has broken. The beam, a piece of driftwood they had found farther down the beach according to Nansen's diary, is truly gigantic; I can't imagine it being moved and set into place by only two men, especially men who had been half-starved for two years. Nansen really must have been a giant, or else desperate.

For some reason a strain of music comes into my mind, a line of Stephen Sondheim's: "There are heroes in the world . . . Princes, and heroes in the world . . ."

JULY 31

---‖‖‖---

After breakfast at 8:30 I go out for a stroll around the ship. As I stand for a moment on the open bow deck facing forward, face into the wind, I hear a solitary voice and a soft whirring, sounds which have become a normal accompaniment to this cruise. Andrée's was the first polar expedition to carry a camera along; ours is the first to carry camcorders, and the sound of their operation is nearly constant in these silent seas. It is a two-part syncopation: the soft whirring of the mechanism is low, and floating above it is the voice of the operator, talking into the microphone and describing what he is seeing.

As I stand there Frank Seeley heaves into view around the superstructure, camcorder to his eye, turning slowly as he pans around the horizon. Frank and his brother Harold are heavy, jolly Australians in their early and late fifties, the life of the party on board. They are hard-working men who take vacations every few years together, leaving their families behind while they see the world. Now Frank pans and catches me in his lens. "And this is my good friend David Fisher," he recites in what is almost a travesty of an Australian outback accent, "standing on the deck in the cold northern wastes."

"Are you talking to your thing or to yourself?" I ask him.

"To my thing," he replies, not taking his eye from the lens or his finger from the trigger.

"That's funny. I've known men who played with their thing, but never anyone who actually *talked* to it."

He laughs so hard that he nearly drops his thing overboard. He and Harold are always laughing. I envy them.

The sun is aft off the port side. This means that we can't be moving north, but west. I go up to the bridge and, sure enough, we're on a heading of 280°. We're now at 80°30′ North latitude; when I went to sleep last night we were at 81°. Our longitude is 42°42′.

By midmorning we turn back to a heading directly north; evidently we headed west to avoid a thick concentration of ice ahead, reported by the helicopter. Nevertheless, by early afternoon we begin crashing through serious ice.

I spend the day talking to several of the guests. They are a pleasant but curious lot. Most of them know each other from previous cruises. It turns out that there is a whole travel industry, small compared to those that offer the usual cruises to Bermuda, the Bahamas or Hawaii, but still larger than I had ever expected, specializing in trips to out-of-the-way places, offering a soupçon of excitement along with the vol-au-vent and beef Wellington as they go sailing up the Amazon, to China and Tibet, to Antarctica, to the festival in Rio, to Turkey, Iran and the jungles of Borneo.

Mrs. Thelma Lewis of San Diego, for example, is a charming woman who has been to the high plateau of Tibet to look for the black-necked crane. Today Frank Stanton, a biological consultant and fellow at Sea World, gives a lecture about his travels in Antarctica. He tells us that the orange-billed dovecote emits a smell like citrus, and shows a slide of himself crawling around on a cold rock island among the guano sniffing for the smell of oranges so he can find a nest.

In this sense the people are interesting, with fascinating

stories to tell. But the stories quickly pale, because they are all basically the same: a trip to nowhere, where no one one knows has ever been before, with the thrill of danger in the air, but organized by a cruise or expedition leader, with colorful tags for the baggage so it won't get lost at Kennedy or Heathrow, and with everyone carefully protected from the outside world they voyage through. Aside from these trips the people seem to have no interest in life; they talk about nothing else. This is the summer of 1991, but not one person has uttered a single word about the outside world. It's as if we don't dwell in the same universe. Nothing about Iraq or the Soviet Union; the only reference to the rest of society has been the standard chant of the rich: how California is being ruined by the influx of Mexicans and Florida by the Cubans and New York by—well, New Yorkers do a good job of ruining it all by themselves, don't they? Not a word about the Supreme Court or even the Atlanta Braves; no one in my hearing has ever asked anyone else if they know what's happening out there. Weird people. All they ever talk about are their other expeditions; they remind me of tennis nuts in Miami.

At 9:20 P.M. we're at 82°29′ N and 37°43′ W, on a heading of 5° at ten knots through heavy ice, but still with occasional large patches of clear water.

Dinner tonight is vol-au-vent *and* beef Wellington.

The first serious thought about reaching the North Pole came with observations made at this latitude. In 1773 Britain's Royal Society had suggested that China could be reached by traveling straight across the pole. The navy responded by sending captains Constantine Phipps and Skeffington Lutwidge out to take a look. They sailed north by northeast and passed Spitsbergen, but ran into pack ice shortly above 80° N. Trapped in the ice, they abandoned their ships and prepared to camp out on the ice until—well, until they died, one supposes. But somehow the ice never crushed their ships, and in the spring it released them and they sailed home. Among the crew, incidentally, was a young coxswain by the name of Horatio Nelson, and among the observations that Lutwidge made while marooned on the ice was that the ice to the north, examined through his telescope, seemed "smooth and unbroken, bounded only by the horizon. . . . A coach and four could have driven unimpeded to the pole."

This sounds too good to be true, and of course it was, but it encouraged the idea of simply skiing or sledding up the face of the "smooth and unbroken" ice to the North Pole, and then sliding down the opposite side to the riches of Cathay.

It's funny. We human beings, in public life as in private, in groups as well as in individuals, seem to have an innate need to justify what we really want to do just for the sake of doing it. When we went to the moon in the 1960s, John Kennedy pretended that it was a race to beat the Russians, necessary because of the military value of establishing bases there. The scientific community was embarrassed by the idea of mobilizing all its resources for a military end, and so it waffled until a University of Chicago geochemist, Harold Urey, came up with the idea that the moon was a primordial body left over from the earliest days of the creation of the solar system. Going there and bringing back pieces of the moon for study, he told us, would enable us to decipher the riddle of creation. The moon was to be the Rosetta Stone of space exploration. Then when we sent our rockets to Mars in the '70s we decided it was because we wanted to search for life there.

Well, we've been to the moon and back again and we still don't know any more about the creation of the solar system than we did before. Moon rocks turned out to be interesting, but they were created half a billion years too late to tell us anything about the creation of our planets. And we've been to Mars and have tested the soil there for signs of life

without success, but we haven't been able to say defini-
tively that there isn't any life there, either.

None of this really matters. The important thing about
going to the moon and Mars was not the reasons we gave
ourselves, but simply the fact that we went there. We want
to do things because we want to do them, and all the high-
blown moral justifications are only stuff and nonsense. The
real reason is fun and games.

Of course, getting to the North Pole isn't fun in the usual
sense. (Apsley Cherry-Garrard, who served with Scott at
the South Pole, explained it best: "Polar exploration is the
cleanest and most isolated way of having a bad time which
has ever been devised.") In 1827, when William Edward
Parry tried to follow the Phipps-Lutwidge suggestion of
driving a coach and four to the pole, he ran into a few
problems.

Parry was an interesting man. The *Arctic Navy List* describes him: "Acted Sir Anthony Absolute in *The Rivals*.
Discovered the passage into the Polar Sea." On one of his
early voyages he discovered the polar Eskimos, who until
that time had thought themselves to be the only people on
earth. He and Sir John Ross had led an expedition northward and were at the very top of Canada, crossing a part of
the frozen Arctic Ocean which they named Melville Bay,
when they saw in the distance what appeared to be black
dots on the white ice. Parry stared at them through his
telescope, trying to make them out. They couldn't be rocks,
for there was no solid land there, and as he watched, he
saw them move. They couldn't be seals, for there was no
open water there. As he watched they came closer, and to
his amazement he saw that they were people, dogs and
sledges.

It's easy to understand Parry's astonishment, seeing a
horde of people materialize from a region so frozen and
barren of all signs of life. But the amazement of the Es-

kimos was even greater. As far back as their tribal memory reached, there was no hint of any other people in the world. Where had these strangers come from? they wondered. As they came together on the ice they floundered for words, and finally one of them made himself understood, asking this question.

"From the south," Parry answered, gesturing off in that direction.

The Eskimos laughed, and when they saw that he was serious they huddled together to confer. Then their leader came back, shaking his head. "That is impossible," he said. Why? Well, it was obvious. No one could live down there. To the south of where the Eskimos had lived all their lives there was nothing but shifting, drifting ice. They could see it for themselves. Every summer when the ice packs began to break up, the currents pulled the ice shoals southward and they disappeared over the horizon. "All of our ice goes off in that direction," the Eskimos said. "It must be filled up with ice by now!"

In his elder years Parry became one of the first naval men in England to argue in favor of that new development, the screw propeller, instead of the old reliable paddle wheel. According to contemporary descriptions he had a serene confidence in himself, and took exemplary care of his men. In several Arctic voyages he kept them healthy in body and mind, cooking for them soups made from herbs and plants he grew himself in his cramped quarters, organizing plays, ship's newsletters and reading classes to get them through the long winters. He was a bit paternal by today's standards—"All sailors are somewhat like children, and require constant looking after," he wrote—but he kept his men healthy, alert and alive during the long Arctic winters.

Parry's 1827 voyage was not successful in getting much nearer to the pole. By other standards, however, it was one of the most successful polar voyages in history, for not a single man was lost. Further, he learned three lessons which have proved invaluable to later explorers.

One, never trust the Arctic. The "smooth and unbroken" ice of Phipps and Lutwidge didn't exist. Instead Parry found broken terrain, pressure ridges, hummocks and lakes, for it rained incessantly during the day when the temperatures rose above freezing. The water accumulated in freshwater pools, filling shallow indentures in the ice never quite deep enough to enable them to use the boats they dragged along, so that they had to slosh through knee- and thigh-high water for hundreds of yards at a stretch. The rain did worse: it melted the ice, which refroze along sharp ridges christened "razor-ice" by his men, sharp enough to slice right through their boots and slit their flesh to ribbons. It was bad enough for their feet, partly shielded by their boots, but when they fell—and they often did as they laboriously dragged their loads across the ice, upward of 250 pounds per man—their gloves and coats were no protection at all, so they rose from the razor-ice dripping large red drops which froze behind them.

Secondly, Parry learned never to trust a clever idea. An admiral at the Admiralty had had the notion of taking along reindeer as pack animals. They were used to living in the Arctic, after all, and were as strong as horses. The problem turned out to be that they were dumber than horses and as stubborn as admirals, a deadly combination. At least they made good food.

Thirdly, in the Arctic you can't even trust the ground you walk on. On the 22nd of July, 1827, Parry noted in his diary a puzzling fact which he had begun to notice a few days before and could no longer ignore: "According to celestial observations [of latitude] we have made four miles to the Northward since yesterday's observation, yet we have travelled at least ten miles by direct observation." He was the first to discover what would later defeat Nansen and (though he would never admit it) Peary: the ice they crossed was drifting southward even as they walked northward. Pack ice freezes to a thickness of fifteen or twenty feet, and one can walk on it as solidly as if it were a granite mountain. But it is not embedded in the earth, it is only floating on water, and where the water drifts the ice must surely follow. To those weary men dragging their loads across seemingly solid ground, its drift is impossible to fathom, but drift it does, driven by the random winds above and the unknown currents below.

Four days later, when Parry realized that they had gained only one mile northward despite ten hours marching every day, he gave up and turned for home. He had reached a farthest north latitude of 82°45′ N, a mark that would remain for half a century.

After the beef Wellington I wandered up to the bridge. The sun no longer set at all, but wandered around the horizon in a great circle. The inertial navigation guidance system said we were at 82°47′ N.

AUGUST 1

‑‑‑‑‑‑‑‑‑‑‑‑ ⑾⎮⎮⑾ ‑‑‑‑‑‑‑‑‑‑‑‑

We passed through 83° N last night while I slept, snuggled under the heaviest quilt I have ever seen. My roommate, John Tolson, and I keep the porthole open day and night now, and the cold winds compensate for the heat of the radiator. Luckily John is one of those Englishmen who enjoys a fresh cold breeze at night. He is also an experienced polar explorer. He began his travels with the Royal Merchant Navy as a navigating apprentice, and later joined the British Antarctic Survey where he began producing home movies. Ten years ago he went with an expedition to the South Pole as official cameraman, and when he returned he thought he had the pole out of his system: he got married and settled down with a local construction firm. He lasted several years there, until he was asked to join another polar expedition as cameraman, and off he went again. He hasn't stopped since. He's filming this voyage as part of a BBC series called *Classic Adventures*. He's a lovely man whom I've never heard say no, whether he's asked to dangle out of the door of a helicopter to take a shot of the *Soyuz* breaking through ice, or to have another beer at the bar, or to leave the porthole open all night for the winds to come in, even though his bunk is directly beneath it.

These winds are truly cold. In the morning when I leave John with his head under the quilt and go out for a breath of air I put on underwear, shirt and pants, a sweater, a thermal vest and the incredibly thick red parka they gave us for the trip. I wear gloves and a hat, pull the parka's hood up over the hat, button it across my mouth, and I'm warm enough until I round the stern of the ship and come into contact with the wind. Then my eyes water, my nose runs and I soon turn and head back the other way.

On the lee side, sheltered from the wind, I lean over the railing and watch the ship crashing through pack ice which must be at least ten feet thick. It splits in gigantic sheets which are thrust down by the weight of the ship; they tip up and over in spectacular slow motion, and come crashing down on their fellows as we pass, spraying great geysers of water and snow fifty feet in the air. Occasionally a minnow is ejected along with the water; it lands on the ice, squirming and flopping around frantically in an effort to find its way back to the water as we plow on and leave it behind.

At breakfast I sit with Sue Ann and Ralph Teller, and George Acklins and his friend Steve. George is a middle-aged Canadian with a head of thick white hair and a full gray beard, who is a Buddhist priest. His friend is, I suppose, an acolyte. George is a friendly giant of a man who lumbers around softly, exuding an aura of gentleness and calm under all circumstances—such as right now, when the ship is crashing heavily and jerkily through the ice. He lifts a spoon of cold cereal to his mouth, but just as it reaches the vicinity of his lips and he leans forward to suck it in the ship bangs, we all lurch and the spoon jerks away and spills the soggy mess on his lap. He smiles and waits for the motion to subside, then takes another spoonful, while around us we hear the anguished cries of discomfited tourists announcing to their companions that this is not what they paid for and can't the captain do something about it? I catch George's eye as one particularly loud complaint reaches us, and he smiles gently: he loves us all.

But then there is the matter of the tables. There are no assigned seats, and we all sit anywhere, meeting new people at every meal. But George and his friend always sit at the same table; in fact they take the same seats at the same table for every meal. Does this indicate a lack of security? Self-consciousness? An anal fixation that does not jibe with the complacency peculiar to one who has no fear of death, for it is merely the gateway to another life, who has no great expectations of this life nor any anxiety about it, for it is merely one stage of a long road?

As we finish breakfast an announcement comes over the loudspeaker that we are plowing through ice so thick that it can easily support us, and we are going to find a smooth place to stop and disembark. There will be a party on the ice; Bloody Marys will be served in an attempt to ward off scurvy.

Everyone laughs, but I notice that several people on their way out of the dining room, reminded of the scourge of the Arctic, nervously pour themselves a quick extra glass of orange juice from the sideboard and drink it down.

Scurvy. The name conjures up an image of debilitating filth, poverty and degradation, of sailors lying huddled in fetid quarters below deck, shivering and shaking in airless squalor, discomfort and lonely misery. The truth is much worse; it is a disease not only debilitating but deadly. It was conquered not once but twice, which is not as unusual as it sounds, particularly with armies and navies.

Take cholera, for example. In 1896 the British army was fighting what Winston Churchill called "The River War," moving up the Nile to retake the Sudan. In June of that year an epidemic of cholera struck the troops. "To all, the time was one of terror . . . Death moved continually about the ranks; a silent, unnoticed, almost ignominious summons, scarcely less sudden and far more painful than the bullet or the sword-cut . . . To find the servant dead in the camp kitchen; to catch a hurried glimpse of blanketed shapes hustled quickly to the desert on a stretcher; to hold the lantern over the grave into which a friend or comrade was hastily lowered . . ."

A thousand soldiers died needlessly, for cholera had been conquered almost half a century earlier in, of all places, England. In 1850 John Snow showed that the disease was spread by drinking contaminated water; he stopped an epidemic in its tracks simply by removing the pump handle of a well that was producing polluted water. In 1865 Sir John Simon demonstrated that cholera could be defeated by simple and inexpensive sanitary means, and that the old policy of quarantine was both unnecessary and useless; the disease was infectious but not contagious. In 1883 Robert Koch discovered the causative agent, the bacterium *Vibrio cholera*, and after a twenty-five-year series of international conferences arguing the point, England finally won: in 1893 sanitation replaced quarantine as a formal policy in Europe, signed off by—in addition to England—France, Germany, Austria, Belgium, Italy, Russia, Switzerland, Luxembourg, Montenegro and the Netherlands.

So what did the British army do when cholera struck on the Nile three years later? They ignored sanitation and instituted the old policy of strict quarantine. They "hustled the sick quickly to the desert on a stretcher, and hastily lowered the dead into their graves . . . ," allowing the filth of the latrines to flow uninterruptedly through the camp, and the cholera with it. They did this even though the quarantine ruined their preparations for battle: "The necessity of enforcing quarantine hampered movement up and down the line of communications . . ."

They did this because the simple knowledge of how to combat cholera had not penetrated in fifty years from Harley Street to Sandhurst; nor had the victory over scurvy penetrated from their own ships through the thick walls of the Admiralty. The disease was a terrible one for sailors. The legend of the Flying Dutchman probably originated with stories, all too true, of more than one galleon found drifting aimlessly on the seas which, when boarded, carried a crew of dead men: all killed by scurvy, every last one of them.

No one knew what caused it—vitamins had not yet been discovered—until in 1747 a Royal Navy surgeon named James Lind carried out a perfectly controlled experiment on human guinea pigs. He took twelve scurvy victims on his ship, the HMS *Salisbury,* and fed two of them a daily mug of cider, two of them a daily mug of seawater, two of them vinegar, and two of them an orange and a lemon every day. The last two lived and made a total recovery; the others died.

It took the Admiralty only fifty years to learn of this experiment, but when they finally did they assigned a daily ration of lemon juice to their sailors and the disease disappeared. Then they forgot their lesson . . .

It is an insidious disease, for the onset is marked by symptoms resembling fatigue and boredom, those twin accompaniments of Arctic exploration, so it was often misdiagnosed as something to be cured by "cheerful spirits"—or if that didn't work, by the lash. The first symptom is gloom, accompanied by weariness. The sailor afflicted becomes irritable and quarrelsome. That is nothing new to people locked in a frozen ship for months on end. Every chore becomes difficult and the victim just wants to be left alone. If startled so that he jumps up, he might become dizzy, light-headed. Then come the pains, at first in the joints so that they seem to be rheumatic.

At this stage the sufferer would probably be diagnosed as having cabin fever, or its Arctic equivalent. He would be told to cheer up, get the lead out, stop complaining, get some rest, have a cup of tea and shut the bloody hell up. As the disease progresses the gums begin to swell and become inflamed, but still the disease would not be recognized. As late as 1901, on Scott's expedition to the South Pole, the surgeon on board wrote: "The gums of many are red and swollen, but it is the redness and swelling of slight inflammation rather than scurvy, and to my mind is to be attributed to clay pipes, strong tobacco, coarse feeding, neglect of the tooth brush and the constant use of foul language."

But soon the pain gets worse, the joints begin to swell, and the gums begin to bleed and soften "to the consistency of cheese. A man picking his teeth with a wooden toothpick will likely bring out a piece of gum, thinking it a chunk of food. The teeth grow so loose that the patient, feeling of them to see how they are, may pull one out without quite realizing he is doing it. . . . The smaller blood vessels break under the skin . . . there is bleeding from the nose and throat. Death . . . comes from internal hemorrhage."

The *Encyclopaedia Britannica* reports: "The regulated administration of lime juice in the British navy, which was begun in 1795, had the effect of virtually extinguishing scurvy in the service." This is not quite true—they administered lemon juice but called it "lime"—but it did work, at least for a while. To such an extent had it been eliminated, in fact, that when a great expedition to discover the North Pole was set in motion in England nearly a hundred years later, Sir Clements Markham, secretary of the Royal Geographical Society, wrote: "It is to the advanced state of knowledge in naval hygiene; to the attention paid to the cleanliness, warmth and ventilation of the ships, to the good quality of provisions, and especially to the preservation of cheerfulness among the crews, that this immunity from scurvy is due and so rare has it become that the naval surgeons who possess any knowledge of this disease, derived from actual observation . . . may be counted upon one's fingers."

The immunity enjoyed during those past hundred years, however, was not due to "the cleanliness, warmth and ventilation of the ships," and certainly not to "cheerfulness among the crews," but to the administration of lemon juice and its hidden vitamin C. That vitamin is also present to a large degree in fresh meat, but on this voyage, as on all ocean-going voyages of that century, the meat was salted and stored, and salt meat is incapable of keeping its vitamin C. Actually, all meat shares this problem, and we share it too, for we are nothing but living meat. We too cannot keep vitamin C in our bodies; it breaks down into simpler compounds and loses its efficacy, which is why we must keep replacing it with fresh intakes. The planners of the 1875 British expedition to the North Pole knew that salt meat was no antiscorbutic, but figured the loss would be made up by fresh meat obtained by hunting parties during the voyage.

Of course there was always the lemon juice. For some reason lost in history, the British navy called it "lime juice," and its constant inclusion among provisions is what gave the British the nickname "Limeys." The standard supply of juice came from Mediterranean lemons, but in preparing the supplies for this voyage someone in the Admiralty's office of the budget came up with a brilliant idea: that year Caribbean limes could be bought for less than Mediterranean lemons, and since the tradition had always been for "lime juice" anyhow, what harm could be done?

Well, a good deal, actually, illustrating the shallowness of Shakespeare's comment, "What's in a name? That which we call a rose by any other name would smell as sweet . . ." Lime juice, it turns out, may smell as sweet but has only about half the vitamin C of lemon juice. The combination of this substitution with the unforeseen lack of success by the hunting parties in obtaining fresh meat was to prove disastrous to the 1875 expedition.

Scurvy had been absent for so long that the tradition of "cleanliness, warmth and ventilation of the ships . . . and the preservation of cheerfulness among the crews," had become in the navy's mind the basis of their antiscorbutic action. And of course these in fact work wonders, as long as a daily ration of lemon juice is included. But without the lemon juice all the cleanliness and cheerfulness in the world aren't worth a damn.

Of particular importance was the lack of vitamin C in the sledging parties which were to leave the ship at its highest latitude and proceed overland to the pole. Also of importance was the lack of experience among the men recruited. Although the commander, George Nares, was an experienced Arctic hand, no one else was; nor had the commanders of the sledging parties any experience at all in such work. They did have other qualifications: Albert Markham was a cousin of Sir Clements, and Pelham Aldrich was not only a water-colorist of some reputation but also had an uncle who had once sailed in the Arctic. Aside from this genetic experience the only advantage the expedition had was enthusiasm: the crew of 111 was chosen from thousands of volunteers.

The entire country was enthusiastic. When the full tragedy of the Franklin expedition had been reported in the popular press, a national revulsion had ensued. Why was it so important to go to the pole? What would be accomplished that was worth the loss of 129 lives? It was similar to the revulsion that followed our loss of the Vietnam war: suddenly everyone was asking what business a civilized nation had in such an inhospitable part of the world.

But time is a great molder of memories, and by 1875 England was once again thinking that the oceans of the world were her natural province. Once again she believed that it was unthinkable that any ocean, even one crowned with impassable snow and ice, should forbid entrance to her ships.

This patriotism was elevated by the sudden thrustings of a new force. By the last quarter of the nineteenth century, science had made her entrance on the world scene, and there was nothing she could not do, no obstacle she could not conquer. Victorian England, borne upward and onward by the stubborn pride of her navy and the brilliant force of her scientific intellect, could conquer poverty and despair, the far-off continents of Africa and India, and all the scheming powers of Europe; could dominate the trade of the world; could harness electricity and turn her nights to day; could conquer the pox and the plague; could celebrate in her individual citizens the wonder and glory of heaven on earth. Could she do all this and not have the crown of the North? Tut! Were it further off, she'd pluck it down!

On May 19, 1875, the coal-powered, steam-driven sloop *Alert* and the whaler *Discovery*, both newly outfitted and refurbished with the newest discoveries of maritime science—including not only the replacement of sails with coal-driven steam power but doubly strengthened hulls to withstand any ice pressure, insulation to keep out the cold, and that newest and most controversial invention, the screw propeller—left Portsmouth harbor to the sound of their own steam whistles, an army band, the cheers of a crowd estimated at more than 100,000 and the sedate blessings of Queen Victoria. One year later they steamed into the polar sea and anchored at the highest latitude ever reached by a ship, 82°30′ N. As the summer ended the men settled in for the winter, and the sledging parties began their explorations.

Commander George Nares's experience in previous Arctic sledging had been with the British custom of hauling the sledges with manpower; teams of British navvies and officers slung ropes over their shoulders or around their waists and dragged the sledges along. Other nationalities had learned to use dogs for this purpose, copying the practice from the native Eskimos. Always eager to learn new tricks, the British had taken along dogs for this purpose. But the dogs were not the pleasant creatures we know in our temperate climes; they were more savage than domesticated, more wolves than dogs. The American explorer Elisha Kent Kane had written in 1853: "More bother with these wretched dogs! Worse than a street of Constantinople emptied upon our decks; the unruly, thieving, wild-beast pack! Not a bear's paw, or an Esquimaux cranium, or basket of mosses, or any specimen whatever, can leave your hands for a moment without their making a rush at it, and, after a yelping scramble, swallowing it at a gulp. I have seen them attempt a whole feather bed . . ."

Danish explorers had learned the Eskimo way with dogs, and sang their praises, but the Brits were not, by their ingrained natures, able to follow the Danes' advice on how to get the dogs to do their work. "Don't feed them more than twice a week," the advice had been. "And if they show any sign of insubordination, knock them down with a marlinspike. If they attempt to come near you, kick them; it is the only way to prevent them from biting you."

Can you imagine the typical Englishman purposely starving his dog? Or knocking him down with a marlinspike? He would rather die . . . and so he did.

The crew spoiled the dogs on the voyage out, feeding them with scraps from their own food as they would have at home, holding them in their laps and petting them, talking to them and playing with them, so that when the time came to harness them and expect them to work the dogs simply looked back over their shoulders and laughed, wondering what kind of new game this was. With the men sitting on the sledges along with the provisions and the dogs laughing in their harnesses, the command finally went out to use the whips, and when finally one or two men were found who were willing to do so, they were found to have had no experience. The whips were not easy to handle; their slashing tips hit more men on the sledges than dogs in the harnesses, and the idea was quickly dropped. The dogs were unharnessed and returned to their snug quarters on board while the men took their place in the traces.

The load they had to pull was enormous, because of necessity combined with stubborn stupidity. They hoped to find game along the way, and so carried guns and ammunition, but they also had to carry food in case there was no game. They had to carry their housing too, for they could not camp out in the open in temperatures which routinely dropped to 30 or 40 degrees below zero and in the dead of winter hit 73 degrees below.

This was to be a source of trouble, for though previous explorers had learned from the Eskimo that a snow house large enough to hold half a dozen people could be constructed in less than an hour, the British would not accept this lesson. Instead they carried along their own canvas tents and poles. During the night the canvas would catch the expelled breaths of the men inside, moisture would condense and freeze, and by morning the weight of the tent would double. Soon the weight load rose to more than two hundred pounds per man, to be pulled over ridges and hummocks and through snow in which they sank to their waists. The men splashed through knee-deep pools of water which then froze to their legs; they labored, struggled, pulled and sweated profusely, and the sweat froze their clothing so that they became solid suits of armor which clinked, cracked and cut into their flesh, becoming heavier and heavier with every step.

The men also became weaker and weaker with every step, as the debilitating symptoms of unsuspected scurvy invaded their bodies. Fatigue was the first symptom, and was greeted with scorn by those as yet unaffected: *malingerer*, they thought of the man who first complained, *shirker, weakling.* Then they saw the complaint spreading, and one by one they succumbed.

On board ship they had been well enough. The daily ration of lime juice had kept the scurvy at bay, though just barely. But now that they were out on the snow this daily ration had stopped, for they could not carry lime juice with them; it would freeze and break open the containers. Not to worry, they had been told by the naval medical officers at home, scurvy was a thing of the past. ("So rare has it become that the naval surgeons who possess any knowledge of this disease, derived from actual observation, may be counted upon one's fingers.")

True enough, but all this meant was that when the symptoms appeared there was no one to diagnose them. The first signs had actually been seen aboard ship, but had been diagnosed as a mild case of fatigue, probably due to insufficient "cleanliness and cheerfulness" among those affected, and so was judged a matter for further discipline rather than medication.

Now, however, the men were out on the ice and their lime juice was back on ship. The hunting parties found no game, and the expedition was reduced to eating salt meat and biscuits; not only were these rations devoid of vitamin C, but they were not nutritious enough to support life— particularly not the energetic life of hauling two hundred pounds of frozen luggage across icy boulders.

The first seaman reported pains in his legs. Another chimed in a day later, and then another. The commander of the sledging party, Albert Markham, made light of this. Muscular aches and pains were to be expected after months of enforced inactivity aboard ship, followed by the strenuous exercise of sledge hauling. "All of us were very tired," he wrote in his diary. No one suspected scurvy.

They could have learned from previous expeditions. Elisha Kent Kane, the American who had written of his troubles with dogs, had also told of problems with Arctic rats, and of how he ultimately turned them to his use in combating the plague. He began by excoriating the ugly monsters: "If I was asked what, after darkness and cold and scurvy, are the three besetting curses of our Arctic sojourn, I should say, RATS, RATS, RATS. A mother-rat bit my finger to the bone last Friday, as I was intruding my hand into a bearskin mitten which she had chosen as a homestead for her little family. I withdrew it of course with instinctive courtesy; but among them they carried off the mitten before I could suck the finger.

"Last week, I sent down Rhina, the most intelligent dog of our whole pack, to bivouac in their citadel forward: I thought she might at least be able to defend herself against them, for she had distinguished herself in the bear-hunt. She slept very well for a couple of hours on a bed she had chosen for herself on top of some iron spikes. But the rats could not or would not forego the horny skin about her paws; and they gnawed her feet and nails until we drew her up yelping and vanquished . . .

"We have moved every thing movable out upon the ice, and, besides our dividing moss wall between our sanctum and the forecastle, we have built up a rude barrier of iron sheathing to prevent these abominable rats from gnawing through. It is all in vain. They are everywhere already, under the stove, in the steward's lockers, in our cushions, about our beds . . ."

Kane tried to get rid of them: "Some days ago, we made a brave effort to smoke them out with the vilest imaginable compound of vapors—brimstone, burnt leather, and arsenic—and spent a cold night in a deck-bivouac to give the experiment fair play. But they survived the fumigation. We now determine to dose them with carbonic acid gas." But he had to give up when he nearly burned down his ship in the effort. Instead, he made use of them to combat the scurvy which he ranked as even a greater curse than the rats: his solution was to eat them.

"Before I pass from these intrepid and pertinacious visi-
tors, let me add that on the whole I am personally much
their debtor. . . . [They provide] another article of diet,
less inviting at first, but which I found more innocuous
[than bear meat] . . . The repugnance of my associates to
share with me the table luxury of such 'small deer' gave me
the frequent advantage of a fresh-meat soup, which contributed no doubt to my comparative immunity from
scurvy."

Kane wrote in detail about the scurvy which afflicted
those men whose repugnance kept them from the "small
deer": "December 2, Saturday.—Had to put Mr. McGary
and Riley under active treatment for scurvy. Gums retracted, ankles swollen, and bad lumbago. Mr. Wilson's
case . . . a still worse one. Morton's is a saddening one: I
cannot afford to lose him . . . His tendon Achilles has
been completely perforated, and the surface of the heel-
bone exposed. An operation in cold, darkness, and privation, would probably bring on locked-jaw. Brooks grows
discouraged: the poor fellow has scurvy in his stump, and
his leg is drawn up by the contraction of the flexors at the
knee-joint . . ."

But in 1875 the British were only a hundred years re-
moved from the nastiness of the American colonies' rebel-
lion, and they were not about to pay attention to an American's musings. So Markham and his men struggled on, past
the 83rd parallel, further north than any men had ever
managed to reach, until finally they skidded to a stop. They
weren't halted by the terrible Arctic terrain or by hunger.
The terrain was bad enough, but the ice in front of them
was no different than that which they had endured, and it
held promise of nothing worse to come. They were hungry,
of course, but their provisions were sufficient to last several
weeks longer. It was scurvy alone that stopped them. It
was the sight of his men bleeding not from wounds but
simply from blotched patches of skin that convinced Mark-

ham to call a halt and turn for home; it was the swollen and purple ankles, teeth falling out of bleeding gums, old scars turning into bloody ulcers, bellies bloated and discolored, the sight of men seemingly struck with leprosy, weary and falling in their tracks, rising again and leaving the snow red with their blood and yellow with their rotten skin, that convinced him.

The expedition held a party on the ice to celebrate its achievement. They had reached further north than any men before them, and if they were still hundreds of miles short of their goal, were sick and dying, and still had a horrific journey between them and the sanctuary of their ships, still they had done something no one else had ever done, and they partied gallantly and loudly.

Then they headed back for their ships, with two thirds of them barely able to shuffle along. They struggled to within thirty miles of the *Alert,* and then had to give up; they could move no further. One of the party, Lieutenant Alfred Parr, volunteered to go for help. Equipped with only a walking stick, he made the distance without stopping in less than one day, and immediately Nares led a rescue party back. By the time Markham's men were brought to their ship only two officers and one man were fit to walk by themselves.

Nor was the shipboard crew immune. The daily ration of lime juice provided less than 10 percent of the minimum requirement of vitamin C, and Nares saw clearly that they could not spend another year in the Arctic, as they had planned. "The Pole was impractical." Sadly he set sail for home, to a welcome of disapprobation and disappointment.

At first the newspapers lauded the hero, and Queen Victoria knighted him, but opinions soon turned ugly. The Admiralty wanted to know why he had turned for home short of his objective, with his crew intact (only four men had died) and with his ships still in one piece and loaded with provisions. When he reported that though his men were alive they were sickened near unto death with scurvy, the Admiralty bristled. Didn't he know that scurvy was a scourge of the past? All one had to do was keep the men clean and cheerful and free of profanity. When his answers were unsatisfactory they talked of a court-martial, but settled for simply not promoting him to admiral.

Parliament asked questions on the floor, the newspapers questioned the bravery and loyalty of modern spars, comparing them unfavorably to the men of Franklin's expedition who had given their all for God and country, and the public soon turned its interest to what was happening in the Crimea.

So ended Britain's strongest and last attempt to reach the North Pole with an official force of naval personnel.

Like the officers and men of Albert Markham's sledging party, we celebrated our achievement of passing the 83rd parallel by partying on the ice. Markham had brought with him a bottle of the finest Scotch whiskey, donated by the Dean of Dundee, to be opened and drunk at the point of their furthest north, whereas we had with us more than one bottle of whatever spirits one could possibly imagine.

There were a few other differences. Throughout the morning the ship would shudder to a stop, rock a few times, then back off and move forward again, searching for the right conditions: ice soft enough to allow the ship to slip into a snug berth, yet thick and strong enough to hold it tight and provide a firm "ground" for us to walk on. Finally, close to noon, the captain found the right spot and the engines stopped. The gangplank was lowered and several members of the crew disembarked. We stood on deck and watched them walking around, stomping on the ice, jumping up and down. Finally they waved back that it was safe.

Half a dozen of the crew took up positions in a circle of a

few hundred yards diameter surrounding the ship, armed with shotguns in case a polar bear should wander by. There was no land within hundreds of miles, but these beasts travel over ice and through icy waters without any hesitation. They are always hungry, and they eat whatever they want—seals, walrus, fish, *anything*. People would be a particular luxury. Nothing frightens them: though they walk through the valley of the shadow of death they fear no evil, for they are the toughest sons of bitches in the valley.

Elisha Kent Kane described the unexpected appearance of a bear which "intruded itself" on one of the sledging parties he had sent out. "It was about half an hour after midnight, and they were all sleeping away a long day's fatigue, when McGary either heard or felt, he could hardly tell which, something that was scratching at the snow immediately by his head. It waked him just enough to allow him to recognize a huge animal actively engaged in reconnoitering the circuit of the tent. His startled outcry aroused his companion-inmates, but without in any degree disturbing the unwelcome visitor; specially unwelcome at that time and place, for all the guns had been left on the sledge, a little distance off, and there was not so much as a walking-pole inside. There was of course something of natural confusion in the little council of war. The first impulse was to make a rush for the arms; but this was soon decided to be very doubtfully practicable, if at all, for the bear, having satisfied himself with his observations of the exterior, now presented himself at the tent opening. Sundry volleys of lucifer matches and some impromptu torches of newspaper were fired without alarming him, and, after a little while, he planted himself at the doorway and began making his supper upon the carcass of a seal which had been shot the day before.

"Tom Hickey was the first to bethink him of the military device of a sortie from the postern, and, cutting a hole with his knife, crawled out at the rear of the tent. Here he extricated a boat-hook, that formed one of the supporters of the ridge-pole, and made it an instrument of a right valorous attack. A blow well administered on the nose caused the animal to retreat for the moment a few paces beyond the sledge, and Tom, calculating his distance nicely, sprang forward, seized a rifle, and fell back in safety upon his comrades. In a few seconds more, Mr. Bonsall had sent a ball through and through the body of his enemy. I was assured that after this adventure the party adhered to the custom I had enjoined, of keeping at all times a watch and fire-arms inside the camping tent."

We on the *Soyuz* followed Kane's practice, and never ventured out on the ice without a protective circle of men with shotguns. (I found out later in the voyage that the man in charge of the guns was our KGB man, on board for security purposes. "Oh yeah," Mike, the tour leader, told me. "He's not here to spy on us, but for security. One of their considerations was, you guys are on a nuclear icebreaker with a hundred rich Americans and Europeans, so is there a probability of a terrorist attack? No, but is there a *possibility?* Sure. So he's here to keep an eye out to see that nothing develops.")

Large holes were dug in the ice, and buckets of Bloody Marys were inserted. Chunks of ice were broken off from extending crags and whittled into great stirring rods. Though the ice was formed by the freezing of salty ocean water, the process squeezes the salt out of the solid so that the ice itself is composed of fresh water. This is a process that was known but not well understood a hundred years ago. Simply by experience Arctic hands discovered that the ice surrounding them was not salty. It took further experience to convince them that nevertheless it was not suitable for eating; the problem was simply that it was too cold. Normally we can put a piece of ice in our mouths; it melts, and the water can safely be swallowed. But when the ice is at a temperature of 50 degrees below zero it chills the mouth to such an extent that a total lowering of one's body temperature follows, and to men already on the brink of freezing this can be deadly (as von Payer had noted). But in the summer of 1991 the temperatures at 83° N were hovering only slightly below freezing, and the ice posed no dangers. We broke off chunks as we wandered around and used them to stir our drinks, then licked them happily.

I had followed my wife's warning and dressed warmly: thermal underwear, a turtleneck shirt, a flannel shirt, insulated ski pants, a sweater, a down vest and the parka. On my feet were two pairs of woolen socks and a pair of $185 polar boots from L. L. Bean. On my head I wore a woolen balaclava beneath the parka hood, and on my hands I had thermal undergloves and snow-resistant mittens. I was warm enough.

After a couple of Bloody Marys I was too warm. I knew, as the uneducated navvies of 1875 did not, that alcohol doesn't really warm you: it dilates the blood vessels, affecting most easily the blood vessels lying close below the skin. This draws the blood outward toward the skin, and since that's where our temperature sensors are (which makes sense, since that's where we make contact with the external environment) the influx of blood into those near-surface blood vessels makes us feel warm. When you add to the equation the feeling of God's-in-his-heaven-all's-right-with-the-world induced by a slight tipple, it is easy to understand how the daily tot of rum Markham's sledgers carried along with them was thought to be more important than the lime juice they had left behind.

But we're not really any warmer drunk than sober. In fact we're colder inside, in the regions from which the blood has flowed, and so are more susceptible to freezing. Of course you couldn't tell this to Markham's men; nor could anyone tell it to us as we stood smiling happily on the ice. Slowly hats and gloves began to come off, parkas were unbuttoned, and life became gloriously warm and friendly.

I found myself in a group including Sue Ann and Ralph Teller and the two large and raucous Australian brothers, Frank and Harold. They were reflecting on the rapid rate of progress in our century, on how we were standing here in complete comfort atop ice that had required so much hardship and so many deaths to reach not many years ago. Somehow—I'm not sure exactly how, since the Bloody Marys were being quaffed generously—this led to how these Arctic regions were so vital in the cold war that was (though we didn't yet know it) collapsing even as we spoke, and from this to the progress that had been made not only in voyages of oceanic exploration but in the conquering of the oceans for military purposes as well.

I remarked how when I was a child Pearl Harbor had been attacked, and what a feat of stretching across an ocean this had represented. "Most people didn't realize it at the time," I said. "The newspapers were full of how the Japanese were going to keep right on coming and invade California." I laughed. "No way. It wasn't even remotely possible to send a battle fleet and invasion supplies across the Pacific, much less to keep enemy soldiers supplied once they landed. But everyone was frightened." I laughed again; the remoteness in time, the transfer of the real world through our own remoteness in space and, I suppose, the additional insulating aspect of the Bloody Marys made it all seem hilarious. "I remember reading in the papers of a big Japanese invasion on the West Coast. We were shooting off cannons and antiaircraft guns and mobilizing the army, and of course it was all nothing. Someone spotted a gull and thought it was a Mitsubishi, so everyone started shooting. Then everyone else started shooting because all the others were shooting. Pretty funny," I said, shaking my head and chuckling.

No one else was laughing and I became aware of feet

shuffling. Ralph said, "I think you're mistaken. They certainly did attack us in San Diego."

I shook my head, wondering why they were all so serious about this. "The record's clear," I said. "There's nothing in any of the Japanese documents to show that their battle fleet ever sailed past Pearl Harbor. They turned around and headed back as fast as they could."

Frank said, "Ralph here was just telling us how he helped fight off the Japanese invasion. He was right there in San Diego, manning one of the cannon. Or was it antiaircraft, Ralph?" he asked with a straight face.

There was a moment of silence. Then Ralph said with dignity, "I'm sure David has some reason for saying what he has," and he turned with Sue Ann and walked away.

Frank and his brother thought it was pretty funny. "Have another Bloody Mary," he suggested, so I did. By the time we staggered back to the ship I had forgotten the Japanese, Elisha Kent Kane, Markham and Nares. I remembered the rats, though, and looked carefully in the closet and under my bed before I collapsed on it and passed out.

AUGUST 2

—— ·ı|||||ı· ——

I woke up thinking about scurvy, science, ocean-going ships and warfare, remembering a meeting I had attended many years ago. Albert Szent-Györgyi, a Nobel-winning biochemist, had given a talk on his discovery of vitamin C in 1927. The point of his talk was the responsibility of scientists when asked by their governments to participate in war-related research, and the temptation to take the largesse that governments hand out to those who cooperate. "I am humbly proud," he said, as I recall, "that I have never given in to that temptation. Nothing I have ever done has ever borne the slightest possible resemblance to warfare, nor can any of my discoveries be twisted to that purpose."

Afterward, as we were all standing around talking, a German participant came up and introduced himself to Szent-Györgyi. He had served in the German *Kriegsmarine*, he said with an apologetic smile. "I was not a Nazi," he explained, "but I thought it my duty to fight for my country. Incidentally," he went on, "we nearly won the war, you know. It was a close thing, in 1943, whether our submarines would be able to cut the Atlantic pipeline to England. Had we done so, there would have been no invasion in 1944, and with the western sections of the Wehrmacht and Luftwaffe freed, we would probably have defeated Russia."

He nodded, smiling to himself, lost for a moment, then turned back to Szent-Györgyi. "Do you know what allowed us to send our submarines to sea and keep them there for weeks at a time, and thus nearly win our war? We had little white pills of vitamin C. There is no room aboard a U-boat for fresh vegetables or meat, and scurvy would have destroyed us if it had not been for your discovery of vitamin C and our ability then to synthesize it." He smiled broadly. "You very nearly won the war for Germany," he said, then turned and disappeared into the crowd.

At 8:20 A.M. we are at 86°36' N and 34°29' W, making six knots through heavy ice at a heading of 11°. The ice is nearly continuous now, with only occasional leads of open water. There is no hint of the sun, not even any way to tell in which direction it lies; there is only gray all around.

At 11:30 A.M. the sun comes out, just in time for a noon party on the aft deck. This is in the form of a ceremony asking King Neptune's permission to proceed to the North Pole. We stand around in the subfreezing wind for an hour because this party is the idea of the ship's crew, and Russians can't organize anything on time.

By 1:30 P.M. there is the blaring of a saxophone—one of our passengers, Liz Harper, the only young single woman on board, plays the instrument beautifully—and out of the hold comes spilling a host of vibrant, colorful characters, if you like that sort of thing. There are women in peasant costumes and other women dressed like mermaids; these are the female members of the staff, either kitchen workers or maids. Surprisingly, this Soviet equal-opportunity ship has no females who actually run anything important.

There are also a lot of males dressed in ways I can't fathom. They come out calling for beer—no fools, they—

and the passengers happily throw them cans of Beck's from the cases brought out to keep us warm. Finally King Neptune emerges and we "have sight of Proteus rising from the sea, and hear old Triton blow his wreathèd horn," but it isn't quite the same. Our captain, a healthily plump man of about fifty who speaks little English, is summoned and dutifully asks permission to proceed to the pole. King Neptune is given a couple of cans of Beck's and gives graceful permission. Then a stereo is plugged in, loud Western music blares forth and everyone dances.

I find the whole business silly and depressing, but everyone else is having a wonderful time. The Russian crew in particular are enjoying themselves. The Russian women dance with each other because the crew are too busy drinking the Western beer and the passengers are afraid to dance with them; you could get trampled to death.

A buffet is set up, with charcoaled and barbecued pork chops, Polish sausages and truly great potato salad. There is also a hot Russian stew or soup which, if gulped quickly before it freezes, is wonderfully warming. In an hour it's all over, and everyone goes inside.

Though we have traveled through the noon hour, all this time the sun has not moved vertically at all; at least I can't see any difference in its elevation from about 11:30 A.M. to 2 P.M. It moves in a horizontal circle around us, at less than a forefinger's width of elevation. At 6 P.M., just before dinner, I go outside and take another look. As closely as I can measure with my finger held close to my eye it hasn't gained or lost at all.

Dr. Frederick Cook claimed he reached the North Pole in 1908. When questioned about how he knew where he was, how he had navigated across featureless ice and snow directly to the pole, since the compass is not much use in these regions, he answered that it was absurdly easy, as simple as following your nose—or, in this case, your

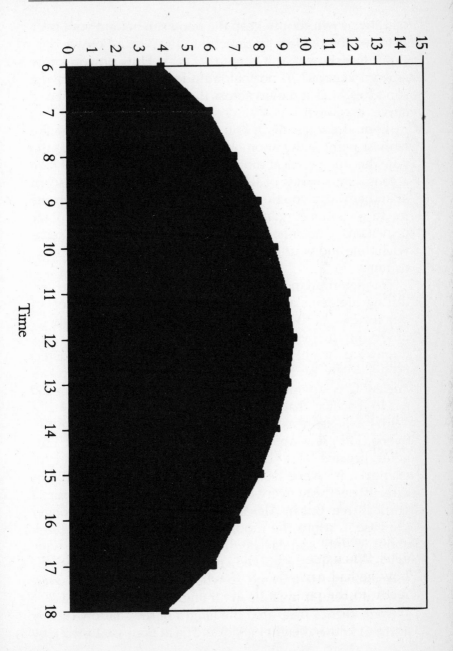

shadow; if you simply keep the noon sun behind you, your shadow points the way directly to the North Pole.

But I see now that it is not that easy. How do you know when it is noon? At normal latitudes you can measure the sun's height as it moves across the sky, and this describes a curve, as shown:

If you draw a smooth line through the observations, the highest point is the noon observation. But this close to the pole the sun's vertical motion is so small that it would take a continuous series of laborious measurements to discern it, and how can you do that when you are slogging over the ice in a footrace against time and the depletion of your provisions? The only other way is to know the exact Greenwich time and your longitude, and that is not an easy proposition.

The determination of longitude has been one of the enduring problems of oceanic navigation throughout most of our history. Early on man learned to measure latitude by observing the height of the sun at its apex, since the sun's noonward height on any given day of the year is determined solely by the latitude of the observer. In fact, an ancient Greek named Eratosthenes used this method in 250 B.C. to discover that the earth wasn't flat.

Eratosthenes was born in the southern Egyptian city of Syene. He grew up there, but later, under Ptolemy Eurgetes, became Royal Librarian at the Grand Library in Alexandria. In Syene he had noticed that the noon sun was directly overhead every June 21 and cast no shadow from a vertical tree. But in Alexandria he saw this was no longer the case. Curious, he thought, and he continued to think about it, until one day he finally realized the reason why: the earth must be curved, not flat. Alexandria was 480 miles due north of Syene, so when the sun is directly overhead at Syene it must lie at an angle over Alexandria.

Eratosthenes measured the length of the shadow cast by a tree of known height in Alexandria at noon on June 21; by

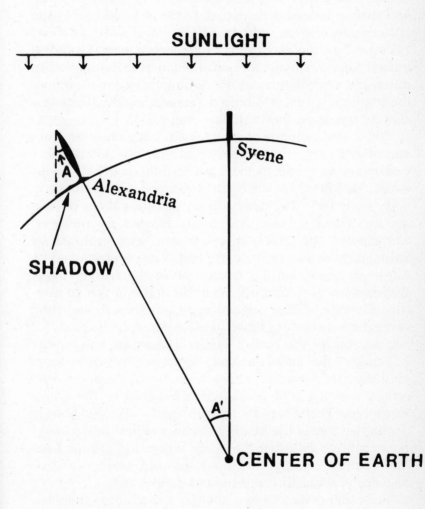

SUNLIGHT

Syene

Alexandria

SHADOW

A′

CENTER OF EARTH

trigonometry this gave him the angle A, which turned out to be 7°. Since alternate interior angles of parallel lines are equal, A is equal to A'. The measured distance from Syene to Alexandria was 480 miles, and therefore—since Ptolemy had earlier defined a degree as 1/360 of a full circle—the circumference of the earth had to be 360/7 × 480, or about 24,000 miles (the earth's circumference is actually 24,989 miles). Since Eratosthenes used the Greek *stadia* instead of miles, and since there is some argument about the length of the stadium, his exact value for the earth's circumference is cloudy; this is our best estimate.

This is interesting enough by itself, but as Damon Runyon used to say, a story goes with it. In 1492 Christopher Columbus sailed off to India because he didn't know his Greek. He knew that the earth was round—by then everybody knew this—but he was in serious error about its size. Ancient Greek science had been replaced by medieval Christianity, the Greek language had been replaced by Latin, and the size of the earth had been redetermined by Cardinal Pierre d'Ailly, chancellor of the University of Paris, who was no Eratosthenes. He didn't bother to measure distances or use trigonometry to discover the truth; instead he studied his Bible. In the Apocrypha he read that one seventh of the earth's surface is covered with water. Looking at the maps currently in vogue, which covered only the Mediterranean region and coastal Europe, he accepted that the Biblical statement referred to the whole earth. From this it was a simple matter to extrapolate from the known size of the Mediterranean and the known land/ocean ratio to find that the ocean separating Europe from Cathay must be only four thousand miles wide. (The true distance is about fifteen thousand miles.)

If Columbus had known how far it really was from Europe to Cathay he would have realized that he couldn't make it before he and all his men died of scurvy, and he never would have tried. I have always thought that this is a good story to bring up whenever someone tries to argue that religion is useless; without the ignorance it engenders, America would not have been discovered in 1492.

Anyway, to find your latitude in the middle of the ocean all you have to do is turn Eratosthenes' method around. You measure the angle of the sun at its apex, and knowing the circumference of the earth you reverse the calculations and figure out your northward distance from any chosen place, such as the equator. In actual practice, all you have to know is where you keep your copy of the *Nautical Almanac*. You look up your measurement of the sun there, and it tells you your latitude; it has been publishing these tables since 1767. Close to the pole, where it is hard to measure the hourly differences in height, it matters less; essentially, if the height doesn't vary from hour to hour, you can measure it at any time and get the correct latitude. But the measurement of longitude is more difficult, and is one of the keys to understanding why Cook and Peary never reached the North Pole, despite their claims.

The whole idea of latitude and longitude began with Claudius Ptolemy about A.D. 100, or at least he gets credit for it; no one is sure who really came up with the idea, so the credit goes to the man who wrote it down and preserved it. The Greeks already knew that the earth was spherical. They also knew that a flat two-dimensional map would be handier to carry around for navigational purposes than a three-dimensional sphere, so they came up with the idea of projecting the sphere onto a plane. They needed a system of coordinates to locate positions, and for simplicity they wanted a rectangular, or mutually perpendicular, pair of axes, the familiar X-Y graph. A series of parallel horizontal and vertical lines was the obvious answer, but Ptolemy went this idea one better by considering the concept of a spinning earth, which wasn't generally acknowledged for another fifteen hundred years.

As soon as people realized that the earth was spherical

instead of flat, the idea that it might be spinning must have been born out of the observation of night and day. Before this, the passage of the sun across the sky seemed to imply that a new sun was created every morning in the east and died every evening in the west. Once the earth was understood to be spherical, it was clear that the sun could simply revolve around it; this had the advantage of only one sun existing, instead of a new one being created each day. At the same time it must have been clear that instead of the sun revolving around the earth, the sun might be standing still and the earth might be spinning. For various reasons this concept wasn't accepted until the Copernican revolution in the sixteenth century, but it led immediately to the concept of a possible axis of rotation and its natural consequence, the existence of North and South Poles.

Ptolemy's chosen system of coordinates consisted of parallel horizontal lines (the latitudes), and a series of great circles passing through the poles of rotation (the meridians of longitude). While these latter are not parallel to each other, since they intersect at the poles, they *are* parallel in a two-dimensional planar representation of reasonably small sections of the sphere—that is, in the maps that Ptolemy prepared.

These two coordinates, latitude and longitude, unequivocally define every spot on the surface of the earth, so if a sailor could measure them he would know exactly where he was. But how to do it was another story.

By the eighteenth century the *Nautical Almanac* was being published and the measurement of latitude had become routine, but longitude was still a mystery. Jonathan Swift thought of its determination as an unattainable goal, an impossibility only to be dreamed of: "I should then see the discovery of the longitude, the perpetual motion, the universal medicine, and many other great inventions brought to the utmost perfection," Gulliver sighs during his voyage to Laputa.

The problem is in the measurement of time: for latitude a calendar is precise enough, but for longitude an accurate clock is necessary. This is because time affects the latitude measurement through the variable tilt of the earth's axis relative to the sun, which changes in time periods of months; so an error of minutes, hours or even a day or two is not crucial. But the longitude measurements vary with the movement of the sun across the sky each day, or with the spin of the earth—that is, a time scale in which hours and minutes become important. An error in time of just four minutes results in an error of one degree of longitude, which at the equator is about sixty-nine miles.

Still, if you have an accurate clock, the determination of longitude is as simple as that of latitude. At longitude 0°, along the Greenwich meridian, the sun reaches its apex at 12:00. If you set your clock to this time and move west, you will find that the next day when your Greenwich clock reads 12:00 the sun will not yet have risen to its full height. In other words, in local time it's still morning. So, for example, when it is noon in London it is only 7 A.M. in New York. All you have to do to determine your longitude as you sail across the ocean, then, is to have an accurate clock set to Greenwich Mean Time and see what time it is when the sun rises to its noon height; each difference of four minutes means one degree difference from Greenwich. If your clock reads 11:20 A.M. when the sun hits its apex, for example, you are forty minutes before Greenwich noon or ten degrees West longitude. Simple.

The difficulty lies in getting a clock to keep accurate time, and the importance of this difficulty was recognized long ago. In the seventeenth century a Spanish ship discovered the Solomon Islands, but didn't know it. Because of a slight error in longitude—a matter of several thousand miles or so—the captain thought he was in the already discovered Marquesas and so didn't claim the Solomons for Spain. They were later claimed by France.

You can hardly blame the poor Spanish captain for his error. Navigation was a difficult art at best, black magic at worst. The master of a ship setting out from port would mark his initial passage from known landmarks on shore, and would roughly confirm his direction by the setting sun. At night he would look for the Polar Star or use his compass to tell him his direction, but he could have no idea where he actually was. He kept his ship aligned across the swells if he could, and calculated the direction he was pushed by the wind, but oceanic currents are impossible to detect. He might know the general tendency of the currents in areas he had sailed before, but in general terms only, and as he ventured into unknown regions even this slight knowledge evaporated.

Winds, currents and the direction of swells change, and although these are related it is not a one-to-one relationship. The patterns among them will change, and the master of the ship had to estimate how all of this might have changed his course, but in open seas the errors in these estimates are enormous and unavoidable. Then there are storms to blow him off course.

In sum, looking at the errors made by early navigators, one is reminded of Dr. Johnson's comment on lady preachers: "Sir, a woman preaching is like a dog's walking on his hind legs. It is not done well; but you are surprised to find it done at all."

The Spanish captain's error was not looked on with such equanimity by his king; it so irritated Philip III that he offered a reward of a thousand crowns to anyone who could determine longitude at sea. The French upped the ante to 10,000 florins, and in 1714 the British Admiralty set up a Board of Longitude which offered £20,000 as "A Publick Reward for such Person or Persons as shall discover the Longitude at Sea." They realized that they were talking about a clock mechanism, and specified that it should have an accumulated error of less than two minutes—or less than half a degree longitude—on a voyage to the West Indies and back.

As indicated by Swift's comment, most people were not optimistic that such accuracy was possible. Sir Isaac Newton, the great man himself, had strongly implied that it was not. But as noted in a delightful book about the subject written in 1941 by W.J.V. Branch and E. Brook-Williams, two Englishmen trying to escape from the boredom and inactivity of the early months of the war, "The Board of Longitude was in one respect extremely modern. It . . . was very large, and very few of its members knew anything at all about the subject under discussion." Hence they thought that it was possible, and they offered the money and waited for someone to claim it.

Fourteen years later a young carpenter from Yorkshire named John Harrison made the journey to London with a set of technical drawings under his arm. He said he could make a chronometer accurate enough to satisfy the Board if they would help him with expense money. They refused.

So Harrison built it himself. It took him six years, and when the Admiralty tried it out they pronounced themselves satisfied. But the Board refused to pay him the money; though Harrison's clock had satisfied the Admiralty, they weren't the ones with the money, and the Board wanted more proof and better accuracy.

Harrison continued to work on his clock, and thirty years later produced the most famous clock in maritime history: Harrison's No. 4. The Board instructed the Admiralty to take it to Madeira and back to see how good it was. "The ship's crew were terrified lest they should miss the island, the consequence whereof would have been Inconvenient as they were in Want of Beer," a contemporary account put it, but the navigation was perfect and they found the island and made their way home again. The total error on the voyage was one minute and fifty-four point five seconds of time. So the Board of Longitude generously gave Harrison

£2500, or slightly more than 10 percent of what they had promised. When he complained, they replied that they still didn't believe his clock was as good as it seemed to be. So the Admiralty sailed with it to Jamaica, and then again to Barbados; each time the clock kept time as accurately as before. The Admiralty noted as much to the Board, which was too bored to reply. Harrison wrote letters, beseeched and argued, and the next year the Board kicked in with another £5000. In 1775, nearly fifty years after he had first come to London, they finally acknowledged that he had done what he claimed, and gave him the rest of the money. Having no further reason to stay alive, Harrison promptly died. (As Branch and Brook-Williams put it, "The shock when they finally consented [to pay him] must have been overwhelming.")

When Cook and Peary separately traveled to the pole in 1908–9, or said they did, they made no measurements of their longitude along the way, or brought back no records of having done so. When checked afterward, Peary's several chronometers were found to vary among themselves by more than ten minutes, so he couldn't have made an accurate measurement even if he had tried. Cook never brought his chronometer back for verification. So while it is clear that each of them endured an incredible journey, it is not at all clear just how close each of them may actually have come to the North Pole. But more of that later.

Like most modern ships, the *Sovetskiy Soyuz* doesn't have any problem with navigation. It uses a satellite system. We can divide the history of navigation into three periods: before and after Harrison's 1714 chronometer, and after the advent of satellite systems. Before the chronometer navigation was by guess and by God; with the chronometer, longitude measurement was accurate but laborious. Today, with satellites, the subject is boring: on the *Soyuz* we simply look at the dial and it tells us exactly where we are. Precisely timed radio signals from a fleet of satellites in known orbits are received by the *Soyuz,* and triangulation by an onboard computer instantly calculates the ship's position to within better than a mile. The United States has a system capable of much greater accuracy—to within a matter of inches, actually—but the signal is purposely scrambled slightly by the military to prevent anyone taking advantage of it to pinpoint targets accurately enough for missile attack.

This doesn't bother us, of course. The system is just one more reason why this voyage to the North Pole is a piece of cake. We simply look up at the cathode display to see where we are and where we're going.

Another reason our trip is so easy is the nuclear propulsion system. Living aboard this ship is like going back to another century, before pollution and worries about energy conservation, when labor was cheap and everyone had servants.

The latter point is Russian rather than nuclear. The Soviet economy, based on the philosophy of "From each according to his abilities, to each according to his needs," translates into a system of managed jobs and no unemployment. The ship is run by more than a hundred people taking care of a similar number of paying guests. Hence the rooms are cleaned to perfection every day, the towels and linen are crisply clean, the ship is spotless. John Boon, a Louisiana Cajun who captains an American icebreaker and is here to see how the Russians do things, is horrified by it all. "Ah don wan t'b' curtcl ahv nuthin, bu' th's har popple don' know sheeit 'bow howt' run'a'shi, y'll know wha' ah min?" he asks over a beer.

I look at him; I can't understand a word he's saying. He has the thickest Southern accent I've ever heard (and the wildest beard I've ever seen).

This afternoon I met the Soviet nuclear engineer, and his English is perfection compared to this cracker's. I was

heading down one of the interior passageways on my way
to the basketball court after the King Neptune party. So far
I hadn't found anyone playing there, but I thought I'd take
another look; if they have a court, they must have people
who play. Coming the other way along the passageway
was a large Russian in the white terry-cloth bathrobes the
crew wear. He stopped me and asked, "American?"

"Yes," I said. "Russian?"

"Da. Please, you come with me. Do you understand?"

I thought, what have I done now? My mother never
wanted me to visit Russia because she was afraid they kept
records of everything forever, would know that she had left
illegally, that therefore they would consider me a Russian
citizen, and so they'd kidnap me. I used to laugh at her, but
now, following this man down the passageway, I was beginning to wonder a little bit. "Aren't I allowed in this part
of the ship?" I asked.

"Please," he said. "You come with me," and he kept
right on walking until he reached one of the doors. He
opened it and gestured me inside. "You go in," he said.
When I hesitated he asked, "Do you understand? My English has not very good. You go in."

I went in. It was a small cabin, similar to the one I had
but smaller. The porthole was open and a small fan blew
cold air in while the radiator sent out waves of heat.
Ranged next to the open porthole were fruits of a kind I
didn't recognize.

"Sit," he said, pulling over the one chair. He sat on the
bed and glowered at me. Evidently he had just come from
the swimming pool or shower. He found a towel and
rubbed off his wet hair, then reached down under his bunk
and pulled out a bottle and one dirty glass. He poured a
shot of vodka and offered it to me. That is, I assumed it was
vodka; I also assumed that the dirty lip of the glass contained new varieties of bacteria that my immune system
had never encountered before. I shook my head.

He looked disappointed, but drank it down himself. "Igor Oparin," he introduced himself.

"David Fisher," I admitted.

"You are American," he said. "You live where?"

"Miami," I said. I started to add, "Florida," but it wasn't necessary.

"Oh, Miami!" he exclaimed ecstatically. "That is my dream, to live in Miami. Do you understand? Russia is a poor country, for the now moment very poor. Maybe tomorrow moment will be better . . ." He shrugged. He didn't really believe it.

"I am nuclear engineer," he said. "In charge here. Very big job." He shrugged again. "You want maybe buy picture?"

"What?"

He stood up, reached behind me and pulled down a white sheet. Behind it was a picture, an oil painting about three feet by four, of an ocean scene. There was a beach and a rowboat and high waves. It was all very dark.

"This is painting by my friend Ostrophsky. I live in Crimea. You recognize?" he asked, pointing at the painting.

I didn't know if he meant did I recognize the Crimea or the name Ostrophsky. Since I hadn't recognized either, I shook my head.

He sat down, obviously disappointed. "Ostrophsky is very big in New York. Do you understand big? Very big man. No one knows him. He lives in Crimea, we are friends. He is very big man, but very poor. In Soviet Union is not good things for artist. Not like New York."

I tried to interrupt. "Sure. Let me tell you about artists in New York—"

But he wasn't listening. "When Ostrophsky dies, soon, he will be very famous. Very sick. Very famous. Good painting. You like it? Nine hundred rubles. You take it. Do you understand?"

I was not about to take it. I don't know much about

monetary exchange in the Soviet Union, but from what I've heard you don't mess with it. Instead I tried to ask him why he was selling the painting. He looked at me as if I was stupid. "Make money," he said.

"But if you're the nuclear engineer on the big ship—"

"Oh," he waved me away deprecatingly. He is proud of his position, but it doesn't pay much. He lives in a small apartment with his wife and two children. His son is studying to be a master sailor and will be captain of a ship like this someday. In the meantime, life is not easy. Igor has four months on board, twelve hours on and twelve off, and then four months ashore. He would work at another job during those four months, but it isn't allowed. Sometimes he moonlights as a janitor in one of the private markets that are springing up everywhere in the Soviet Union.

When I asked him about the ship, his attitude changed and his eyes lit up with pride. I am to call him this evening, when he is on duty from midnight till noon, and he will show me through the ship.

"Is that allowed?" I asked.

"I am nuclear chief engineer," he said. "Do you understand? I say *da*. Yes," he explained.

When my daughter was three years old and my son a year and a half, he spoke in a baby dialect that no one could understand except his sister. She would bend over, listen to him babbling and then turn around and tell us that he wanted a cookie or a toy or whatever. In the same manner, I find out later today what John Boon, the icebreaker captain, was trying to tell me. Howard Moggen, who is from Georgia and therefore understands Boon's old-fashioned Southern dialect, yet speaks clearly enough for me to understand him, says that Boon feels that this ship is straight out of the nineteenth century, notwithstanding its nuclear technology. It is run by a crew of more than one hundred. Boon will run *his* new American icebreaker with a crew of twenty, and the Japanese have a ship in the works that is run by a crew of one.

I don't believe that. "True," Boon says. (By the third beer it is becoming possible to understand him; I'm not sure if it's his third beer or mine that is the important one.) "They've got it all computerized. One man, that's all. But they'll never get it built 'cause no one trusts it."

But his own ship has a crew of only twenty, and he insists this is all that is necessary. "You put this damn ship here on the open market and it would be bankrupt in one voyage. No way the Russkis can compete. They don't know sheeit 'bout running a ship."

The *Soyuz* is too labor-intensive, he says. "They steer th' damn thing by hand, 'f'you c'n b'lieve tha'. Y'all go up in th' bridge, there's one man steerin' an' 'nother handlin' th' power an' one more sumbitch lookin' out through binoculars!"

Boon's new ship which is being built now will be run by computer, like the Japanese, but will have a crew of about twenty because of union regulations. Still, that's a lot better than a hundred. It can shift ballast and juggle the engines by computer and is therefore faster and better. The Commies can run this ship, he explains, because essentially they have slave labor: our waiter gets $15 a month, most of the officers about $30. When they come up against the world economy they won't be able to afford the wages necessary to run the ship. This is going to be a problem for them, because with it they can keep the northern Siberian sea-lanes open about 275 days a year; without it what are they going to do?

Boon's argument is persuasive; nevertheless it is hard to not be impressed by this ship. It is half again as long as a football field and about half as wide. It weighs 20,000 tons, its two nuclear reactors generate 75,000 horsepower, and it can crash through ice fifteen to twenty feet thick. It has an internal ballast system, so if it gets stuck on the ice it can slosh a few thousand tons of water around inside, from side to side and front to back, and literally shake itself loose. Because of the nuclear propulsion system the energy output is virtually infinite, at least as far as the passengers are concerned. The reactor can generate more hot water than we could possibly use, more electricity than we can consume, and it doesn't care how profligate we are because it will just sit there in the bowels of the ship splitting uranium atoms for another five years or so; by then it will have contaminated itself with radwaste and have to have its fuel rods replaced, no matter whether we use the energy it puts out or not. It couldn't care less.

The lovely part of it is that it doesn't spew out any kind of crud into the environment as it plows through the Arctic. When we stand out on the deck it doesn't matter if we're moving or not, if a breeze is blowing or not: the air is as clean as it was before we got here. There is no smell of oil, gas or smoke swirling around; it's like magic. When it works right, nuclear power is the most beautiful thing in the world, yet everyone is afraid of it. There is good reason to be afraid of it—one thinks of Chernobyl—but the fears go beyond rationality.

Some thirty years ago, when I went to Brookhaven National Laboratory on Long Island for a postdoctoral appointment in nuclear chemistry, I spent the first couple of days with a realtor looking for a place to live. It was all country living then, and as we drove through the woods I saw a sign warning that this was a deer crossing. I was a city boy, and thought this wonderful. "Do you ever really see deer?" I asked.

She nodded and told me, quite seriously, that it used to be a problem, particularly at night, when they might come crashing out of the woods and onto the highway without warning, but that it wasn't a problem any longer because now all the deer glowed at night and so could be seen easily. "Because of the radiation," she said, and then remembered that I was a scientist. "But you know all about that," she finished, and started chatting again about the house we were going to see.

It's amazing how responsive a chord this business about glowing in the dark strikes. The first few days aboard ship, when we were meeting people, the first question asked was where you came from and the second was what you did. Soon everyone knew that I was a nuclear chemist, and they sought me out to question me about the ship's nuclear reactor. They took what I said seriously, and for the most part I tried to talk seriously because radiation *is* a serious problem, but once in a while you run up against an ignorance so abysmal that the temptation to fool around is too great to be resisted.

Over cocktails tonight someone said jokingly that we would never know if we began to glow in the dark because the sun never goes down up here, so there isn't any darkness. Then Howard Tetler, my old Helsinki roommate, said that he was checking it. Every night when he washes up before going to sleep he closes the bathroom door and doesn't turn on the light. These are the only rooms in the ship where there is total darkness. He looks to see if the tips of his fingers are glowing, especially under the nails. That's where his doctor at home told him to look for it, right under the nails.

I thought this was pretty good. In these days of multi-million-dollar malpractice suits, you don't often find a doctor with a sense of humor. But the temptation to gain a little revenge for that first night of horrors in Helsinki was too great to resist. So I pointed out to him that because of the lack of rod-shaped receptors in our eyes it takes us a while to adapt to varying conditions of darkness. Cats can't really see in the dark, I explained; it's just that they can go from light to dark without being blinded because they have rods that can adapt instantaneously to conditions of low light—thus the superstition that they can see in the dark.

"So we have this problem," I explained. "If we go from a well-lit room into a dark room we're blinded for a while until our eyes adapt. Like when you go into the bathroom and turn off the lights. Any glow from your fingernails isn't going to be bright like a searchlight, you know. It will be a dull, bluish green, and you'll never see it until your eyes adapt to the darkness."

Howard looked worried. "What you have to do," I said, "is give your eyes time to become acclimatized. After you close the door with the lights out, you've got to stand there a good ten minutes. Then you'll be able to see if there's anything glowing in the dark."

He nodded; he felt better already. So did I, at the thought of him standing in the dark bathroom every night for ten or fifteen minutes, waiting to see if his fingernails glowed bluish green.

It is amazing how distrustful we are of radiation. Or perhaps not; it is, after all, invisible, with no smell, taste, sound or any other manifestation of its presence, and it certainly is dangerous. It would actually be a wonderful thing if our fingernails *did* begin to glow; a built-in radiation detection system would be useful.

Since we don't have one, people are going to look for something. It has always been this way. Back in the late 1930s a group of British scientists were working on what was to become radar, and the people living in the vicinity of Bawdsey Manor, a magnificent estate on the eastern coast, were uneasy at the stories of "radiation from the Manor" and the mysterious consequences thereof.

Nearly everyone had a story to tell about what had happened to them or to a friend. They (or their friend) would have decided one night to drive up and take a look by moonlight at what was going on in the old manor. As they drove up the slight hill and approached the place their automobile would stall. Nothing they could do would get the engine started again. Eventually a soldier would appear out of the dark woods and ask them what the trouble was. They would tell him about their stalled engine. He would nod, look at his watch and tell them to wait ten minutes—or five or eight or fifteen—and then their engine would be all right. He would stand there with them in silence, and then he would look at his watch and at the appointed moment would tell them to start up—and with no trouble at all their engines would start. Then the soldier would watch as they turned around and drove away home.

These stories were due not to any mysterious radiation leaking out of the manor, but just to the fear of it. The stories would all begin with someone coming out of the pub after an evening of heavy drinking, daring themselves to see what the military camp was up to. It's easy to see how they might stall the car, even easier to see how they would flood the engine in their frantic attempts to start it and get moving again before they were discovered. When the sentry found them their problem would be clear to him; he would tell them to wait a few minutes to give the carburetor time to drip clear. Then when he gave them the signal the car would start easily. It had nothing to do with any radiation from Bawdsey Manor.

At about 1 A.M. I call Igor on the ship's telephone and he tells me to come right down. I find the control room and there he is, welcoming me like an old friend. He shows me around—it looks like a combination of a normal reactor control room plus a ship's operating room—and then takes me through a bulkhead door into a sort of locker room. He points to the clothing there and starts to put it on, so I do so, too. We put on cloth shoes, white lab coats, gloves and hats, and in an inner room soft slippers over the cloth shoes, and then we go down several flights and through several doors, each of which is clanked and locked shut behind us, to get into the reactor room. Igor wants "the good people of U.S.A. to know about our equipment, our good icebreaker."

I am emboldened by that to ask if I can come again and take a few pictures.

"No," a voice says from behind me, and I turn to see a bearded man standing there. "It is not allowed," he says.

Igor barks at him in Russian, and the man barks back. Igor rears up—he is a very big man—and barks again, and the man turns and walks away. "Come see me to take picture," Igor tells me. "I allow you. Do you understand? I am nuclear chief engineer."

AUGUST 3

When I signed on for this voyage, I had expected that I would be the novice among a group of initiates; that the people willing to spend $30,000 for a few weeks' voyage to the North Pole would at least be amateur explorers—amateurs, people who do things for the love of it, being the most knowledgeable and enthusiastic of all. But my expectations were dashed on the very first day, before we even left Murmansk. I was on the foredeck, walking around to have a look at the port and the ship, and fell into conversation with my first passenger, Tess Mannix of Brookline, Massachusetts.

"Do you play bridge?" she asked.

"No," I said.

"Oh," she replied, and her eyes immediately shifted focus, found someone else twenty yards away, and left me without another word. I later found out, in talking with her husband Tom, that she is a world-class bridge player and, like most world-class practitioners of any art, it is the only art she practices. The two of them sail on cruises continuously because of Tom's love for the sea, but the only time she goes out on deck is on the first day when she scouts around for bridge players. Once she has her foursome she is set for the rest of the cruise. Since then I've seen her every afternoon in the library lounge playing bridge. She has never seen me again since I said "No."

The others seem much the same. Not quite so monomaniacal as Mrs. Mannix, but all of them disappointing to my expectations in one way or another. They have all heard of Admiral Peary, for example; that is, they recognize that the name has something to do with the North Pole, but most of them aren't sure exactly what.

We are passing the 87th parallel now, where Peary first made his appearance on the public scene. Robert E. Peary was the prototypical American hero: "Tall, erect, broad-shouldered, full-chested, tough, wiry-limbed, clear-eyed, full-mustached, clear-browed complexion, a dead shot, a powerful swimmer, a first-class rider, a skillful boxer and fencer, perfectly at home in any company yet always bearing an indefinable atmosphere of the wildness and freedom of the woods and mountains, master of German, Spanish, and French . . ."

An altogether admirable description, and it must be accurate since it is Peary's own, taken from a letter he wrote to his mother in 1880 when he was twenty-four years old. To be perfectly fair, he was not describing himself as he then was but as he saw himself to be in five years' time. He finished the description by adding that by then he hoped to have acquired "a knowledge of the Isthmus equaled by no man living."

The Isthmus? Yes. The Isthmus of Nicaragua, for Peary began his career after graduation from Bowdoin College as a civil engineer hired by the navy, with the equivalent rank of lieutenant, to assist in evaluating the proposed site for an interoceanic canal. He immediately became infatuated with the romance of the navy, and never in all his life got quite accustomed to the fact that he merely worked "for" the navy and was not quite "in" it; certainly to real sailors he was never "of" the navy. But he was inordinately proud of his rank of lieutenant, and furious when the local naval personnel whom he regarded as fellow officers insisted on addressing him as "Civil Engineer Peary."

It was in Nicaragua that Peary first went exploring. Since the proposed route for the canal led through unexplored jungle, it became his job to get out there and take the navy's first look. He left civilization behind and set out through the tropical wilderness, forging through swamps which housed snakes and leeches, enduring—in fact ignoring—mosquitoes carrying malaria and yellow fever and dengue, living with natives in their own style, and loving every minute of it. "In situations requiring great powers of endurance and capabilities for resisting hunger, thirst, exposure, and fatigue . . . an intelligent educated man will hold out longer than an ordinary one . . . it is will power that does it, the superiority of mind over matter. [It is] a direct, conscious, painful exertion of the will, saying to the body 'you shall not give up,' 'you must keep on,' 'I will make you.' . . ."

Peary did his job well and earned a strong commendation from his superior, who praised "the untiring energy, skill, and devotion to duty of Civil Engineer Peary, who, under the discomforts and hardships endured through many rainy days in the field and many nights with only a few palm leaves for shelter . . . and scanty rations, never flinched while there was work to be done."

Oh, that must have rankled! Why did they insist on calling him "Civil Engineer" instead of Lieutenant Peary, he wondered as he returned to civilization and rested from his ordeal. But as he recuperated from his recent past, his entire future beckoned to him, for it was while browsing through a secondhand bookshop in Washington one evening that he happened across a little pamphlet of Baron Nordenskjöld's, *Exploration of Interior Greenland*.

Baron Nils Nordenskjöld had set a record furthest north

of 81°42' in 1864, and in 1883 had set off to find paradise in the interior of Greenland. The interior of the island at that time, and even when Peary read his account, was totally unexplored, and somehow the Baron had fixed on the idea that it would prove to be free of ice, covered with vegetation, suitable for habitation, perhaps even already inhabited by tribes unknown to Christianity. What a prize! He failed to find this fabled land, managing to penetrate less than a hundred miles inland, but the account of his experiences fired the imagination of the young American.

Peary later said that his interest in the Arctic world dated back to this chance occurrence, but he had obviously fixed on the Arctic even earlier, for on the previous Christmas, sailing to Nicaragua, he had written to his mother that he was passing the "birthplace of the New World," which looked to him just as it did "nearly four hundred years ago when it smiled a welcome to [Columbus] whose fame can be equaled only by him who shall one day stand with 360 degrees of longitude beneath his motionless foot, for whom East and West shall have vanished; the discoverer of the North Pole."

Undoubtedly Peary's dreams went back even further. As a child growing up in the snow-covered wastes of Maine, staring out over the rocks and the tempest-tossed shore to the nearly freezing surf beyond, he must have dreamed of the further north where the waters actually were frozen, forever and ever. The book by Nordenskjöld crystallized his romantic dreams of the north with his implacable desire for fame—"Remember, Mother," one of his early letters home reads, "I *must* have fame!"—and he saw his future, his mission, his karma: the North Pole.

Peary wanted the pole not for itself, nor for any scientific or geographical importance it might hold, but simply because it was seen to be both important and difficult; its attainment was like the search for the Holy Grail, a job for a hero. "I am after the Pole," he wrote in 1898 for *McClure's*

Magazine, "because it *is* the Pole; because it has a value as a test of intelligence, persistence, endurance, determinated will, and perhaps courage, qualities characteristic of the highest type of manhood; because I am confident that it can be reached, and because I regard it as a great prize which it is peculiarly fit and appropriate that an American should win."

And Peary wanted it not as a normal man wants something, but as a monomaniac wants; he longed for it as Tess Mannix longed for her daily bridge game, he wanted it with every fiber of his being, and he simply would not take no for an answer. Not if it meant risking his life, sacrificing his health and his body piece by piece, strewing his steps to the goal with his own frozen toes as they dropped off; not if it meant stepping on others with those shattered feet; finally, not if it meant refusing to accept failure, and lying to achieve in form what he had not quite achieved in substance.

As the twentieth century began it was finally clear, from the failures of so many men—Franklin, Parry, Andrée, Nansen, Kane, De Long, so many men who had left so many of their comrades frozen forever in the ice—that the passage to the North Pole did not lie along a route that would ever be followed by others. The man who would finally discover the North Pole would not be opening up new lands for mankind, nor would he be connecting old lands; he would simply be reaching the most inaccessible spot on earth.

That was enough for Peary. As diamonds are desirable not because they are useful but simply because they are hard to obtain and therefore expensive, the North Pole was desirable because no one else had been able to reach it, because people had died trying to reach it, because it was in most people's eyes unattainable. Fame and glory would come to the first person to set foot there, and this was what

Peary wanted: fame and glory, for whatever purpose, at whatever cost.

His campaign for the pole would be, according to a letter Cook would write to the president of the United States in 1911, "the dirtiest campaign of bribery, conspiracy, and black dishonor that the world has ever known." According to others, it would be the supreme achievement of the human race, a triumph of perseverance, courage, foresight and the ultimate limit of human endurance.

It was, perhaps, a bit of both.

Peary studied reports of all previous expeditions and decided that the British method, which had failed so often, was doomed to fail. The British attacked the Arctic as if it were a sentient enemy. They gathered together scores of men for an invasion force, loading their sleds with provisions which then had to be hand-dragged for hundreds of miles over ice hummocks and open leads of water and through thigh-deep slush, and carrying heavy tents for shelter instead of building igloos as they went. They took their civilization with them as a barrier against the alien cold and the hostile hunger.

Peary realized instead that the Arctic couldn't be as terrible as it seemed, since there were people who actually lived up there. Eskimos were born and bred, they lived and died, they hunted, found food and clothing, housing, warmth and sustenance in the frozen far north. What a native could do, surely a white man could do! He decided to reach the North Pole not by invading the foreign land with a great army but by applying for citizenship, so to speak—that is, by learning to live as the Eskimos did. The first step, then, was not to mount a great campaign for the pole but somehow to get up to the Arctic regions and learn to know the Eskimos and their ways, learn to make friends with the frozen inferno, or at least come to terms with it.

Peary asked for six months' leave from the navy, to ex-

Henrietta Island, De Long's last sight of land before the *Jeannette* sank.

Zodiac approaching Cape Flora, Franz Josef Land.

Polar bear enjoying
a meal and a stroll.

Approaching the North Pole.

Sovetskiy Soyuz "docked" at the North Pole.

Santa Claus at the North Pole.

Circumnavigating the earth at the North Pole.

Looking south from the pole.

Helicopter landing us on the island where I nearly got left behind.

The nameless island.

Left: The Russian meteorological station on Henrietta Island.

Bottom left: Arctic version of Stonehenge on Arakamchechen Island.

Below: The walrus-watcher's hut on Arakamchechen Island.

The harbor of Provideniya.

The movie theater in Provideniya.

plore northern Greenland. (At the time it was not known whether Greenland was an island or part of an undiscovered Arctic continent.) Permission was readily granted since the navy didn't really have full-time work for him. Then he thought better of his idea, and went back to them with another proposition: wouldn't this exploration be a suitable project for a naval officer? In which case shouldn't he stay on active duty in the navy while taking on the task? This would enable him to keep his salary during his travels, and perhaps even to get some financial and logistical support from the military for the mission.

The navy didn't bother to point out that Peary was not, in fact, a naval officer but only a civil engineer. They contented themselves by saying merely that such a project was not in the best interests of the navy. He could have unpaid leave if he wanted it; he would have their blessings, but not their money.

Money was to haunt Peary all his life, and later in his career he was not above stealing from his "loyal friends," the Eskimos, to obtain it—although he always managed to convince himself that the trinkets he gave them were more than satisfactory payment for the skins, dogs, ivory and meteorites he took from them. At this first stage he was able to get started with the aid of a $500 gift from his mother. Thus do remarkable careers sometimes begin.

Peary sailed to Greenland that summer, 1886, and with one companion penetrated over a hundred miles inland—finding no land of lush vegetation, but achieving a certain degree of fame for his exploit. He had traveled on the Greenland ice, as he pointed out in his book *Northward over the Great Ice*, "a greater distance [inland] than any white man previously." It is a choice of words not uncommon a hundred years ago: explorations, travels, exploits conducted by other than a "white man" simply didn't count.

The fame Peary received was modest, but he reveled in

it. The trip "has brought my name before the world," he wrote to his mother. It meant "an enduring name and honor" together with "social advancement, for with the prestige of my summer's work . . . I will next winter be one of the foremost in the highest circles in the capital, and make powerful friends . . . Remember, Mother, I *must* have fame . . ."

But his leave of absence from the navy was up, and they sent him back to Nicaragua. He went happily; armed with his fame and secure in his bravery in foraging through the jungles, he was a great social and professional success there. Thoughts of the North receded as he began to think he would make his name in Nicaragua after all, connecting the oceans. But then it was decided to build the canal in Panama instead of Nicaragua, and suddenly he was out in left field, his work unimportant and ignored.

Worse followed almost immediately, for news came that Nansen had crossed the Greenland ice cap from one coast to the other. Still, he had done so at a narrow point in the south; Peary now determined to cross it near its northern-most known stretch, and to determine if in fact there *was* a northern coast, if it was an island or part of a continent—if, indeed, it might stretch all the way to the pole.

In 1891 he sailed from New York with a group of seven, including three who would become, after his mother, the most important people in his life. On his way to Nicaragua he had stopped in at a Washington store to buy a tropical helmet; he ended up not only with the helmet but with a valet. Matthew Henson was a twenty-one-year-old black man who had shipped around the world since he was a child, when he had been befriended and informally adopted by an old sea captain. He had been just twelve years old at the time; an orphan, he had run away from the traditional mean stepmother and walked from Washington to Baltimore, where Captain Childs found him, hired him as a cabin boy, and brought him up to read and write and do anything that had to be done on a ship. After years of sailing with the captain he had ended up stagnating in a Washington clothing store, where Peary found him and hired him on the spot.

The second person to accompany him on the 1891 voyage was his new wife, Josephine Diebitsch Peary, whom he had married three years before. Taking a woman on an expedition to the Arctic was unheard of, but Peary always believed in the necessity of having a woman along: on later trips, when his wife didn't come, he would share his sleeping blanket with Eskimo women, at least one of whom would bear him two children.

The third person was a charming young doctor, fresh out of medical school, who yearned for a life more exciting than could be provided by a family practice in Brooklyn; his name was Dr. Frederick A. Cook.

They left New York in July and sailed to McCormick Bay on the western tip of Greenland, where they spent the winter. The following April Peary sledged across the ice cap to the northeast coast, naming the point Independence Bay. Standing there he looked northward and saw ocean, and beyond it another island. With characteristic modesty, he named the northern waters the Peary Channel, and the island beyond he named Peary Land. He returned home to announce that he had established the fact that Greenland had a northern coast and was therefore an island; "It was evident that this channel marked the northern boundary of the mainland of Greenland," he reported.

Years later, when other explorers followed his path, they found that the Peary Channel did not exist. Peary Land is simply an extension of Greenland, and so he had not accomplished what he proclaimed; though Greenland did indeed turn out to be an island, he had not proved it.

What had Peary accomplished? Nothing that would attract the attention of the newspapers; he had merely made the longest and most difficult sledge voyage of all time. For comparison, Nansen's longest trek had been 235 miles; Peary's was 1100. But this was not the sort of record that papers headlined; he had not accomplished a furthest north, he had discovered no new areas except Peary Channel (which doesn't exist) and Peary Land (which turned out to be nothing more than Greenland). He had proved nothing except that Greenland was an island (which, though true, he had in fact not proved).

Still, Peary garnered a further measure of fame based on his supposed discoveries. He came home to the United States and went on a lecture tour. In one period of less than four months he gave 165 speeches, collecting hundreds and even thousands of dollars per lecture. He visited wealthy patrons and charmed and beguiled them. He was indeed, as he had prophesied, "clear-eyed, full-mustached, clear-browed in complexion . . . perfectly at home in any company yet always bearing an indefinable atmosphere of the wildness and freedom of the woods and mountains." Who could resist such a combination? The money flowed in, and the following year he left once again for Greenland.

This time Peary sailed with one person fewer and half a person more. The Brooklyn surgeon, Dr. Cook, did not accompany him, for the two men had had their first falling out. When he volunteered for the previous expedition, Cook had willingly signed an agreement stating that Peary was the sole leader of the expedition, and specifying in detail what this meant. Among other conditions it was stated that no one would write or lecture about the trip except Peary. But when they returned Cook informed Peary that he had kept an ethnological diary of the trip, and that he was going to publish an article based on it in a medical journal.

Oh, no, you're not, Peary responded. "No one publishes anything except me."

"But it's merely a medical journal," Cook explained. He

promised that he would publish nothing about the exploration or the expedition itself, and would confine himself to his own scientific studies.

Peary shook his head. Cook had signed the agreement, and agreements mean what they say or they don't mean anything. There were to be no exceptions. Cook gave in, but when asked to travel again with Peary he refused. He had his own plans.

For the moment Peary couldn't care less, though the time would come when he would. For now he hired another surgeon and sailed off in the summer of 1893 to seek a route to the North Pole by way of the Greenland ice cap and Peary Land. With him again was his wife, and in her belly a not-yet-formed person. The child was born while they wintered again in McCormick Bay, the first white child ever born there; named Marie Ahnighito after an Eskimo god personified in the great Cape York meteorite, she was known to the Eskimos as the "Snow Baby," and they came from miles around to see her.

In the spring of 1894 Peary set off from his base camp for the northeast, but this time he failed. He returned to McCormick Bay without having crossed the ice cap, let alone having found a way to the pole. When their transport home came in the summer, he declined to leave. He sent his wife and baby home, but he stayed on with Matt Henson and one other man, Hugh Lee, to have another try the following spring.

On the last day of March, 1895, Peary wrote to his wife. He wasn't able to mail the letter, of course; he left it at the camp for her to find when she came back in the summer with the boat to pick him up. That is, she would find the letter if she did not find him.

My Darling,

It is the eve of our departure for the great ice, and I sit down to write to you what I know I shall later hand you myself . . . The winter has been a nightmare . . . The enormous snowfall of last summer lost me everything on the icecap, biscuit, milk, pea soup, cranberry jam, pemmican . . . I can carry full rations only for the outward and return trips to Independence Bay . . . beyond . . . I must depend entirely upon the game of the country.

The papers and records are in the steamer trunk . . . under the floor of our room . . . I have promised [the Eskimos] a portion of the house . . . Should I not return the rest of the house should go back on the ship. Put on exhibition it will make you independent. All the keys I have put back of the books on the very top shelf.

Good-bye my darling.

Bert

The next morning, April Fool's Day, Peary set off with four Eskimos, Henson and Lee, sixty-five dogs and two sledges, which he named *Josephine* and *Chopsie* (his pet name for the Snow Baby). He carried food enough to reach Independence Bay; beyond that—since he hoped to go all the way to the pole—he would have to depend on whatever game he could find and kill.

The Eskimos went along as a support party, but only as far as the ice cap. He wasn't sorry to see them go; there wasn't enough food for all of them, and there had been no game so far and none expected once they were on the ice. By the time they reached the crest, halfway to the targeted encampment at Independence Bay, they had eaten more than half the food and killed more than half the dogs. Lee was too sick to continue, so they built him a snow igloo, left him what food they could, and Peary and Henson continued on alone.

Somehow they made it to Independence Bay, reaching it finally in mid-May, but they went no further. The caches of food left along the way the previous summer had been lost, and they straggled into their base on the bay nearly starved. Peary's plan to augment provisions there and then to continue north to the pole were frustrated by terrible weather and ice conditions, and most importantly by a lack of food. In two weeks of hunting they found only one group of musk-oxen, and the animals they killed provided barely enough meat to enable them to hope to return to McCormick Bay. (Incidentally, when writing about this trip Peary never mentioned seeing the channel or the land he had named after himself on his first trip. His description of the weather tells of days clear enough to see them, yet he ignores the subject. He must have realized that his "discovery" had been merely a mirage, but he simply ignores the fact.)

On the first of June they started back, battling weather and winds, picking their way over crevices they barely saw in the fog, jumping for their lives over crevices that opened beneath their feet, racing constantly in an effort to get home before their scanty provisions ran out. They found Lee on the way; miraculously he was still alive. They hurried him along with them, and when he called out that he couldn't keep up and begged them to leave him behind in the swirling snow—all he wanted to do was sit down and die peacefully—Peary hauled him to his feet and half pushed, half dragged him along. There was neither time nor food nor energy left to search out the best way through the treacherous ice in order to avoid the possible hidden crevices; Peary simply took them straight on, always forward, through the blinding wind and fog, over the skin of the ice which might at any moment open and plunge them to a death hidden from all humanity.

But the ice did not open. By some chance their feet found firm footing without seeking it, and they made it back to camp by the frostbitten skin of their blackened noses, with one dog left, no food in their packs and no energy in their bodies.

He had made it, Peary recognized, but he had failed to

find a way to reach the pole. He had discovered no new lands, had covered a route which he had already trod before, and had no wonderful new tales to tell, no stories that would bewitch the rich and raise money for another try. It must have been the lowest moment of his life. "I shall never see the North Pole unless someone brings it here," he said. His body was shattered by the ordeal, and so was his mind; he couldn't keep his food down, and thought someone in the party was trying to poison him. Who could it be? He looked around at the Eskimos, at Hugh Lee, at Matt Henson . . . Yes, Henson, he thought.

Then his delirium passed and cold logic took its place. No one was trying to kill him except the North itself, and he wouldn't let it. Nor would he let it defeat him. He sat down to plan, and by the time the relief ship returned in the summer he had his solution: he would steal Ahnighito, the living meteorite after whom he had named his daughter.

Peary didn't think of it as stealing, of course; he would simply take it. Why not? It was just sitting there in the ice, belonging to no one. It was an iron meteorite of more than a hundred tons which had fallen from the skies so long ago that no one alive had seen it. It was the only source of iron in the frozen north, and all their lives the Eskimos had visited it, begged its pardon and chipped pieces off to use as tips for their knives and implements. It was the most important object in their lives. More than that, they venerated it and thought it was alive in some mysterious way. Peary himself tells why: "If a sledge, ill aimed in the darkness . . . chanced to strike it, a spouting jet of scintillating sparks lit the gloom and a deep note [like] . . . the half-pained, half-enraged bellow of a lost soul answered the blow."

But despite the religious significance of Ahnighito, despite its material importance to the Eskimos and despite the difficulties of lifting the tremendous mass and moving it to the ship, Peary took it. He told himself that the Eskimos were well compensated by the trinkets he gave them; what need had they for iron when he gave them knives, pots, runners for their sledges, even guns? He never asked himself how long these gifts would last, and what the people would do when finally they rusted and broke; he simply took their only supply of iron and sailed home.

He also took six live Eskimos and several dead ones with him: "The cask contained Quajaukitsoq and his wife and the little girl . . ." The meteorite was sold to the American Museum of Natural History for an immense sum, and so were the Eskimos, alive and dead. The meteorite, called by the museum the Cape York meteorite, was put on exhibit and is still there. The bones of the dead Eskimos were also put on exhibit, as were the live ones themselves: Qisuk, his son Minik and friend Usaakassak, Nuktaq, his wife Atanga and their young daughter Aviak.

But not for long. They had been given a small space in the basement as a home. After all, why not? It was cold and dark and damp, but they were used to such conditions, weren't they? Evidently not. They began to cough and sneeze, then to choke, and soon all except the two boys Minik and Usaakassak were dead of pneumonia. The bodies were dismembered and these bones too were put on exhibit by the museum, but the feelings of the boys were spared; they were shown a fake burial ceremony. Usaakassak managed finally to get home to his tribe; Minik died in the great flu epidemic of 1918.

But there was a happy ending for Peary; the money he raised from the museum and from others who were impressed by his trophies enabled him to return to the North. On the 4th of July, 1898, he set sail once more. He was to stay in the Arctic four years, and in 1902 would achieve his own furthest north, 84°, but these were not years of triumph. Rather they were years of despair, tragedy and bedroom farce. In his first winter, out on the ice scouting possible routes, he literally bumped into another white man, the Norwegian explorer Otto Sverdrup. He immediately (and wrongly) suspected that Sverdrup was out to beat him to the pole, and so scuttled his plans and set off immediately, in the dead of winter, leaving camp on December 20 with Matt Henson (and against Henson's objections), several Eskimos and of course the dogs. Traveling through the Arctic night at temperatures that dropped well below 50 below zero, the party finally reached a small hut left by a previous expedition. Though it had been abandoned more than twenty years earlier, the constant freezer-like conditions had preserved everything; the food left behind was edible and even a cup of coffee left on the table could be drunk once the frozen liquid was melted.

But the forced march through the terrible cold had taken its toll. As they rested in the hut Peary complained that the feeling wasn't coming back to his lower legs. As he pushed his body to the utmost, his muscles would often overload their sensory systems and would simply fade from his consciousness, their cries of pain never heard by his brain. The terrible cold intensified this desensitization. But always before when he rested and got warm the muscles would begin to tingle, then ache in a strangely comforting way. Today they did not.

Henson kneeled and pulled off Peary's sealskin boots, then looked up and shook his head. Peary's skin had always been whiter than Henson's, but this was a different kind of white—a white without any blood flow, a dead white. When he pulled off the inner lining Peary wore under his boots, two of Peary's toes stuck to the lining instead of to his foot; they broke off, cold and bloodless, frostbitten and useless.

"Why didn't you tell me, sir?" Henson asked.

"No time to pamper sick men on the trail," Peary answered.

Henson tied him onto a sledge and hauled him back to the ship, where the doctor, Tom Dedrick, amputated Peary's toes on the spot. The journey was over for this year.

Peary returned to the hut the following summer, hobbling on his toe-less feet, but made no further advance. In 1900 he tried again, and this time reached the very top of Greenland and looked out on the polar sea. During these years his mother, to whom he had been devoted, had died, and a second daughter had been born and had died. His ship, the *Windward*, had returned home, picked up Mrs. Peary and their daughter, and now, in the summer of 1900, it was returning with relief supplies. But it couldn't find him. The Eskimos at his base camp thought he had gone one way, but he had actually taken another, and so the *Windward* searched for him through the summer and was caught by the onset of cold weather and the ice. Mrs. Peary would spend another winter in the Arctic.

This winter was to place its own peculiar strain on her. On board the *Windward* was Allikassingwah, an Eskimo woman who came up to her to introduce herself and her son, Peary's child. As Peary's mistress, she was happy to have the honor of meeting his white wife, she said. Josephine Peary was not as happy, and certainly not honored, but she made no outward fuss. "You will have been surprised, perhaps annoyed," she wrote Peary, "when you hear I came up on a ship . . . believe me had I known how things were with you I should not have come." There is no record of what went on between husband and wife when he joined the ship the following spring.

In 1902 Peary tried again for the pole, setting off with Henson and a party of Eskimos across the frozen polar sea. When they encountered a vast open lead—a stretch of unfrozen water extending to the horizon in both directions, right and left—they were forced to halt. They spent several days waiting for it to freeze over and let them cross; during this period they marched both right and left to try to find its end. But there was no end, and it did not freeze, and when Peary finally took a longitude measurement he found that the ice they were waiting on was drifting east: they were already 12° further east than when they had left. Since his base was to the southwest, this meant they were drifting further and further from home. As summer approached it was clear the lead would not freeze over this year, so reluctantly he gave the order to turn for home.

Peary had reached 84°17′, but in the meantime an Italian expedition sent out by the Duke of Abruzzi had gone even further, so his achievement was meaningless. He had accomplished nothing. "My dream of sixteen years is over," he said. "I have made a good fight but I cannot accomplish the impossible. . . . I close the book. . . . I accept the result calmly. . . . The goal still remains for a better man than I . . ." He later described himself as "a maimed old man, unsuccessful after the most arduous work, away from wife and child, mother dead, one baby dead . . ."

Three years later Peary tried again. The problem wasn't that he was a maimed old man, he decided as soon as he had rested and gotten warm and well-fed; it was that he had started from too far south with the wrong plan. What he needed was a way to get further north, and a better plan. He devised both.

First, he needed a ship that could break through the ice to a higher latitude than any before it. For this he needed a hull designed like the *Fram*, a powerful engine and screw propellers. He wrote down the detailed specifications and helped design the *Roosevelt*; then he set out to raise the $100,000 that would be needed to build it.

He turned to Morris K. Jesup, a banker, railroad man, chief founder of the American Museum of Natural History (for whom Peary had brought back Ahnighito and the six Eskimos), current president of the American Geographical Society, and the man for whom Peary had named his first discovery. In 1903 Otto Sverdrup had returned from the

Arctic to report the existence of a new island which he named Axel Heiberg Land. Whereupon Peary announced that he had seen this land in 1899 and named it Jesup Land. He had never reported it, however; obviously he hadn't been sure he had really seen anything back in 1899. But now that the land had been seen by someone else, he tried to claim the discovery.

No one believed him. Some even insinuated that he was not only trying to claim discovery for a land so dimly seen that he hadn't been sure it was there, but that he was making the whole thing up. But explorers are a gentlemanly lot —or were in 1903—and no one wanted to accuse Peary of lying; they simply didn't believe him.

No one believed him, that is, except Morris K. Jesup, who now gave $50,000 toward the cost of the *Roosevelt*. With this seed money and his indefatigable energy Peary soon raised the rest, and the *Roosevelt* was built to specification. She was the first ship since the *Fram* to be designed for Arctic work, and like the *Fram* the sides of her hull were egg-shaped so that she might ride up on the ice and escape crushing if caught. But this was to be a last resort; unlike the *Fram* she was designed to break through the ice rather than to sit passively in it, to be in control of her fate and to choose her own destination. The hull was wooden on the outside because steel was more susceptible to large-scale damage by sharp-edged ice (as in the *Titanic*), but under the wood was an interwoven layer of steel beams.

The *Roosevelt* had a steam-routing system that allowed all the power generated by the boilers to be concentrated into one cylinder; this was extremely dangerous (the cylinder might explode under the pressure), but for a short time would allow tremendous power—for example if they were caught in the ice and needed to blast their way through. The propeller and shaft were oversized, and she carried on her deck windlasses and winches with which she could literally pull herself up by her own bootstraps and shake herself loose from enveloping ice. She was thick and strong, reinforced and powerful, and Peary signed on a man just like her to skipper her.

Bob Bartlett, a Newfoundland captain, was fast becoming a legend in Arctic sailing circles. He was a short, thick, powerful man who could scamper around the sheets and crow's nest of a schooner, take care of the logistics of stocking her or lay out a course with equal facility. When offered command of the *Roosevelt* he eagerly accepted; it would be a fine thing, he told Peary, to reach the North Pole. The thought of standing on top of the world would be reward enough for risking his life. Peary shook his hand and promised him that indeed he would one day stand on the North Pole and look down at the rest of the world.

Peary's new plan called for a staggered series of efforts. He would send out teams in relay. The first, loaded with supplies, would break a trail as far as it could go and leave its supplies at the furthest point. The second and third would follow on its heels, conserving energy by following the trail, then take over in turn and extend the trail and cache of supplies still further. At the end, Peary would coast along to the furthest point; then, continuing on his own with the accumulated supplies, he would break virgin territory and attain the pole.

Alone. With no one to share the honor, the glory, the prestige of reaching the North Pole.

But there was no need to tell Bob Bartlett that just yet.

Peary also needed another leave of absence from the navy. It came through once again, but this time with a no-nonsense clause attached. "The attainment of the Pole should be your main object. Nothing short will suffice."

On Sunday, July 16, 1905, the *Roosevelt* set forth, bound for Etah, Greenland. On Wednesday, August 16, they resupplied there, picked up Eskimos and dogs, and left civilization behind. They began plowing through heavy ice, and the ship behaved beautifully until the ice proved almost too much even for her; from this point on it was Bartlett's mastery that drove her forward as he conned the ship from the crow's nest and picked out lanes of new or thinner ice for her to break through.

At one point she was nearly caught. As she was crushing through the ice a sudden current brought her up against a giant floe, thicker than she could manage. The ice stopped breaking below her keel, and since something had to break, it looked as if it would be the *Roosevelt*. She was caught in an ice vise, squeezed and nearly shattered. But suddenly she rose straight up, as she was designed to do, rode over the ice, and dropped again onto thinner ice on the other side, crashing through and making her way once again.

She sailed up to the northeast tip of Greenland, on the edge of the polar ice, and there put into harbor. All winter the Eskimos went out hunting and brought back supplies which Peary arranged in proper order to have ready for the spring. On Monday, February 19, 1906, they left the ship and began their trek to the north. Peary divided them into half a dozen support groups, each led by a member of the expedition with a few Eskimos. Bartlett went off first, then Ross Marvin of Cornell University, and so on. Each was to move fifty miles ahead, then set up a camp. As each successive party came in, the supplies would be transferred. Peary would bring up the rear. In this fashion they would hop, skip and jump to the pole. "Nothing short would suffice."

There were a couple of problems. The plan called for each party not only to bring up supplies, but to ensure that the path they broke was kept open and could be followed both up to the pole and back by the others. This was possible on firm ground, but not on a shifting surface. Although on his previous try Peary had noticed the ice shifting him eastward, he somehow did not account for the possibility of such drift in his plans.

Then there were the open leads of water. An advance party would come up to one, and would simply have to halt and wait for it to ice over. Then the second party would come up against it, and the two would have to sit there and wait. It was like trying to race along an interstate during rush hour; unpredictable and unavoidable bottlenecks developed. The difference is that on the interstate you sit, drum your fingers on the wheel, watch your temperature gauge climb toward overheating and know you're going to have to call the AAA. On the Arctic ice you sit, curse and consume your provisions down to the starvation point, but there is no AAA. "Each day the number of my dogs dwindled and sledges were broken up to cook those of the animals that we ate ourselves," Peary wrote.

By the middle of April he realized he was beaten. The party had reached 87°06', further north than "any white man" had ever been, but their provisions were low, he and his men were weak, the dogs were starving and unable to pull steadily, the ice was terrible and getting worse as temperatures began to rise and the leads widened. He had to turn back. He had gone further north than any explorer before him, but he had not reached the pole, and nothing short would suffice.

Meanwhile, Dr. Frederick A. Cook was playing his own version of succeed and fail. The Arctic bug had bitten him on his first trip north with Peary in 1891, and he would never again be the same man. He was a physician, but the social and economic life of a doctor in the late years of the last century was not as rewarding as it is a hundred years later, particularly the economic aspect. Despite Peary's description of him as "having practiced his profession in New York City for several years," in his first six months of practice in Brooklyn, fewer than six people had opened the door to his surgery. So he sat there and read books about the Far North, the Far South and every inaccessible spot in between. One of the closest of which, yet still among the most inaccessible, was Mount McKinley, the highest mountain in North America.

From the *Encyclopaedia Britannica:* "Mount McKinley, a peak of the Alaska range in south-central Alaska . . . is the culminating point of North America (20,300 ft. above sea level) and rises higher above the surrounding country than any other mountain in the world. Its crest gives rise to numerous glaciers of gigantic size, and it is claimed that the entire surface above 19,000 ft. is a field of snow and ice."

Mount McKinley had never been climbed—in 1897 the Duke of Abruzzi, who had set the furthest north record that Peary was to beat in 1905, had tried and failed—and as Dr. Cook sat in his Brooklyn office it seemed the answer to his ambitions. Close enough to reach without the need of enormous financing, and with conditions on its upper reaches severe enough to remind one of the Arctic north, it beckoned him like a serenading siren: "Climb me and become famous. Conquer me and the world will hasten to your doorstep, bringing riches and praises."

Why not? It was worth a try. In 1903 Cook set out like a seasoned explorer. He hired guides and support groups, and spent the climbing season reconnoitering his enemy, traveling around it, climbing the lower slopes and selecting possible routes to attack. Finally he decided to climb it from the west, but he failed. In 1906 he tried again, and once again failed. Or did he?

"We took twenty pack horses from Seattle for our difficult cross-country transportation, and for the river we built a powerful motor boat," Cook wrote in his book *To the Top of the Continent.* "We forded and swam icy streams, pushed through thick underbrush and over gloomy marshes, only to find that the part of the mountain which we finally reached was impossible for an ascent. A good deal of pioneering work was done at this time, but . . ."

But they had failed. They had not climbed the mountain. The group of five people and twenty pack horses broke up. One went back to New York, a couple of others busied themselves by finishing incidental work such as collecting museum specimens, and Cook took the assistant horse packer to wander around to the south side and see if that route looked any better.

Six weeks later those of the expedition party still in Alaska met once again, and Cook laconically announced that he had climbed Mount McKinley all the way to the top with his friend Edward Barrille, the horse packer. He sent a telegram to his chief backer: "We have reached the summit of Mount McKinley by a new route from the north."

The north? He had last been seen heading around to the south. Moreover, only six weeks had gone by; as one member of the dumbfounded expedition later remarked, it was somewhat like "walking from the Brooklyn Bridge to Grant's Tomb in ten minutes."

Never mind. The man said he had done it, and had even brought back pictures. One in particular showed his companion, Ed Barrille, standing bravely on the summit beside an American flag he had planted in the snow.

Three months later, on December 15, 1906, Dr. Cook was the featured speaker and one of two men being honored at a National Geographic Society banquet. The other honoree was Robert Peary, for achieving the world's highest north. Peary was to be given a special gold medal struck by the society for the occasion, and since it was to be awarded by President Roosevelt himself he certainly had the right to think of himself as the "point of light" of the occasion.

He could not have been happy, however, sharing the stage with Frederick Cook. For one thing, he never liked to share anything with anyone, least of all the focus of attention, and least of all with Cook. The two men had begun as colleagues on Peary's 1891 expedition, and had returned from it nearly friends. Later Peary wrote that he had picked

Cook from hundreds of applicants because of his "intelligent willpower, youthful elasticity, and enthusiasm," and
by the end of the expedition he had found no reason to
change his mind. "I owe much to his professional skill,
unruffled patience and coolness in an emergency," he
wrote. "He was always helpful, and an indefatigable
worker . . . In his special ethnological field . . . he has
obtained a large mass of most valuable material concerning
a practically unstudied tribe."

But when Cook had brazenly asked Peary's permission
to publish those "most valuable" ethnological notes and
Peary had refused, the friendship had died. The two men
had met only once since then. When Peary lost his toes but
refused to abandon his 1901 expedition, Cook had been
prevailed upon by Peary's friends and supporters to make
the hazardous journey to Greenland to offer his services as
a physician. He had done so, and had found Peary a nervous, discouraged, crippled wreck. His advice: "Give up.
You are through as an explorer."

One can imagine Peary's reaction, which would not have
included gratitude that Cook had made the arduous voyage to help him. Now he had to sit at the head table at a
banquet which should have been his alone, and share hon-
ors with this man. Moreover, while waiting for the president to arrive and present his medal, he had to listen to
Cook give the main speech of the evening. And he had to
endure the introduction given by Alexander Graham Bell,
who rambled on and said, "We are glad to welcome Commander Peary of the Arctic regions, but in Dr. Cook we
have . . . the only American . . . who has been to the
top of the American continent, and therefore to the top of
the world."

That must have hurt. But Cook was most gracious as he
began his speech, going out of his way to share credit with
Peary, telling the audience, "I would prefer to tell you tonight of the splendid achievement of Commander Peary,

and of the noble character of the man . . . but your chairman has put me to the task of getting to the top of our continent. . . . In the conquest of Mount McKinley," he continued, "success was mostly due to our use of the working equipment of polar explorers, and among polar explorers Commander Peary has worked hardest to reduce the outfit to its utmost simplicity. Thus, indirectly to Commander Peary should fall a part of the honor of scaling the arctic slopes of our greatest mountain."

What conquest? Peary must have been wondering. Had this man really conquered McKinley? Peary had heard rumors that Ed Barrille, the horse packer who had accompanied Cook, had been telling friends in bars that they had never even attempted to reach the summit.

But Cook stood confidently now in front of the assembled group and gave his usual brilliant speech. He had them on the edge of their seats. "Hour after hour we dug our feet and hands into the snow in desperate efforts to get from crevasse to crevasse, from grottos to cliffs, always gaining a little altitude and rising farther and farther into cloudland, with its awful cold and stormy agitation . . . Here, on a cornice, we built a snow house and within we found rest and comfort, amid the cloud and storms." On and on he went, describing the tortures of the damned but rising in volume and pitch as they rose in altitude further and further toward the summit, and then triumphantly concluding with the words: "The summit at last—the top of the continent. Our North Pole had been reached!"

Oh, infamous boast! Was it an ingenuous tribute to the man sitting at his side, or a slyly calculating reminder that Peary had not reached *his* North Pole?

The applause for Cook was deafening, and it never quite died down even when the president of the National Geographic rose to introduce the president of the United States. The applause rose again to a crescendo as the president presented the gold medal, and Peary was inspired to tell them all: "President Roosevelt, for over three centuries the world has dreamed of solving the mystery of the North. Tonight the Stars and Stripes stand nearest to that mystery, pointing and beckoning . . . To me the final and complete solution of the polar mystery which has engaged the best thought and interest of the best men of the most vigorous and enlightened nations of the world for more than three centuries, and today quickens the pulse of every man or woman whose veins hold red blood, is the thing which should be done for the honor and credit of this country, the thing which it is intended that I should do, and the thing that I must do."

There it was. He was *not* finished. He might be an old, battered, maimed man, as Cook had told him and as he had admitted to his own diary, but he would not fade away. There was only one goal in his life, the North Pole, and he would stalk it until he was victorious or dead. Nothing would stop him. *Nothing*.

Frederick Cook nodded and applauded with the rest of them. If he was smiling, no one noticed.

By early afternoon we are passing the 88th parallel. The ice is continuous now. From the bridge one can see the unbroken mass of white stretching in all directions, the only relief being formed by pressure ridges. As the *Soyuz* surges forward and rides up on the ice, cracks appear and spread outward; as we come crashing down the cracks widen, spreading out like lightning flashes caught in slow motion. The ice under the bow breaks into huge fragments that tip up and over, reaching heights of fifteen or twenty feet, sliding back into the sea slowly as we pass.

And pass we do. We are maintaining a steady eight knots, the ice seemingly powerless to stop us. This is not quite true; we are here only because it is summer; in winter not even the *Soyuz* could come this far north. In fact, the Soviet nuclear icebreaker fleet can't even keep the northern coast of Siberia clear of ice throughout the long winters. But today there is nothing that can stop us.

This morning during breakfast the Klaxon sounded: "Polar bear off the port bow. Attention, please! We are approaching a polar bear eating a seal off the port bow." Everyone jumped up and ran back to their cabins for their camcorders and cameras. By the time I reached the foredeck it was jammed, and ahead of us on the port side a polar bear was wandering casually on the ice, trailing red spots of blood. Hanging from its mouth was the remains of a seal, and as we pulled up silently behind it and it turned to look at us the red streaks on its mouth made it appear to be grinning.

But it was not amused, nor was it frightened by our approach. It ignored us, enjoying its food while a small crowd of birds appeared from nowhere and circled around, diving down to the ice to snatch up fallen pieces of seal much as they do at the beach when children throw them pieces of stale bread. After a while the bear wandered off across the ice, disappearing into the white background as we watched.

By evening there are no more sightings of polar bears, nor of anything else. A solitary fulmar is seen in midafternoon; otherwise there is no sign of life. We are absolutely alone. The mood is intensified by the fog, a white veil that settles over us. Sometimes the sun comes out, in the form of a whiter light; it is never visible as an entity. Once we see a fog bow, a colorless rainbow, whiter against the white fog.

The fog rolls back a bit and the Klaxon announces that helicopter flights will be laid on, but before the first one gets airborne the fog comes stealing back, racing in on giant polar-bear feet, and once again we are caught in it. The flights are canceled, and steadily we crash ahead.

At six o'clock several of us get together for volleyball in the gymnasium. Among the players on my team is Huntington Bradley of Manhattan (the East Eighties) and Cape

Cod (East Dennis). One has the impression that he wouldn't even visit the west side of anyplace. He and his wife Elisabeth are one of the young, modish couples on board; they are known as Bunny and Puffy. He is in his fifties, she is thirty-five-ish—a dangerous age combination. She is pretty, smiling and vivacious, a bubbling, effervescent personality with supreme self-confidence. She is always touching someone—all the young people anyhow: Taffy Mostyn, the Welsh historian, Mike McDowell, the Australian geophysicist, Bill the bartender and all the Russian dining-room waiters. The Russians appear nervous when she comes near them; they don't know what to expect and they're afraid of losing their excellent $15-a-month jobs. The others seem to enjoy her touching them. I would, too.

Bunny and Puffy are not inveterate travelers to exotic climes; this is their first such trip. You can imagine what must have happened: "When should we go out to the beach house, Puffy?"

"Oh, it's the same old crowd every summer. Let's go to the North Pole instead. Wouldn't that be a hoot?"

You can see them every evening walking and talking together on the deck. What about? Their friends on the Cape and what they must be saying?

"Where are Puffy and Bunny this summer? I haven't seen them."

"Oh, haven't you heard? They've gone to the North Pole."

"Oh, that Bunny! It must have been her idea. She's awfully good for Puffy, don't you think? She'll be the making of him."

Of course it may be Puffy who's good for Bunny; I never did find out which of them is which. At any rate, Bunny (or Puffy) is a good volleyball player except that he simply refuses to pass the ball off. Every time he hits it he tries for a killer spike, even from the back court. He makes some of them, but not enough; we lose every game.

Dinner is at 7:30: avocado pear with baby shrimps, mahi Madras style, vegetables, salad and fruit salad. Most people skip coffee because the crashing of the ship through the ice makes the pouring dangerous.

Alcohol, however, is a different matter. Every evening before and after dinner we gather in one of the ship's two lounges for drinks. One of the lounges is reserved for smokers, one for non's. Unfortunately, while it is a truism that smoking is an obnoxious habit, only one or two rungs higher than farting in public, it is also true that the people who tend to be victims of the habit also tend to be more social and extroverted. The discrepancy between the ambience in the two lounges is exacerbated by the fact that the nonsmokers' lounge is also the ship's library and bridge-players' haven, and any tentative conversation there is quickly snuffed out by belligerent stares from the readers and dealers. Combining this with the deciding factor that the smokers' lounge is adjacent to the bar, it usually turns out that despite the polluted air the smokers' lounge is the place to be.

I spend the evening there with Motilal and Kamala Nishtar, the Indian doctors from Manchester. Motilal, the Mr. Dr., is charming and fun, but a bit loud, brash, overwhelming. He is fond of telling stories like the time he had lobster in California and it was so good that he had two of them and then ordered another for dessert. "Oh yes," he chortles, "if I like something I must have it. Nothing will stop me." As if ordering a third lobster for dessert challenged the basic tenets of democracy and exposed him to physical danger from outraged diners on all sides.

Mrs. Dr. Nishtar, Kamala, sits quietly through all this and only smiles serenely at him, as at a spoiled but favorite child. She obviously adores him, while recognizing his silliness. I have always thought her much the wiser of the two, until tonight when for some reason she begins to talk, and sets me straight about living conditions in India, which I tell her I know about only from Richard Attenborough's *Gandhi*.

She laughs. "Well, you know these people in India who are living in shantytowns, they are not actually poor people. If you go into those shacks you will find they all have color televisions."

I express amazement.

"Oh, yes," she assures me. "You know in India we have a system of part-time helpers. They will come in for an hour in the morning to do the breakfast things, and then an hour in the evening. My sister has these people to do that. But on Monday they will *not* come. Oh, no. You see, on Sunday they all rent video movies, three or four of them, and they stay up all night watching them and then they sleep on Monday. They will not come. So they are not poor —well, of course they are poor, but they are not starving; they all have television."

"You're talking about big cities, though. If you go into the countryside are they still so well off?"

"Oh, in the countryside they are much *better* off. They have fresh vegetables. They are happy there in their simple life. They do not have the bad habits, you know?"

Tomorrow the pole.

AUGUST 4

᛫ı|||||ı᛫

I am awakened at 6 A.M. by the announcement that we are approaching the pole. But last night I stayed too long in the lounge, and it is impossible to wake up; finally at seven I get out of bed and find that the dining room is already empty. After a quick breakfast I go up to the bridge, where everyone is crammed around the satellite navigational system, holding drinks, laughing, joking and keeping a watch on the digital display while the captain maneuvers the ship back and forth to get it to say that we're at exactly 90° North. It is like New Year's Eve, with the crowds all watching the ball on top of Times Square, holding glasses of champagne, ready to shout and drink a toast at the exact instant when we hit.

The weather is as usual: cloudy, not a trace of the sun. It is odd to realize that the times I mentioned have no meaning outside the convenience of the people on this ship. All time merges here.

One woman asks half jokingly (only half) as the ship creeps forward, "It won't suddenly slide down the other side, will it?"

At 0825 hours the display hits the magic figures—90°00'00"—and a cheer goes up. Next moment the cham-

pagne corks pop and we all rush down to the bow deck.
The ship has come to a halt and there is no wind. A few
snowflakes are falling and the fog hangs heavy over us.
The temperature is just below freezing; with the absence of
wind it seems almost tropical. We wander around, disappointed that there isn't more to see. It all seems so normal.
After all this traveling it is almost banal. Gertrude Stein's
remark about her hometown of Oakland pops into my
head, and I quote it to Tess Mannix, who has been dragged
by her husband from the bridge table in honor of the occasion, and who clearly is waiting with an outward show of
patience until she can decently return.

"What?" she asks.

I gesture out over the vast white nothingness. "There is
no there, there," I repeat.

"Where?" She looks at me as if I'm addled. I look at her
but can't think how to explain; she walks away and I let her
go. All the same, it's true. When they climbed Mount Everest or landed on the moon, they knew they were *there*. They
stood on the highest peak and looked down on the world
or they stood in a new place and looked up at the world,
and they knew they had arrived at their journey's end, at a
place where no one had stood before. But when the first
men reached the North Pole, where were they? It all looks
the same here; one spot is no different from another. There
is nothing here, and there was never really any reason to
come here—no reason for Franklin to lose all those lives,
for Nansen to risk and nearly lose his own, for Lutwidge,
Parry and von Payer and all the others to suffer so terribly
in order to reach this non-spot. No reason at all except to
test the limit of human endurance, to stretch the power of
human imagination and to reach beyond our grasp.

Now that we're here, it seems anticlimactic. There is no
here, here. Nothing but, as Cook called it, "a white vacantness." Puffy (or Bunny) Bradley comes along, champagne

in hand, and I decide to try the line on her. "There's no there, there," I gesture out to the snow.

"Oh, *God*," she bubbles. "Does *any*one *really* still read Gertrude Stein? Spare me," and she bounces away.

We are all walking around the deck, singly and in small groups, smiling slightly at each other as we pass, waiting for something to happen, something momentous to mark the moment, as in Poe's "MS. Found in a Bottle": "The ship proves to be in a current, if that appellation can properly be given to a tide which, howling and shrieking by the white ice, thunders on . . . with a velocity like the headlong dashing of a cataract . . .

"To conceive the horror of my sensations is utterly impossible; yet a curiosity to penetrate the mysteries of these awful regions predominates even over my despair, and will reconcile me to the most hideous aspect of death. It is evident that we are hurrying onwards to some exciting knowledge . . . whose attainment is destruction. Perhaps this current leads us to the pole itself.

"The crew pace the deck with unquiet and tremulous step . . . The ship is at times lifted bodily from out the sea —Oh, horror upon horror! the ice opens suddenly to the right and to the left, and we are whirling dizzily, in immense concentric circles, round and round the borders of a gigantic amphitheatre, the summit of whose walls is lost in the darkness and the distance . . . We are plunging madly within the grasp of the whirlpool—and amid a roaring, and bellowing and thundering of ocean and of tempest, the ship is quivering, oh God! and—going down."

That would be more like it. Of course Poe was talking about the South Pole, but surely one might expect something of the same sort of thing. Or how about the ideas of United States Congressman Robert Bruce Macon (Democrat, Arkansas, of the House Committee on Naval Affairs) who, while investigating Peary's claims, stated on the floor of the House: "I am advised by a school of scientists that it is a physical impossibility for man or beast to reach the North Pole for the reason that . . . the diminishing centrifugal action and, in proportion, the increasing center of gravity near the Pole causes a complete failure of man and animal energy that produces a kind of paralysis of the senses and of motion, a paralysis of sensation in any part of the body, including the exercise of the faculty of the mind . . . So that it would be almost impossible for them to exercise their independent functions so that anybody could ascertain a real fact.

"It is contended by scientists . . . that the thing that they call the North Pole is a hole that extends into the interior surface of the earth . . ."

Which I suppose is what Poe was talking about, and without being as fantastic as Poe or as silly as the congressman, each of us was half expecting something of the sort. At least we were expecting *something* out of the ordinary. Perhaps not that we might suddenly "slide down the other side" or get caught in the meridians which meet at this spot or fall insensibly through a hole in the ice, but that at least the winds would howl, ice would surge around us and giant icebergs come careening out of the mist to crush us . . .

But no, nothing. The *Soyuz* sits nestled in the calm ice and we stroll around the decks with our glasses of champagne and wait for something to happen.

Things were different in 1908 when Peary once again determined to make for the pole. He would make a final attempt; he couldn't resist it. "The lure of the North! It is a strange and a powerful thing. More than once I have come back from the great frozen space, battered and worn and baffled, sometimes maimed, telling myself that I had made my last journey thither, eager for the society of my kind, the comforts of civilization and the peace and serenity of home. But somehow it was never many months before the

old restless feeling came over me. Civilization began to lose
its zest for me. I began to long for the great white desola-
tion, the battles with the ice and the gales, the long, long
arctic night, the long, long arctic day, the handful of odd
but faithful Eskimos who had been my friends for years,
the silence, the vastness of the great, white lonely North.
And back I went . . ."

The ship Peary had designed for his last trip, the *Roosevelt*, had barely made it home the previous year. After
wintering in the ice she had broken out and "had squeezed
down along the shore past Cape Union when she was
smashed against the ice-foot just south of the cape, tearing
a blade from the propeller and breaking off her stern post
and rudder." From Peary's point of view, once he had
reached the sanctuary of his ship he was as good as home
again. From the captain's perspective it wasn't that easy.
Bob Bartlett wrote about this voyage home as a life-and-
death struggle every moment of the way. "I used to go on
deck and decide that we would sink in a few minutes and
then go down and make a last entry in my diary. Then I'd
come up again and we'd still be afloat and I'd try to explain
how it was possible for a wreck like ours not to sink . . .
all the time the rudder we had rigged was being punished
worse and worse and the bottom was getting more holes
punched in it. Most of our men had given up hope long
ago."

At the very end, when seemingly all their troubles were
finally behind them, Bartlett wrote: "Going through St. Peter Canal in thick weather I ran the *Roosevelt* into a fence
which was built down into the water, and jammed her nose
hard and fast into the bank. This happened because our
rudder could not operate fast enough to let us maneuver in
narrow waters. I remember a girl was milking a cow behind the fence. When she saw the *Roosevelt* headed straight
for her she grabbed the stool on which she was sitting and
dashed screaming up the hill. The cow galloped after her.

The poor old *Roosevelt*, as well as ourselves, was ready for the insane asylum or the dump heap."

But Peary would never admit this. All he said about the ship in a telegram to his supporters back home was the laconic: "*Roosevelt* magnificent ice fighter." For it was his design and his ship, and therefore the right design and the right ship to carry him close enough for a dash to the pole. He loved that ship: "In all my experiences I recall nothing more exciting than the thrill of hurling the *Roosevelt*, a fifteen-hundred-ton battering-ram, at the ice to smash a way through . . ." All that was needed was to effect a few small repairs and it would do the job one more time.

In fact, none of Peary's plans were much different from those of last time; there were merely a few improvements. He would try to leave from further north; he would keep his supporting parties closer together so they wouldn't get separated by intervening movements of the ice; he wouldn't set up his main rear base until they were north of the largest stretch of open water that had detained him in 1906—the Big Lead, as he called it at first, or the Styx, as he called it at last—and he would cache supplies for the return trip along several different routes in case they were moved east or west by the drifting ice. (In light of his later claims at navigation, this last point is an interesting one and should be remembered.) Aside from these small changes he would do as he had done before, for the plan was good. He would simply try again, and this time he would make it to the pole!

Why this determination? Why this insane desire to reach this ridiculous spot? Was it that he was infected with that fervent, jingoistic brand of patriotism personified by the then president of the United States, Teddy Roosevelt? When Roosevelt had presented the medal to him at the conclusion of his last voyage he had responded that "the final and complete solution of the polar mystery . . . is the thing which must be done for the honor and credit of this country . . . Should an American first of all men place the Stars and Stripes at that coveted spot, there is not an American citizen at home or abroad but what would feel a little better and a little prouder of being an American; and just that added increment of pride and patriotism to millions would of itself be ten times the value of all the cost of attaining the Pole . . . President Roosevelt, you have planted the Stars and Stripes at Panama and . . . God willing, I hope that your administration may yet see those Stars and Stripes planted at the Pole itself [for the glory of] that giant whose destinies you guide today, the United States of America."

Or was it Peary's own personal devil, the "lure of the North," which he couldn't resist? Or perhaps it was the thought of Frederick Cook, who wanted to get to the pole as a simple sporting proposition. Peary made light of Cook; when, in 1907, someone told him that Cook was on his way to the pole by Peary's route, he dismissed the suggestion with the reply that Cook was an honorable man, and no honorable explorer would impinge on "his" route. As if he had it copyrighted or patented. At least that is how he talked to others; when he and his wife discussed Cook their attitude was a bit different, referring to him as a fake and a scoundrel, a man who could not be trusted. It would kill him to have Cook reach the pole first, despite the fact that, should this happen, "the Stars and Stripes" would still be planted at the "coveted spot" by an American.

No, it wasn't patriotism that guided Peary. It was the passion Joan of Arc knew for God, the passion Paris and Menelaus knew for Helen, the passion of Faust for knowledge and power, the passion of Ho Chi Minh for independence and of Lyndon Johnson for success. It was simply *passion:* blind and unreasoning, indefatigable and ultimately irresistible.

By this time Peary had given all that most men have in their lives to give, and more. He had been absent from his

mother's death and his daughter's. He had missed the birth
of his second son. His daughter, the Snow Baby, knew him
as a stranger, almost a myth. She wrote to him: "My dear,
dear Father, I read that the Peary Arctic Club are trying to
get your consent to go north again. I think it a dog's shame
. . . I have been looking at your pictures, it seems ten
years, and I am sick of looking at them. I want to see my
father. I don't want people to think me an orphan . . ."

None of that mattered. Peary loved his wife and daughter as much as a monomaniac can love anything beyond his
mania; he loved them, but he *must* have the pole. On July 6,
1908, he boarded the refitted *Roosevelt,* backed out of the
East Twenty-fourth Street pier, and steamed up the East
River toward the north.

It was early afternoon when he left, and the scene was
tumultuous—depending on whom you talk to. "A cheer
that echoed over Blackwells Island went up from the thousands who had gathered on the piers to see us off, while
the yacht fleet, the tugboats and the ferryboats tooted
their good wishes. . . . President Roosevelt's yacht, the
Mayflower, and her small gun roared out a parting salute,
while the officers and men waved and cheered. Surely no
ship ever started for the end of the earth," Peary wrote in
his book *The North Pole,* "with more heart-stirring farewells
than those which followed the *Roosevelt.*"

Watching from amidships, Matt Henson saw a different
scene. "An indescribable blending of sincerity and hypoc-
risy, boos and cheers, confidence and disdain, bid the *Roosevelt* farewell. . . . Men in the streets brawled among
themselves over the degree of disaster the expedition
would meet. Gamblers accepted fabulous odds on their
success, while women wept for no reason. It was tense and
exciting, yet it was ugly and vicious."

Whatever, it must have been something to see. (When
the *Sovetskiy Soyuz* left Murmansk on July 27, 1991, we
were sent off from an empty dock by a bedraggled six-man

Russian naval band which played the "Internationale" followed by "The Star-Spangled Banner," "The Marseillaise," and the anthems of the several nations represented on board. When they paused, our young woman passenger, Liz Harper, echoed them on her saxophone and then serenaded the band by herself with "The St. Louis Blues" as we moved silently up the Kola River and out of sight.)

The trip north was a typical Arctic nightmare, though Peary's cabin and private bathroom on the *Roosevelt* were a model of comfort that would have appeared incredible to earlier polar explorers. It was roomy and well-furnished, with a wide bunk on which his daughter had placed a fragrant pine-needle pillow; beside it were several bookshelves with a complete Arctic library, novels and magazines, a writing desk, and a Pianola featuring the music of Gounod and Strauss, but including a gallimaufry of marches, songs and even a few ragtime pieces.

The rest of the ship, however, was a Hieronymus Bosch nightmare. It was built to house a ship's crew of fifteen, plus an exploring party of half a dozen, but now it also had stuffed on board five dozen Eskimos of assorted sizes and sexes and more than two hundred snarling dogs, and in every crevice was stuffed tons of walrus, whale meat and blubber. The captain, Bob Bartlett, who had come along again because he was determined to stand on the North Pole, later remembered that voyage: "To my dying day I'll never forget the frightful noise, the choking stench and the terrible confusion . . ."

They spent a miserable few weeks plowing through ice so thick that they frequently thought they would be stuck, with Bob Bartlett up in the crow's nest trying to pick out a ziggedy-zaggedy route through the thinnest of the ice and Peary at the helm exhorting the coal stokers to give them more steam, always more steam. The chief would bellow up through the voice pipe that the boilers couldn't take any more, and Peary would bellow back down that if they didn't get another burst of power *right now* they would be crushed by the ice and it wouldn't matter if the boilers lasted another thousand years because they would all be dead in ten minutes. So the coal would be piled on, the fires would roar and Bartlett would scream at his ship from the crow's nest, "Rip 'em, Teddy!"—he called the *Roosevelt* by her first name—"Bite 'em in two! Go it! That's fine, my beauty! Now—again! And once more!" And the ship would squeeze through another narrow lead, and somehow the boilers didn't quite split apart. It was all perfectly routine. As Peary said, "The life is a dog's life. But the work is a man's work."

Almost from the beginning what marked this voyage apart from the normal was the absent but seemingly ubiquitous Dr. Cook. When they reached Etah, docked and began transferring provisions from their supply boat to the *Roosevelt* for the last push up to the forward base, a sick and frantic white man came up to Bartlett, begging to be taken home. He was Rudolph Francke, and he told Bartlett that he had come up to Etah with Dr. Cook, who was on his way to the North Pole.

Two years earlier Frederick Cook, still flushed with his victory over Mount McKinley, met a wealthy yachting sportsman and hunter named John R. Bradley, who was planning an Arctic hunting trip aboard his yacht and invited him along. Cook agreed to go, ostensibly to complete his ethnological studies of the Eskimos begun on his first trip with Peary.

The next step is clouded with mystery, having been told many times by different people with different plots. But it seems that at some point Bradley said, "I just want to hunt a bit, but wouldn't it be a lark if you went off to the North Pole?"

Well, why not? It wouldn't be much more than a 2000-mile hike over "unknown and uninhabitable wastes of moving ice," without any of the preparations or thought that Peary had put into it. The idea appealed to Cook—if in fact it was Bradley's idea instead of Cook's from the beginning. He didn't attach much importance to the pole, he later wrote. The thought of attaining it was merely a "crazy hunger [he] had to satisfy." It didn't represent a patriotic cause, as with Peary; it was just an "intoxication . . . to go on, and on, and ever onward, where no man had ever been." The feeling grew as the yacht sailed northward, evidently with none of the drama Peary wrote about aboard the *Roosevelt*. Cook stood on deck, stared out over the ice and began to feel "the indomitable, swift surge of awful goading determination within me—to subdue the forces of nature . . . to reach the silver-shining vacantness which men call the North Pole."

It was a lark, a jaunt, a dash into excitement, the sort of thing that other men seek to accomplish by taking a ride on a ferris wheel or embarking on an affair. "I felt the intoxication, the intangible lure of the thing exhilarating, buoying me gladsomely, beating in my heart with a singing rhythm."

So on February 19, 1908, when the yacht reached its northernmost limit, Cook left Bradley and set off with the ship's cook, Rudolph Francke, and nine Eskimos. "My heart was high. The natives were naturally excited. The dogs caught the contagious enthusiasm and barked joyously. At eight o'clock in the morning our whips snapped, the spans of dog teams leaped forward, and we were off."

Six months later Rudolph Francke, sick with scurvy and in a serious mental state, according to Peary, came staggering up to Bob Bartlett. "He held out a black, grimy fist and slowly opened his clenched fingers, revealing a grubby wad of paper nestled in his dirt-smeared palm. 'Look,' he screamed. 'Look! I can go away. I have permission from Dr. Cook!' "

Francke had broken under the strain of the march northward and had been sent back by Cook to the shack he had left behind with provisions for his return journey and written permission to seek the first passage home. Cook himself, Francke told the Peary party, had kept going, traveling with two Eskimos toward the pole.

So it was no longer simply a matter of Peary reaching the pole, as difficult as this had always been. It was now a race to get there first, for to reach the pole and find another man's footprints there would be worse than useless; it would be ignominious. Particularly if the footprints were those of a clown like Cook who had embarked on the trip without the painstaking preparations Peary had made, and who was now sauntering northward with no supporting parties, alone on the ice with two Eskimos. If he should reach it first he would make a laughingstock of the careful, meticulous Peary. "I believe in you, Peary," President Roosevelt had boomed as he shook his hand and sent him on his way. "And I believe in your success if it is within the possibility of man." To have another man accomplish the feat which was solely within his own realm of possibilities was unthinkable.

But there was worse, Peary realized, for hard on the heels of Cook's announcement of the conquest of McKinley had come the rumors that he hadn't done it after all, that he had simply claimed to have done it. What would stop him from doing this now, from coming home after several months alone on the ice and saying to everyone, "The North Pole? Oh yes, I've been there. Nothing, really. Just a white vacantness. Please don't make a fuss." Then he would stand there facing the newspaper photographers and smile his charming, disarming smile, reluctantly accepting the plaudits of the world, a humble, modest, charming rogue and liar.

Peary couldn't stand the thought. He tacked a notice up on the door of Cook's shack: "This house belongs to Dr.

F. A. Cook, but Dr. Cook is long ago dead and there is no use to search for him. Therefore I, Commander Robert E. Peary, install my boatswain in this deserted house."

But Cook was not dead, and Peary's worst fears were to inspire the gods to laughter and merriment.

In August, 1908, Peary and the *Roosevelt* settled in at Cape Sheridan on Ellesmere Island. They unloaded supplies in preparation for the march that would begin in the spring, and then settled down to wait. "Only the few months of waiting . . . and the long, dark winter lay between me and the final start."

That long, dark winter was not much different from all those endured by all the men who had come north before. "How do we spend the twenty-four hours?" Dr. Kane wrote a hundred years earlier. "At six in the morning the decks are cleaned, the ice-hole opened, the refreshing beef-nets examined, the ice-tables measured, and things aboard put to rights . . . Our breakfast is hard tack, pork, stewed apples frozen like molasses-candy, tea and coffee, with a delicate portion of raw potato . . . At dinner as at break-fast the raw potato comes in, our hygienic luxury. Like doctor-stuff generally, it is not as appetizing as desirable. Grating it down nicely, leaving out the ugly red spots liber-ally, and adding the utmost oil as a lubricant, it is as much as I can do to persuade the mess to shut their eyes and bolt it, like Mrs. Squeer's molasses and brimstone at Dotheboys Hall. Two absolutely refuse to taste it . . .

"Sleep, exercise, amusement, and work at will, carry on the day till our six o'clock supper, a meal something like breakfast and something like dinner, only a little more scant . . . We have cards sometimes, and chess some-times,—and a few magazines to cheer away the eve-ning . . .

"All this seems tolerable for commonplace routine; but there is a lack of comfort which it does not tell of. Our fuel is limited to three bucketfuls of coal a day, and our mean temperature outside is 40 degrees below zero; 46 below as I write. London Brown Stout, and somebody's Old Brown Sherry, freeze in the cabin lockers; and the carlines overhead are hung with tubs of chopped ice, to make water for our daily drink. Our lamps cannot be persuaded to burn salt lard; our oil is exhausted; and we work by muddy tapers of cork and cotton floated in saucers. We have not a pound of fresh meat, and only a barrel of potatoes left.

"Not a man now is exempt from scurvy; and, as I look around upon the pale faces and haggard looks of my comrades, I feel that we are fighting the battle of life at disadvantage, and that an Arctic night and an Arctic day age a man more rapidly and harshly than a year anywhere else in all this weary world."

On the 15th of February, 1909, the time came for Peary to shake off the lethargy of winter hibernation and begin. Bob Bartlett left the ship with the first sledge party, followed in turn by Dr. J. Goodsell, who had taken Cook's place as surgeon of the expedition; then Ross Marvin, a professor from Cornell; George Borup, a young graduate of Yale; and Donald MacMillan of Bowdoin. They would break the trail and store supplies, and on February 22 Peary started his final journey.

"The first serious obstacle of the sledge journey," Peary wrote, "was encountered the second day out from land. The day was cloudy, the wind continuing to blow from the east with unabated violence." Traveling last among the sledge groups, he saw on the horizon an "ominous cloud" —ominous because it meant an open lead. Water evaporating from a lead condenses almost immediately in the cold air, and so a cloud is a signpost. When he reached it he found his advance party stuck there, with nothing to do except build igloos and settle down. At this point they had already beaten Markham's old furthest north record of

83°20', but this was scant consolation if the lead refused to freeze over.

When they woke the next morning they heard the sound of grinding ice, which meant that the two sides of the lead had come together, and they rushed out and hurried across. They traveled for a while without further incident, and on March 5, with the temperature 20 degrees below zero, Peary sent the first supply group home. Donald Mac-Millan was the one chosen to leave, and though he must have been disappointed he knew the arrangement: one by one they would be sent back until the last group made the final dash alone.

On March 20th George Borup was sent back. "I can still see Borup's eager and bright young face, slightly clouded with regret, as he turned away at last and disappeared with his Eskimos and steaming dogs among the ice hummocks of the back trail." Still, as Peary said, he had carried the Yale colors past 85°. Now Bartlett took up the lead, with Marvin, Henson and Peary following.

They pushed onward, making excellent time though the weather was extremely cold. "Sometimes, in opening my mouth to shout an order to the Eskimos, a sudden twinge would cut short my words—my moustache having frozen to my stubble beard." But on they pressed, passing Nansen's record furthest north of 86°13'. On March 25th they passed the Italian record of 86°38', and there Marvin and his sledge party were sent home.

There were just two companions left now besides the Eskimos: Henson and Bartlett. It was Bartlett who took out the lead group the next morning, while Peary and Henson were still sleeping. When Peary awoke he saw another of those ominous dark clouds ahead of him, and sure enough, he caught up to Bartlett six hours later stuck in front of an open lead. Peary and Henson built an igloo and settled down for the night.

As he slept, Peary heard the grinding of ice; this comforted him, for it usually meant that the lead was coming together. Not this time. He was awakened by sudden shouting. Looking out through the igloo's peephole, he saw that a tributary of the lead had sneaked in between his igloo and Bartlett's, which was being carried off into the open lead on a small sheet of ice. He and Henson could do nothing but watch helplessly as Bartlett drifted off toward a cold oblivion, but then the current changed. Bartlett began to drift downstream, inching closer to the main ice mass on which Peary waited. Finally it touched, and Bartlett and his Eskimos jumped across.

"The next march," Peary later wrote, "was to be Bartlett's last, and he let himself out to do his best." There is certainly a strong implication here that Bartlett knew it was to be his last, and that he would not go all the way to the pole. But this is a lie. He had signed on for the 1905 expedition only after being promised that he would go all the way to the pole, and this agreement had never been retracted. Though Peary writes that "the program was for him to go back," it is clear that Bartlett hadn't been told this in advance, for he nearly went crazy with frustration when Peary told him he was to go no further; Henson would be the only one of the party to accompany Peary to the pole. "It was a bitter disappointment," Bartlett told the newspapers when he returned. It was more than that. In fact, he "got up early the next morning while the rest were asleep and started north alone . . . I guess perhaps I was a little crazy then. I thought I could walk on the rest of the way alone."

He couldn't, of course, and soon returned. Peary glosses over this. He writes: "After breakfast Bartlett started to walk five or six miles to the north in order to make sure of reaching the 88th parallel"—which is not at all what Bartlett himself said. Peary finishes by transferring the focus once again to himself: "I felt a keen regret as I saw the captain's broad shoulders grow smaller in the distance and finally disappear behind the ice hummocks. . . . But it was not time for reverie, and I turned abruptly away and gave my attention to the work which was before me."

Henson and Peary set off on a "fine marching morning, clear and sunlit, with a temperature of minus 25° and a gentle breeze." The ice turned hard and level and they sped forward; the fifty-foot-high pressure ridges all had gaps through which they could slip, "the years seemed to drop" from their shoulders, and they traveled for ten hours without stopping.

"On, on we pushed, and I am not ashamed to confess that my pulse beat high, for the breath of success seemed already in my nostrils." For two more days they raced onward, covering more miles on each day than any man had ever before covered in the Arctic, until finally . . .

"The last march northward ended at ten o'clock on the forenoon of April 6 . . . I was actually too exhausted to realize at the moment that my life's purpose had been achieved. . . . I turned in for a few hours of absolutely necessary sleep . . . the first thing I did after awaking was to write these words in my diary: 'The Pole at last. The prize of three centuries. My dream and goal for twenty years. Mine at last!' "

And what about Cook? Ah, Cook, the charming, roguish gentleman, the Errol Flynn of the Arctic. Wouldn't it be wonderful if he really had been first to the pole instead of Peary: the gentleman instead of the posturer, the easygoing, laid-back explorer instead of the pompous patriot who took himself so seriously? Yes, indeed it would be, and indeed it was, for when Cook returned from the frozen wastes in 1909 he announced that he had reached the pole before Peary. The problem was, he hadn't.

Peary retraced his steps, following the trail he had beaten out on his way up and which his support teams had kept open for him on the way back. He reached the *Roosevelt* in Greenland and set sail once again for civilization. His first contact with the outside world came at Etah in August 1909, and the first thing he heard was that Cook was not dead, but had returned from his expedition the previous April, when Peary was just reaching the Pole. When asked where he had been for the past year Cook replied laconically, "Oh, I've been to the pole."

When had he reached it? A year ago. To be precise, on April 21, 1908.

The world went crazy. Cook sailed from Etah to Denmark, hitching a ride on a passing whaler, and was met by a few reporters at his first landfall. His next stop was Elsinore in Denmark, where a mountain of cables and telegrams from newspapers all over the world begging for his account awaited him. As he made his way to Copenhagen his story, like Cyrano's nose, traveled half a league before him, and by the time he reached the city he was met at the dock by the crown prince and a wild, cheering mob. "As we approached the city, I saw far in the distance flags flying. Like a darting army of water bugs, innumerable craft of all kind were leaping toward us on the sunlit water. Tugs and motors, rowboats and sailboats, soon surrounded and followed us. The flags of all nations dangled on the decorated craft. People shouted, it seemed, in every tongue. Wave after wave of cheering rolled over the water. Horns blew, there was the sound of music, guns exploded. All about, balancing on unsteady craft, their heads hooded in black, were the omnipresent moving-picture-machine operators at work. All this passed as a moving picture itself, I standing there, dazed, simply dazed."

Tut-tut, the amiable Dr. Cook said. Why all the fuss? His cheerful, bemused face looked out over the crowd modestly. The Copenhagen celebration burst on him "like a bolt from the blue. I was utterly bewildered by it," he wrote. "In the wildest flights of my imagination I never dreamed of any world wide interest in the Pole. . . . I regarded my entire experience as purely personal. I supposed that the newspapers would announce my return, and that there would be a three days' breath of attention, and that would be all. . . ."

And if you believe that, I've got a lovely bridge in Brooklyn I'd like to sell you.

The stage was set for the battle of the century, a battle in which the victor was quickly crowned, then a tie was decided upon, then the first winner was declared bogus, then the second winner was renounced, then . . . a battle which is still going on to this day, with the momentum ebbing and flowing every few years.

In one corner stood the pugnacious, pompous Peary, civil engineer by the grace of the United States Navy, "Commander" by the grace of an honorary appellation by Congress which he used as his lawful title. In the other corner was the modest, charming Cook, willing to shake hands with Peary and call it a draw. "There is glory enough for both," he suggested.

Never! "It is my destiny to plant the Stars and Stripes at the Pole," Peary had said. There could be no gentlemanly sharing of the prize, especially since Cook, if he had done it at all, had done it first. No, Peary's position was clear: Cook had *not* done it, could not *possibly* have done it. It would have been an insult to Peary's manifest destiny, which translates as God. Therefore Cook must be shown to be a liar.

Which was not that hard to do. The Peary camp began with the Mount McKinley incident. Rumors had been flying for some time that although Cook had accomplished a great deal—certainly he had been the first person to explore the complete circumference around the base of the mountain—he hadn't actually climbed it. There were no two ways about this: if he hadn't reached the summit he had faked it. At the end of September *The New York Times* published a letter from one of Peary's supporters claiming that Ed Barrille, the assistant horse packer who had supposedly accompanied Cook to the summit, was telling his friends back West that they had faked the whole affair.

On October 4 a lawyer hired by the Peary group brought home from Montana a notarized statement by Barrille, swearing that the peak photographed by Cook with Barrille holding the American flag was not the summit but a lower peak; in fact it was only 8000 feet high and was at least twenty miles from the top of the mountain. Barrille also swore that the description in his diary of how they had climbed to the peak was dictated by Cook after they returned, and was pure fiction.

At the end of the month Cook, on a lecture tour, challenged Ed Barrille to meet him in Hamilton, Montana, to debate the matter in public. What he was thinking it is impossible to understand. What happened was that Cook gave his usual North Pole lecture and then, turning to the McKinley controversy, told the audience that they should read the "mass of testimony" his lawyer had collected, and then left the stage.

But though the meeting was taking place in an auditorium called the Opera House, this was not a polite audience, but a group of Barrille's rough townsfolk, and they roared their disapprobation. Barrille stood up and shouted that he had something to say, and the audience roared its approval. Cook snapped back that *he* had rented the Opera House for the night, and that *he* would decide who would speak.

The audience charged the stage. They had come for a public fight, and they were damned well going to get it. Cook fled backstage, and when coerced to reappear he would do nothing but write down a statement that said he had traveled to the top of McKinley. He refused to answer any questions, and after Barrille had told his story Senator

J. A. Dixon proposed a resolution that was carried by unanimous voice vote: "We, the people of Ravalli County, Montana . . . do declare our belief in the veracity and statement of Ed Barrille . . ."

The following year two expeditions traveled to McKinley. One, sponsored by the Peary Arctic Club, went to find the photographed peak and show that it was not the summit. The other went to follow the route outlined in Cook's book *To the Top of the Continent* and thus prove Cook right.

The Peary group found a peak which they said was the photographed "summit" at an altitude of 5300 feet. No one noticed the discrepancy between this and Barrille's statement that it was at 8000 feet, but it didn't matter, for the other group returned to report that they had followed Cook's route until it "abruptly departed from reasonable accuracy into complete fantasy." With even his putative supporters deserting him, Cook was firmly established in the public mind as a liar.

But all this was a year later. In the meanwhile Peary was bombarding newspapers with telegrams denouncing Cook as a fake, and insisting to everyone that the man should be forced to provide proof of his feat. Peary's insistence was so virulent that the public turned against him; he had the profile of a braggart and bully, hounding the modest, charming Dr. Cook who was perfectly willing to share the glory that he didn't believe either of them deserved. "It seemed silly for such a fuss to be made," he said.

Cook wrote his book and told his story in lecture tours around the world, and a thrilling story it was. He had left the safety of the solid earth behind when he stepped off the north coast of Axel Heiberg Island northwest of Greenland on March 18, 1908, and ventured out onto the polar ice with two Eskimos, Ah-we-lah and E-tuk-i-shook, twenty-six dogs and two sleds. Audiences thrilled as he told of his journey to the top of the earth and of the dangers that beset every step: "With bated breath and my heart thumping, I advanced at the end of a long line which was attached to the first sled, and picked my way through the crushed and difficult ice along shore. With the life-saving line fastened to each one of us, we were insured against possible dangers as well as forethought could provide. Running from sled to sled, from dog to dog, and man to man, it would afford a pulling chance for life should anyone break through the ice. It seemed unlikely that the ice along the entire chain would break at once, but its cracking under the step of one of us seemed probable.

"I knew, as I gently placed my foot upon the thin yellowish surface, that at any moment I might sink into an icy grave. Yet a spirit of bravado thrilled my heart. I felt the grip of danger, and also that thrill of exultation which accompanies its terror. Gently testing the ice before me with the end of my axe, with spread legs, on snowshoes, with long, sliding steps, I slowly advanced.

"A dangerous cracking sound pealed in every direction under my feet. The Eskimos followed. With every tread the thin sheet of ice perceptibly sank under me, and waved, in small billows, like a sheet of rubber.

"Stealthily, as though we were trying to filch some victory, we crept forward. We rocked on the heaving ice as a boat on waves of water. Now and then we stepped upon sheets of thicker ice, and hastily went forward with secure footing. None of us spoke during the dangerous crossing. I heard distinctly the panting of the dogs and the patter of their feet. We covered the two miles safely, yet our snail-like progress seemed to cover many anxious years.

"I cannot describe the exultation which filled me when the crossing was accomplished . . ."

But there was to be no respite, not even in bed at night: "Terror gripped my heart. Loud explosive noises reverberated under my head. It seemed as though bombs were torn asunder in the depths of the cold sea beneath me. I lay still, wondering if I were dreaming. The sounds echoingly died away. Looking about the igloo, I detected nothing unusual. I saw Ah-we-lah and E-tuk-i-shook staring at me with wide-open frightened eyes. I arose and peeped through the eye port. The fields of ice without reflected the warm light of the rising sun in running waves of tawny color. The ice was undisturbed. An unearthly quiet prevailed. Concluding that the ice was merely cracking under the sudden change of temperature, in quite the usual harmless manner, I turned over again, reassuring my companions, and promptly fell asleep.

"Out of the blankness of sleep I suddenly wakened again. Half-dazed, I heard beneath me a series of echoing, thundering noises. I felt the ice floor on which I lay quivering. I experienced the sudden giddiness one feels on a tossing ship at sea. In the flash of a second I saw Ah-we-lah leap to his feet. In the same dizzy instant I saw the dome of the snowhouse open above me; I experienced the suffocating sense of falling, and next, with a spasm of indescribable horror, felt about my body a terrific tightening pressure like that of a chilled and closing shell of steel, driving the life and breath from me. In an instant it was clear what had happened. A crevasse had suddenly opened through our igloo, directly under the spot whereon I slept; and I, a helpless creature in a sleeping bag, with tumbling snow blocks and ice and snow crashing about and crushing me, with the temperature 48 degrees below zero, was floundering in the opening sea!"

His companions dragged him from the water, and they continued onward without dwelling on the horror of what might have been. Indeed, "My two companions saw the humor of the episode and laughed heartily." Onward they drove, ever onward. Yet the strain mounted as they ventured further and further into this strange land where "to the frozen fingers ice cold water was hot . . . In our dreams Heaven was hot, the other place was cold. All nature was false; we seemed to be nearing the chilled flame of a new Hades."

Still onward despite the frozen fingers, treacherous waters, the falseness of nature itself, onward as far as man could drive himself until finally the "absolutely cheerless path" overwhelmed them. "No torment could be worse than that never-ceasing rush of icy air. It gripped us and sapped the life from us. Ah-we-lah bent over his sled and refused to move. I walked over and stood by his side. His dogs turned and looked inquiringly at us. E-tuk-i-shook came near and stood motionless, like a man in a trance, staring blankly at the southern skies. Large tears fell from Ah-we-lah's eyes and froze in the blue of his own shadow. Not a word was uttered. I knew that the dreaded time of utter despair had come. The dogs looked at us, patient and silent in their misery. Silently in the descending gloom we all looked over the tremendous dead-white waste to the southward. With a tearstreaked and withered face, Ah-we-lah slowly said, with a strangely shrilling wail, *'Unne-sinig-po—Oo-ah-tonie i-o-doria—Ooh ah tonie i-o-doria!'* ('It is well to die—Beyond is impossible—Beyond is impossible!')

"I shall never forget that dismal hour. I shall never forget that desolate drab scene about us—those endless stretches of gray and dead-white ice, that drab dull sky, that thickening blackness in the west which entered into and made gray and black our souls, that ominous, eerie and dreadful wind, betokening a terrorizing Arctic storm. I shall never forget the mournful group before me, in itself an awful picture of despair, of man's ambition failing just as victory is within his grasp. Ah-we-lah, a thin, half-starved figure in worn furs, lay over his sled, limp, dispirited, broken. In my ears I can now hear his low sobbing words, I can see the tears on his yellow fissured face. I can see E-tuk-i-shook standing gaunt and grim, and as he gazed yearningly onward to the south, sighing pitifully, shudderingly for the home, the loved one, An-na-do-a, left behind, whom, I could tell, he did not expect to see again.

" 'Unne-sinikpo-ashuka,' Ah-we-lah gasped. 'It is well to die.' "

The pole was one hundred miles away.

Somehow Cook found the strength to urge them on. "Ka-bis-chukto-emongwah. Come walk a little further. Ka, aga. Come, go!" So they went on.

As they approached the pole their despair lifted and joy swept over them. "Bounding joyously forward, with a stimulated mind, I reviewed the journey. Obstacle after obstacle had been overcome. Each battle won gave a spiritual thrill, and courage to scale the next barrier. Thus had been ever, and was still, in the unequal struggles between human and inanimate nature, an incentive to go onward, ever onward, up the stepping-stones to ultimate success. And now, after a life-denying struggle in a world where every element of Nature is against the life and progress of man, triumph came with steadily measured reaches of fifteen miles a day!

"We were excited to fever heat. Our feet were light on the run. Even the dogs caught the infectious enthusiasm. They rushed along at a pace which made it difficult for me to keep a sufficient advance to set a good course. The horizon was still eagerly searched for something to mark the approaching boreal center. But nothing unusual was seen. The same expanse of moving seas of ice, on which we had gazed for five hundred miles, swam about us as we drove onward . . .

"As the day advanced beyond midnight and the splendor of the summer night ran into a clearer continued day, the beams of gold on the surface snows assumed a more burning intensity. Shadows of hummocks and ice ridges became dyed with deeper purple, and in the burning orange world loomed before us Titan shapes, regal and regally robed . . .

"About the horizon the icy walls gleamed like beaten gold set with gem-spots of burning colors; the plains represented every shade of purple and blue, and over them, like vast angel wings outspread, shifted golden pinions. Through the sea of palpitating color, the dogs came, with spirited tread, noses down, tails erect and shoulders braced to the straps, like chariot horses. In the magnifying light they seemed many times their normal size. The young Eskimos, chanting songs of love, followed with easy, swinging steps. The long whip was swung with a brisk crack. Over all arose a cloud of frosted breath, which, like incense smoke, became silvered in the light, a certain signal of efficient motive power.

"Our leg cramps eased and our languid feet lifted buoyantly from the steady drag as the soul arose to effervescence . . . We were thin, with faces burned, withered, frozen and torn in fissures, with clothes ugly from overwear. Yet men never felt more proud than we did, as we militantly strode off the last steps to the world's very top! Cracking our whips, we bounded ahead. The boys sang. The dogs howled.

"Over the sparkling snows the post-midnight sun glowed like at noon. I seemed to be walking in some splendid golden realms of dreamland. As we bounded onward the ice swam about me in circling rivers of gold . . .

"The ice under us, the goal for centuries of brave, heroic men, to reach which many had suffered terribly and terribly died, seemed almost sacred. Constantly and carefully I watched my instruments in recording this final reach. Nearer and nearer they recorded our approach. Step by step, my heart filled with a strange rapture of conquest.

"At last we step over colored fields of sparkle, climbing walls of purple and gold—finally, under skies of crystal blue, with flaming clouds of glory, we touch the mark! The soul awakens to a definite triumph; there is sunrise within us, and all the world of night-darkened trouble fades. We are at the top of the world! The flag is flung to the frigid breezes of the North Pole!"

Wow, Cook's readers said.

Nonsense, Peary said. "Cook has handed the public a gold brick." Peary talked to the two Eskimos who had accompanied Cook, and though they knew nothing of astronomical navigation or longitudes and latitudes, they told him that they had never been out of sight of land. Since the pole is more than four hundred miles distant from the nearest land, this was a denial of Cook's story.

Never out of sight of land? That's what they *think*, countered Cook. They were so frightened at the thought of leaving solid land behind that he had been forced to trick them into thinking they were always close to home. "Both Ah-we-lah and E-tuk-i-shook were sure of a constant nearness to land. Because of the native panic out of its reassuring sight, I encouraged this belief, as I did concerning every other possible sign of land further northward. I knew that only by encouraging a delusion of nearness to land could I urge them ever farther in the face of the hardships that must inevitably come."

Rubbish, Peary repeated. The idea that a white man could fool an Eskimo about conditions in the Arctic, he said, was laughable. They have lived all their lives there. They may be uncivilized and superstitious, but they are not foolish. They know the Arctic better than anyone, and would know better than an amateur like Cook whether or not they were in sight of land.

This defense of the Eskimos' intelligence was not characteristic of Peary. He himself treated them as he did his dogs; he cared for them and fed them, but with the same level of consideration. A writer, Jean Malaurie, talked to some Eskimos who remembered Peary, and in *The Last Kings of Thule* he repeats the words of one of them, who referred to Peary as "the great tormentor" and who still feared his ghost: "People were afraid of him," he said. "Really afraid, like I am this evening . . . You always had the feeling that if you didn't do what he said he would condemn you to death . . . I was very young, but I will never forget how he treated the Inuit . . . His big ship arrives in the bay. He is hardly visible from the shore, but he shouts: '*Kissa Tikeri-Unga!*—I'm arriving, for a fact!' The Inuit go aboard. Peary has a barrel of biscuits brought up on deck . . . Later, the barrel is taken ashore, and the contents thrown on the beach. Men, women, and children hurl themselves on the biscuits like dogs, which amuses Peary a lot. My heart still turns cold to think of it."

One of Peary's two sons by Allikassingwah, Kaali, told Malaurie, "I never heard a word from my illustrious father, nor did I ever receive any money. All I have of his is a photograph I cut out of a magazine."

Peary himself reinforces this impression when he writes of the Eskimos: "They were all as children . . . They had tried our tempers and taxed our patience . . . [But] I had come to regard them with a kindly and personal interest, which any man must feel with regard to the members of an inferior race."

Granted that Peary was not the noblest of men, and that he had motive enough to want to prove Cook's story false, this does not prove that Cook's story is *not* false. (Just because you're paranoid doesn't mean that someone is not out to get you.) Though at the beginning the public had been solidly behind Cook, as more and more discrepancies were brought forward and as less and less proof was produced to counter them, the tide slowly turned. The University of Copenhagen announced that when they had honored Dr. Cook they had simply taken his word as a gentleman that he had accomplished what he said he had done; they had asked for and received no proofs of his voyage. Peary demanded that such proofs be submitted, and Cook announced his intentions to send them to Copen-

hagen. What he did send there finally, after months of pro-
crastination, was nothing at all. The University of Copenhagen announced publicly, "The documents handed the
University for examination do not contain observations
and information which can be regarded as proof that
Dr. Cook reached the North Pole." The commission's chairman admitted that the university had been hoaxed, and
declared that Dr. Cook's claim was "shameless" and
that "it was an offense to submit such papers to scientific
men." One of the experts called in by the Copenhagen
committee said, "It is the most childish attempt at cheat-
ing."

Hampton's Magazine offered Cook a chance to tell his
story directly to the public, and he jumped at it. It turned
out to be like jumping off a precipice in the dark, with no
knowledge of what lay ahead. He might have known better, but he was a curious mix of charlatan and naïf waif: he
expected everyone to believe him without proof, just as he
accepted whatever he was told at face value, never searching for devious motives in others. He should have, since
Hampton's had just paid Peary $40,000 for *his* story. Cook
now thought they were offering him an opportunity to tell
his own side to the same public; in reality they were not
about to jeopardize their investment in Peary.

Cook wrote his story, and thereby learned a lesson in
journalistic ethics. *Hampton's* emblazoned it on the front
cover with the title of "Dr. Cook's Confession!" The story
itself was twisted around until it sounded as if Cook was
apologizing for a mental breakdown. In truth, it nearly
gave him one.

After this, Cook's supporters began to fall away, and
other revelations soon followed. In his picture of the "First
Camp at the Pole, April 21, 1908" the two Eskimos were
wearing musk-ox pants. But according to the account Cook
himself wrote of the journey they had no such pants with
them when they started out, and they did not kill any

musk-oxen until their homeward trip, so the photograph could not possibly have been taken "at the Pole." The *Brooklyn Standard-Union* then published proof that at least two of the photographs Cook brought back with him "from the North Pole" had actually been taken years previously on another expedition.

Finally, Cook's account of what he saw on his journey seemed reasonable, if a bit overblown, until another explorer, Vilhjalmur Stefansson, covered part of the same route a few years later and discovered several islands where Cook had written of nothing but snow and ice. At the time of Cook's trip, everything he described fit perfectly with what was known, but Stefansson's expedition proved that Cook couldn't have gone where he said he went, for the islands rise out of the sea nearly a thousand feet high and couldn't possibly be missed.

After this Cook's life spiraled downward in a dizzying descent. In 1909 he had been greeted by the King of Denmark and honored by people all over the globe. In 1923 he was convicted of fraud and sent to jail for selling worthless oil stock. He had escaped from his former fame, which had become infamy, and sought seclusion and anonymity in the interior of the American continent. He had no patience to practice again as a doctor, and somehow ended up as a petroleum geologist, though he had no formal training. He became president of a company selling land "rich in oil," probably because he believed the tales his fellow owners told him. When purchasers finally complained to the government that the land they had bought was worthless, he was tried and convicted of using the mails to defraud, and was sent to Leavenworth. He was released in 1930, and a few years later oil was indeed found on the "worthless" land he had sold. In 1940, sick and broken, he was fully pardoned by Franklin Roosevelt. He died a few months later.

* * *

So Peary was left as the sole discoverer of the North Pole. It didn't occur to many people for some time that *both* Cook and Peary might have been lying.

AUGUST 5

I awake with a blistering headache, a terrible hangover from yesterday's North Pole party on the ice. The bright daylight streaming through the open porthole sears my eyes unless I clench them tightly shut, and when I do the veins in my temple start throbbing. I open one eye a bit and squint at the clock on the wall. It's blurry at best, and jumps every time the ship crashes into another block of ice, but it seems to be saying two o'clock.

I don't believe I've slept that late. And perhaps I haven't, because for some unexplained reason the clocks are the only things on the ship that don't work properly. They stop, go, jump ahead and fall backward seemingly at random. Usually, however, they're within an hour or two of the right time.

I feel with my fingers under the bunk and finally locate my watch. But my eyes can't yet see anything as small as the digits on its face. I lie back in bed and try to relax, to focus on the little capillaries in my skull that are impeding the flow of blood and causing such pain. It doesn't work. I shift to my toes, and focus my energy on relaxing them. Then I move this feeling up through my legs and thighs, past my stomach and chest, bringing it up to my head.

It works fine until I get to the head. Nothing up there will relax. I sometimes wonder about the nature of God, who gave us sex and AIDS, alcohol and hangovers. I try my eyes again, and they seem to be working a bit better. My watch says that it really is two o'clock. I must have slept forever.

I sit up. My roommate, John Tolson, is not here; the room is empty. The air blowing in from the porthole is cold enough to overpower the flux of heat from the radiator, and as soon as my feet come out from under the quilt they start to chill. I dress warmly and wonder about going outside.

Outside is bright searing sunshine—you can never find some fog when you really need it—but inside the noise is awful. The ship is plowing through heavy ice and the crashing, shuddering and shaking are not recommended palliatives for what ails me. It must be better outside.

Indeed it is. The sun is too bright but the air is clean and sharp, and I walk around for a while until I feel better. Then I go inside and glance into the dining room, hoping it's still open for lunch. The cold air has helped a lot, but I could use a cup of coffee. The doors are shut. The crowd in the bar is heavier than usual for this time of day. The bartender, Bill, asks me if I want a beer as I pass through. I shake my head gingerly. "Too early for me," I say.

He gives me a funny look but doesn't say anything, and I get a sudden suspicion. "What time is it?" I ask.

He glances at his watch. "Two-fifteen."

I look around at the crowd in the bar. They're much more rambunctious than the usual midafternoon group. They're also younger; none of the older ones are here. I begin to suspect . . . "Bill," I say, "is it 2:15 A.M. or P.M.?"

He smiles. "A.M.," he says.

"Shit," I say. I've slept less than two hours. No wonder my head is killing me. I go back to my room, undress in the bright daylight spilling in with the cold air from the port-hole, and crawl back under the thick white quilt.

The party yesterday on the ice was a doozy. It began in midafternoon when the captain decided that the ice was too rotten to pull up and park: whenever the *Soyuz* nudged into a likely place it cracked and split. So he simply parked in the middle of the street, so to speak, and we disembarked by helicopter. The choppers shuttled back and forth from the ship to a spot about a hundred and fifty yards away; as long as the ship didn't move the ice would hold firm, we were told. I decided not to be in the first group to go ashore, but after several flights with the ice holding firm I thought I might as well give it a try, and so I set my foot down on the North Pole.

Well, it wasn't, actually. With the *Soyuz* searching back and forth and up and down for a landing site we had drifted a mile or two from the spot, but everyone pretended that we were right on the top of the world. Certainly we were closer to it than Peary or Cook ever got.

Also, it was easy to believe. It was only an illusion, of course, but standing on the ice and turning around 360 degrees, seeing nothing but the white snow and ice all the way to the horizon in every direction, it *looked* like the top of the world. I could actually see the world curving away from me, going down in all directions. With the exercise of a little imagination I got a touch of vertigo, could almost feel myself slipping down the curve of the earth and rolling all the way to Rio, as the old song goes.

This feeling of dizziness was not helped by the champagne and Bloody Marys being served. I stomped around in my L. L. Bean Arctic boots, occasionally plunging through the ice crust and sinking thigh-deep in the snow. Crew members armed with shotguns were spread out along a half-mile perimeter, looking for polar bears who might want to crash the party. Other crew members strung up two flagpoles and, on a line between them, hung the flags of all the nations represented on the ship: Russian, American, British, German, South African, Texan, Mexican, French, Canadian, Australian, Austrian, Swiss, Greek and Japanese.

Someone put up a red sign, a metal arrow six feet tall with its tip pointed down into the snow and with the words NORTH POLE and its Russian equivalent СЕВЕРНЬЙ ПОЛЮС written in white. They found a big, fat Russian crewman (not hard to do) and dressed him in a Santa Claus suit. Evidently they poured a good bit of champagne into him, for he wandered around laughing, ringing a bell and shouting the Russian equivalent of "Merry Christmas, welcome to my home!" in everyone's face. At least that is what I assume he was shouting.

The atmosphere quickly grew to something like a combination of V-E Day and New Year's Eve. Half a dozen people began shooting off Very pistols and red flares; at first I worried because they were obviously drunk and looked as if they might decide it would be more fun to shoot them at people instead of over their heads, but after a few glasses of champagne and a couple of Bloody Marys I began to wish they would. Above us rockets were bursting in air, and the ship's orchestra—a single man who played an electronic keyboard with a multitude of sounds available—set up shop with an amplifier that boomed our celebration to at least Novaya Zemlya.

The cold came and went. When the wind stopped it was reasonably comfortable, but with every gust my nose started to run. Luckily one didn't have to wipe it off; it froze in a moment or two, and another glass of champagne seemed to make the mess disappear. At least that's how it felt; I have no idea how it looked.

There was a shout from leeward and everyone started to run there. I saw someone splashing around in open water; if it weren't for the champagne we would all have panicked, thinking that the ice was splitting. But no, it was only a few of the younger members of the crew and guests who, on finding a small open lead, had taken off their clothes and plunged in. I thought of explaining how the alcohol which was making them feel warm wasn't really keeping them warm and that they were in danger of hypothermia, but it didn't seem worthwhile. The hell with them.

The hell with all of them. I began to get depressed, looking around at how we were behaving and thinking of all the men who had died trying to reach this spot. I didn't want a church service, but somehow . . . I don't know. We could have had a drunken party anywhere on earth. There is, after all, something special about this spot, the pivot on which the earth turns. I poured my champagne out, drop by drop, onto the ice. Of all the empty gestures I have ever made this was the most ridiculous, but I couldn't think of anything else to do. What the hell; I got another glass of champagne.

Far out in the distance I saw a solitary figure standing with his back to the ship and the party. It was Wally Herbert, who came up here on his own in 1969, on a thirteen-month trip by sled. I staggered out across the ice to him. He turned his head as I approached, and nodded. We stood there, staring out into the distant unending ice and snow, with an unrecognizable blend of Russian and American rock music blaring out behind us. He was trying to recapture the solitude of the North, while I was trying to absorb his spirit by osmosis.

We both failed, smiled sadly and walked apart. You can't be alone with somebody. The hell with it. They had begun to charcoal something back at the party, and it smelled good. I was cold and hungry, that was all.

After a couple of hours of this I returned to the ship. Everyone else was still on the ice, so I had it to myself. I stood on the quarterdeck and saw them all in a circle, marching drunkenly around the red arrow marking the North Pole. Last night Jackie S. was telling us that there was an organization called the Circumnavigators Club, formed exclusively of people who have traveled around the world.

"How do you define 'around the world'?" I asked.

She looked at me as if this was the dumbest question she had ever heard. "You have to go *around the world*," she said, emphasizing the words and speaking slowly, the way you would to someone who didn't speak English well.

"Yeah, but how? Does it have to be around the equator? Or pole to pole? Or a great circle route?"

She took another bite of the grilled snapper, and by this I knew that she was angry because she had been saying a few moments earlier how awful the snapper was. "You simply have to cross every meridian of longitude," she said tightly. "You have to go *around the world*. I went from New York to South Africa to India and Australia, and then home across the Pacific," she added proudly. "Six of us on this trip are members."

"We can all be members," I said. "When we get to the pole tomorrow all we have to do is walk around it and we'll be crossing every meridian of longitude." I was only kidding, to upset her, because clearly she didn't like the idea of just anyone claiming to belong to the Circumnavigators Club. But the other people at the table liked the idea, and it must have spread because it looked like just about everyone on the ship was out there now marching around the pole in a weaving, drunken line. I wondered if the six who were already members were there with them, or were hoping the ice would crack beneath them and plunge them into the polar sea.

I wandered off to the other side of the *Soyuz* and looked out into the distance. There was nothing to be seen but ice and snow. After a while I wondered how long I had been standing there and started to tug at my parka and gloves and sweaters to free my wristwatch, but realized it didn't matter. There isn't any time at the pole; it is the same time everywhere, or it is every time in the twenty-four-hour clock at the same time. Or something. I'd had too much champagne and Bloody Marys to figure it out now.

It didn't matter, though; I could work on it tomorrow. Though there wasn't any tomorrow either, with the sun simply looping around in a big circle and never setting. I leaned on the railing and stared out into the snow and ice, trying to imagine how it must have been to have walked all this way alone, without a satellite navigation system, the first time anyone had ever done it. I tried to imagine myself as Peary, with my black "manservant" and four "faithful" Eskimos, hurrying onward with the dogs in an effort to get here before the food ran out or the ice cracked beneath them. I tried to ignore the rock and roll music echoing over the ice, and the drunken shouts and laughter. I shut my eyes to the rockets' red glare and the cacophony, and tried to see Peary.

I couldn't. Because of the distractions? Or because he had never been here?

In 1909 the *Pittsburgh Press* conducted a poll, asking its readers whether they believed Cook or Peary. Nearly 100,000 people responded, and 96 percent of them thought that Cook had reached the pole; only 24 percent believed that Peary had.

But when the McKinley fake was exposed, and when Cook refused to present any proofs, and when the Copenhagen commission ruled against him and his support dropped away, all the people who deserted him flocked to Peary. After all the fuss, after all the celebrations over *two* people reaching the pole in the very same year after centuries of failure, it simply didn't seem possible that *no one* had reached it. If Cook had failed, then Peary must have succeeded.

Peary's main support was the National Geographic Society, which examined his "proofs" and pronounced themselves satisfied. Of course. One of the members of the three-man examining committee of the NGS was Admiral Colby Chester, who not coincidentally was also a member of the Peary Arctic Club (formed when Peary saw how useful the original Arctic Club had been to Dr. Cook), which had raised money for Peary and sponsored his expeditions. The second member of the committee was Henry Gannett, not only the vice-president of the NGS but also an old personal friend of Peary. The final member was Otto Tittman, supervisor of the Coast and Geodetic Survey, which had long been one of Peary's sponsors. The NGS itself had contributed money to Peary's expedition, and therefore had a stake in its outcome; moreover, all three members of the committee had been voting members of the group which had recommended financial support. Thus, it was hardly a group likely now to repudiate his claims.

The National Geographic Society had—and has—a unique and dubiously polar position, using the word "polar" in a different sense: "opposite in character or nature." By its title it seems to be a national board, with members elected or appointed according to their prestige and position in the field of geography or exploration—that is, an organization on the order of Britain's Royal Geographic Society. Not so. The NGS is a private organization whose primary function is to publish the *National Geographic* magazine. To put it bluntly, it is a profit-making private organization responsible to no one but its board of directors. Its very nature, together with its sponsorship of Peary, rendered it an unlikely candidate to examine his "proofs" without prejudice; yet its public image as an impartial and honorific society lent its deliberations great importance.

What were its deliberations? The three men chosen to examine Peary sat down, chatted with him and immediately pronounced themselves satisfied with his "proofs."

What were those proofs? Nonexistent. The only data remotely suggestive of the North Pole were solar observations that Peary took at his farthest north. These indeed showed that he was very near the pole. But anyone with Peary's knowledge might calculate what the solar observations at the pole *should* be, in the same manner that students cheat in chemistry labs. (In organic chemistry, for example, we had to synthesize aspirin, so we stood around for a few hours, mixed the component chemicals together, boiled and fluxed them, and then when the instructor wasn't looking we swept the whole mess off the tabletop, took out a bottle of aspirin, crushed the tablets up and submitted the powder as our result. Voilà! We all got A's except for one poor sod who used acetaminophen.)

Along with any competent explorer and navigator, Peary knew what solar observations at the North Pole should be, so he could have substituted a crushed aspirin tablet for his synthesis; without independent witness the observations themselves are worthless as proofs. Peary had no independent witnesses because he had taken none to the pole; he had sent back to base all those on the expedition who could have provided independent observations of the solar latitude.

This was a curious thing to have done, for Peary clearly recognized the need for independent verification of his position. Here is what he says about his latitude observations early on the march north. At the 85th parallel he "had the Eskimos build a wind shelter of snow, in order that Marvin might take a meridian altitude for latitude. I intended that Marvin should take all the observations up to his farthest, and Bartlett all beyond that to his farthest. This was partly to save my eyes, but principally to have independent observations with which to check our advance."

A curious statement indeed, for surely the important position to be determined independently was not the various points along the route but the final one itself, the North

Pole, and yet on his final dash he took no one along who could make "independent observations."

Why not? Marvin and Bartlett could have done so; Henson could not. Yet he took only Henson with him. In particular, why did he not take Captain Bartlett, whom he had promised would accompany him to the pole? Why would he renege on his word? Why not send Henson home with the last returning group and take Bartlett instead? No promise had been made to Henson. If Bartlett had been along to take an "independent observation" there would have been no question of whether or not the expedition had actually achieved the North Pole; yet Bartlett was sent home.

Curious.

Nevertheless, the committee accepted Peary's solar observations as proof because he was known to be a gentleman and his word was to be trusted. But this comes under the heading of *faith*, not *verification*. No one on the committee thought to ask how he had managed to find the pole without longitude measurements along the way—in effect, how he had managed to direct his course when he didn't know where he was day by day.

Peary writes in his book *The North Pole:* "The distance which we traveled day by day was at first determined by dead reckoning, to be verified later by observations for latitude. Dead reckoning was simply the compass course for direction, and for distance the mean estimate of Bartlett, Marvin, and myself."

But a compass course is notoriously inaccurate in the polar regions. In a book critical of Peary, the astronomer Dennis Rawlins quotes from the *Bowditch Navigator*, published by the Secretary of the Navy: "[In polar regions] it is good practice to keep the magnetic compass under almost constant scrutiny as it is somewhat erratic in dependability and its errors may change rapidly. Frequent compass checks by celestial observation or any other method available are wise precautions."

One of Peary's companions on the trip, Donald MacMillan, later wrote a book about his own expeditions. In it he debunks the idea that the compass needle invariably points north: "*As true as the needle to the Pole* is but an empty phrase. Actually following such an injunction, no man could be more fickle, more untrustworthy, more uncertain in his purpose in life, or more devious in his wanderings."

Moreover, the magnetic compass is devious and unreliable in *any* area where the local variation is not known. That is, the compass theoretically points due north (magnetic north); in a perfect universe, this would be true. In our own world the compass's direction is modified if, for example, there is a load of iron nearby, such as might be present in a mountain.

There are no mountains on the polar sea, but there are mountains *under* it. In fact, the whole sea floor is riddled with magmatic eruptions from the mantle, which bring iron-rich magmas up to the surface. Peary didn't know about the undersea eruptions, but he did know that magnetic variations exist and are both ubiquitous and unpredictable, so that the magnetic compass is unreliable in any area of the world where the local variations are unknown. In fact, this is one of the primary observations every explorer has made since the use of the magnetic compass became fashionable in the fifteenth century: they measured the local magnetic variations so that those who came after them could use their compasses safely.

But Peary didn't do this; he took *no* measurements of compass variation. Why not? Perhaps because this was one of the few ways a claim to have made a particular journey could be disproven by later travelers. One can claim to see a lot of ice and snow or a little ice and snow, and twenty years later if someone comes along and says that conditions aren't the same it means nothing: ice and snow conditions change year by year. But the magnetic variation of the compass doesn't change, at least not on human time scales, and so a clear record of these variations is an indelible statement which later explorers can check.

There was another problem besides the unknown variations of the compass which would have hindered Peary's dead reckoning. Even if he was confident that he could keep a straight trail over the featureless ice, how could he possibly know if the ice itself was drifting? East or west, north or south, there was no possible way of knowing. And Peary himself *knew this*. He must have, for on his earlier trip north he found that he had drifted eastward without knowing it, and on his first trip he had found that the ice had been drifting silently south beneath his feet as he trudged north over it. This phenomenon had been noted by every Arctic explorer since Parry in 1827, and was as well understood as it was known to be incapable of detection.

Yet Peary pretended to be able to detect it. Earlier in his trek, while waiting for the lead of open water to close, he "was glad to see that there was no lateral movement in the ice; that is, that the two shores of the lead were not moving east or west, or in opposite directions." But all that this meant was that one ice pack was not moving relative to the other; whether both might be moving relative to the solid earth was impossible to know. In fact, the supposition must be that they were, for on the very first day of the march Peary had written: "The day was cloudy, *the wind continuing to blow from the east with unabated violence*" (emphasis mine). Such a wind would be likely to blow the ice in front of it, and Peary knew it. (Eighty years later the NGS decided that he had indeed been drifting west, but later coincidentally drifted east the exact amount needed to counterbalance the earlier western movement!)

Several days after passing the lead Peary found that they had not advanced as far as his dead reckoning showed, because the ice once again had been drifting south as they marched north: "The northerly wind had crowded the ice southward as we traveled over it northward. We had traveled fully twelve miles more than the observation showed in the last five marches, but had lost them by the crushing up of the young ice in our rear and the closing of the leads." Yet he contended that throughout the long march to the pole he was walking straight up the 70th meridian, with no correction for east-west drift necessary. Curiouser and curiouser.

When Peary arrived at the pole, according to his account, he was so exhausted that he fell asleep for a few hours. "The first thing I did after awaking," he writes, "was to write these words in my diary: 'The Pole at last. The prize of three centuries. My dream and goal for twenty years. Mine at last!' "

But A. E. Thomas, the professional writer of fiction who actually wrote Peary's book as a ghostwriter, and to whom Peary had given his diary for this purpose, complained in a letter to him during the time he was writing the book that there was no diary entry at all for the critical date of April 6. Moreover, Dennis Rawlins has shown that the diary was clean when it was presented to Congress in support of his claim to have reached his objective, but such a document, which accompanied Peary throughout his tumultuous journey, ought not to have been clean. Indeed, when later examined by navy people it was suitably dirty.

One begins to wonder about the statements made in Peary's book that have been shown to correspond less to truth than one might expect. How seriously should one take these statements? Well, first one has to recognize that he didn't write the book himself. He didn't write *any* of his books, nor did he consider them important; they were simply a means of making money. So when he returned from the North Pole his work was done and he felt an enormous relief. He turned his material over to his ghostwriter to produce a profitable book, but for Peary it was all over. He didn't read the galleys closely because he was not really much interested, so misstatements and inaccuracies naturally crept in.

But by the time Peary came home he knew that Cook was claiming to have reached the pole first, and that he was going to have to challenge the man's claim. Which meant that he was going to demand hard proof that Cook had reached the pole. Which meant that he would have to produce such proofs himself. Which in turn meant that he couldn't afford any inaccurate or misleading statements in his account of his journey. Yet they are there. Therefore one is forced to the conclusion that he didn't tell a straightforward story without muddles and inconsistencies because he didn't have such a story to tell.

Still, there was no convincing proof that he *hadn't* reached the pole. There was no smoking gun, such as the evidence against Cook, and everyone wanted to believe a man who was, after all, one of the world's foremost explorers and who had never been known to tell a lie. The Royal Geographical Society met in London and presented him with a gold medal, its president in his speech honoring Peary as "the first and only human being who has ever led a party of his fellow creatures to a Pole of the Earth." This was done solely on Peary's word as a gentleman, without even looking at his diary or records. Later in the year, after Peary had sent the society his papers, the president called a meeting to reconsider the matter. Only seventeen of the thirty-two-member governing board showed up. After they examined Peary's "proofs" a vote was taken: eight men voted for Peary, seven voted against him, two abstained. By this margin the verdict of the RGS was sustained; it was hardly an overpowering vote of confidence, but in the public eye it was simply a vote of "Yes."

Peary now appealed to the United States Congress, for he wanted retirement and promotion to rear admiral. Congress met to consider a man who had been honored by the president of the United States, the National Geographic Society and the Royal Geographic Society. Naturally they were overwhelmingly biased in his favor, and of course they were not imbued by background, training or native intelligence with the understanding necessary to evaluate his "proofs." In addition, Peary had one invaluable opponent: Congressman Robert Bruce Macon (Democrat, Arkansas), who proposed that Peary could not possibly have reached the pole because "the diminishing centrifugal action" there rendered humanity senseless, and because the pole is actually "a hole that extends into the interior surface of the earth." He pontificated to the assembled congressmen that "conditions are such in the Arctic that . . . an object that might appear small here would be about the size of a mountain [there]." So, he asked Peary, "How do you explain to the committee that you took a correct observation [of latitude]?" Peary replied that he did "not see how the eye would be affected in that way." Then Macon asked if the compass needle at the pole "answered to the primary or the secondary magnetic pole?" Whereupon a member from California, growing impatient with this nonsense, interrupted and asked Macon where he had "ever heard of a primary or secondary magnetic pole? In Arkansas?"

Macon replied, "I want to say to the gentleman from California that if he intends that as a slur in regard to Arkansas . . ."

And they were off and running in a dozen different directions. With an enemy like Macon you don't need friends. In the end Congress simply accepted the word of the NGS, RGS and Teddy Roosevelt, and in 1911 acknowledged Peary as the discoverer of the North Pole, promoted him to rear admiral and adjourned. He hadn't presented any proofs of his accomplishment, but irritation with the idiot opposing him swept Congress along. That tide of human affairs which, taken at the flood, leads on to fortune, caught Peary and swept him on to worldwide acclaim.

But tides ebb and flow, and the controversy has never died. In 1916 a bill was introduced in Congress which would have repealed the 1911 act of recognition, but early in the next year its sponsor died, and with him his bill expired. For nearly six decades Peary reigned supreme, until in 1973 an American astronomer, Dennis Rawlins, challenged him, claiming that not only did Peary not reach the pole but that he *knew* he hadn't reached it.

Rawlins's book kept the pot bubbling, and then in 1984 CBS presented a TV "docudrama" (what a horrible word, with its implication of truth but its license of fiction) called *The Race to the Pole*, which gave full credit to Cook for getting there first. To be sure, television is not particularly noted for its fascination with truth, and no new evidence was presented, but by carefully winnowing what was presented to be sure it was all from Cook's viewpoint, it undoubtedly left millions with the impression that he had been unfairly treated by Peary and the world.

With this, the National Geographic Society was stung into action. They felt that the television production was obviously false but that to people who didn't know the facts it might *seem* true, so they got the Peary family to release his diaries, which had never been made public. They also commissioned Wally Herbert to examine them and make a new, unbiased study of Peary's trip.

In 1988 the society published his results. Herbert's conclusion was that Peary had never made it to the pole; he had missed his destination because of the drift of the ice and his neglect of longitude measurements which might have enabled him to correct for the drift. Then, a year later, the *Washington Post* carried a headline stating that a newly discovered document showed that Peary had actually cheated.

The document was later shown to have been misinterpreted, but it was the final straw. Enough is enough, the NGS decided. They commissioned the Navigation Foundation, "a Maryland-based group devoted to preserving the art of navigation," to carry out a "comprehensive study of all the evidence regarding the Peary claim and draw a warranted conclusion, let the chips fall where they may." Which sounds fair, until you realize that this is exactly what they had done two years previously when they had asked Wally Herbert to do the same thing. They didn't like where Herbert's chips fell, however, and so they now decided to hire someone else. Presumably they would keep doing this until the chips fell where they wanted them to.

This is not the way scientific questions are properly answered. A group "devoted to preserving the art of navigation" is not the same as a group of scientists who understand the technical problems involved. The Navigation Foundation found among Peary's documents "unimpeachable" proof that he had succeeded in reaching the pole, which to the NGS signaled the "end of a historic controversy and the confirmation of due justice to a great explorer."

But things are not always what they seem. Unimpeachable proofs, like unimpeachable presidents, may be impeached.

The Navigation Foundation first made the unusual claim that Peary was the luckiest explorer who ever lived. They didn't phrase it quite this way, but that was how it turned out. They acknowledged that Peary had never bothered to measure his longitude and didn't correct his dead reckoning for ice drift, but they said it didn't matter: by "examining patterns of ice drift in the Arctic Ocean and the expedition members' accounts" they concluded that Peary first drifted westward without knowing it, and that then this westward drift "was offset by a subsequent rapid eastward movement of the ice." In other words, Peary drifted west of his course and was then brought back exactly to where he wanted to be by pure chance, by an equal and opposite drift of the ice. If this is true he shouldn't have wasted his time trying to reach the pole, but should have played the lottery.

How did the Navigation Foundation come to this conclusion? By "examining patterns of ice drift in the Arctic Ocean and the expedition members' accounts." *What* patterns of ice drift? Measurements taken when? How precise were they, and what relation did they have to ice drifts back in 1909? They don't say. If the pattern they project is accurate, it is different from the drift that Peary encountered on his previous trip just three years earlier. In other words, the drift patterns vary from year to year and month to month, and since there weren't and aren't any data for the year Peary went "to the pole," how accurate could such an assessment possibly be? Not very.

Next on the foundation's list of unimpeachable proofs was a series of depth soundings that Peary took. The first five soundings match well the seafloor depth, but of course it is the later soundings that are important for proving whether or not he reached his objective, and these are not as definitive since on the fifth sounding the wire split and some of it was lost. On subsequent soundings there was never enough wire to touch bottom, so all Peary could manage were minimum limits rather than any measurement of the actual depths. The depths have subsequently been measured, and in each case are greater than Peary's limits, so there is no contradiction here, but that is the most that one can say. To claim that the soundings "support Peary's account of his entire trek to the pole" is to go too far.

The foundation also pointed out that Peary's minimum depth at his claimed North Pole, 2743 meters, was not only less than the true depth but was *greater* than the depth of the Lomonosov Ridge, where Herbert claimed that Peary ended up. This would seem to rule out the Herbert analysis.

I asked Wally about this one night on the *Soyuz* while we were having a few beers at the bar. "The *National Geographic* says Peary's soundings show he wasn't where you said he was," I said.

"Yes, well, they would say that, wouldn't they?"

"But do they or don't they?"

Wally bristled. "A Royal Navy submarine went up longitude 70° [Peary's claimed route] several years ago. Now you can't have better than that. I have their tracks, their records, and Peary is wrong on every single count."

"But the *National Geographic* article shows the soundings he took and the ridges he hit or didn't hit, especially his last sounding at the pole. If he was where you put him he'd have hit bottom at 1500 meters, they say, but he bottomed out at 2743. Are you saying they're wrong?"

Wally shook his head sadly. "Suppose you're in a balloon hovering over Mount Everest," he explained, "and you drop a sounding line longer than your distance to the top of the peak. If you don't hit the exact peak you'd hit nothing, so you'd say there's no bottom, and someone like the *National Geographic* would say there's no mountain there, so you're not where you think you are. But don't you see? If you go just a few feet past the peak, you miss the bloody thing entirely, don't you? Because it's so bloody sharp. It's the same thing with the bloody submarine ridge, the Lomonosov; it's just as sharp as Mount Everest."

The point is that Peary's sounding, or rather his lack of a definite sounding, doesn't mean much as far as locating his true position.

But the Navigation Foundation's chief proof lay in several photographs Peary supposedly took at the pole. The foundation measured the angles and lengths of the shadows cast by the people in the photographs—Henson, Peary, and the Eskimos Ootah, Egingwah, Seegloo and Ooqueah—and gave a confusing explanation of how these angles and lengths related to the height of the sun, which is in turn related to the latitude at which the photos were taken. This was the evidence that the National Geographic Society accepted as unimpeachable, and the end of an historic controversy.

Is it? Not quite. What is not discussed in the *National Geographic* article is the magnitude of the errors which are inevitably involved in any measurement, from the most sloppy to the most precise. Error analysis is an important part of any scientific observation (entire disciplines have grown around it), but the subject is hardly mentioned in the NGS report, and while the mathematics relating the shadow angles to the position of the source—the sun—are precise, the actual measurements are not.

The *Scientific American* discovered that retired rear admiral Thomas D. Davies, who compiled the report for the Navigation Foundation, had originally sought the cooperation of James Williamson, a photogrammetrist who specializes in such analyses, but the cooperation fell apart when Davies refused to understand how important the error analysis was. Williamson later wrote to the *Scientific American* that Davies was a "nonprofessional" who was giving the science of photo analysis a "black eye," and that he had analyzed the photos by a technique which was totally wrong for the type of pictures they had. When Dennis Rawlins did his own analysis of the photos, he concluded that they were taken a hundred miles from the pole.

In the spring of 1991 the U.S. Naval Institute convened a meeting at Annapolis to reopen the question. The consensus of the meeting was that the evidence was indeed fallible. When a computer expert examined the photographs and the errors associated with the NGS analysis he concluded that they indicated that Peary was somewhere within 300 miles of the Pole, but that they couldn't be relied on for anything more precise. Summarizing the meeting,

Charles Burroughs, chairman of the Washington Chapter of the Explorers Club (the club which once boasted Peary as its president), said, "I'd say the evidence was pretty well lined up against Peary."

A few months later I visited the National Geographic Society's offices in Washington, D.C. In the lobby is a display of Pearyana, with signs identifying and explaining the exhibits. The statements in these signs are not as clear and definite as one would expect from Peary's main supporters. With the photo of Peary at his furthest north camp, which he claimed was the North Pole, the caption reads: "On April 6 Peary determined he had reached the pole . . . Although many have challenged Peary's claim to have reached the North Pole, his exceptional courage and boundless determination remain legendary."

So they do. No argument there. By the remains of the flag Peary carried with him on all his trips, and from which he cut diagonal strips to leave as a memento of his presence, it is now written: "Peary left the diagonal strip [of this flag] at what he believed was the North Pole."

The society seems to have decided to hedge its bets a bit. I think this was probably a pretty good idea.

AUGUST 6

We are now plummeting down the opposite side of the world, heading across the polar sea for the northern coast of Siberia, crashing through heavy ice. Taking a pre-breakfast stroll around the ship is like walking on a sunlit beach with gauze strips over your eyes: there is a pervading brightness, but everything is grayish white. Not a sign of the sun, only fog and clouds lit as if by indirect lighting, merging into the grayish white snow and ice without a visible horizon. It is like a scene out of *Ship of Fools*, or *Here Comes Mr. Jordan*; we could be sailing off into infinity, no longer of this world nor yet quite into the next.

I have breakfast with Les Havelka. He is a portly, balding, middle-aged man with a weatherbeaten face and a nicely sad smile. Generally he doesn't talk much, but this morning I mention that I noticed in the passenger list that he comes from Australia and yet his accent is Middle European.

He tells me about it. He left Czechoslovakia in 1948 when the Russians came in, emigrating to Australia because that was the only country that would take him. On his way to join the ship last month he stopped off in Prague for the first time since then. He was disappointed, he told me. Even though he left because he thought Communism would be the end of civilization there, it turned out to be worse than he had ever expected. "Everyone is lazy, inefficient and rude," he says with his sad smile. "I went to buy a railroad ticket to Vienna. I went up to the window and spoke Czech, of course, to ask the woman for a ticket. For a moment it felt good to be speaking Czech again. Then it was not so good. The woman was very rude and impatient when I asked for a first-class ticket to Vienna.

" 'Have you permission?' she asked me.

"I was astonished. Permission from whom? Impatiently she asked if I didn't know that first class was reserved for tourists. 'Unless you have government permission?' she asked, but very sarcastically. Of course, she tells me, since you want to go to Vienna, part of the train journey is in Austria, so part of the ticket price goes to the Austrian government. Therefore I had to have permission from the National Bank to buy the ticket even if I didn't want first class."

Les left the station angrily, then decided he wanted to take the train anyhow, so he went back and without a word put his Australian passport on the counter. The woman was immediately apologetic: "Why didn't you tell me? Of course you can have a ticket."

He went to a nice restaurant for lunch. The place was empty, and he went up to the maitre d' and asked for a table.

"All booked." The man turned his back on him.

"But it's empty!"

"Sorry. All these tables are booked."

He returned to his hotel and asked what was going on. The hotel clerk laughed. "Speak German or English if you want service in Czechoslovakia. The tourists tip well, but the Czechs can't afford to, so the best restaurants save their tables for tourists."

The country has been sold to foreigners, Havelka tells

me. It doesn't belong to the Czechs anymore. "This is the result of socialism, selling your birthright to the capitalists."

And the inefficiency! Everyone depends on the state and no one wants to work. His niece works from nine to five, but he notices that she is home every day by two. "We get our work done by then, so we come home," she says. He suggests that maybe if they put in a whole day's work the factory would be more productive. She looks at him as if he's crazy. Perhaps he is. How would it benefit her if the factory was more productive, and why should she work harder if she gets no benefit from it? "As my grandfather used to tell me, if there's no incentive to work, no one will work."

His niece asks what kind of a car he drives. She is impressed, and asks how much the government contributed to its purchase. "She couldn't understand the concept of my saving and working to buy it myself."

I nod understandingly, lift my coffee, and spill it on my lap as the *Soyuz* crashes to a halt. We all run outside to take a look, and stop and look around in amazement. We have run into a solid wall of ice; it looks like a continent. We back up and ram into it again, then again and again. Grudgingly it cracks a bit and we inch ahead. It looks as if the boat's been grounded; the ice looks absolutely solid. But as we plunge forward again and again great cracks open up, like an earthquake, and the ship inches through. After almost an hour the ice thins back to normal and our speed picks up.

The next race for the pole started nearly twenty years after Peary's and Cook's journeys. At that time it was generally accepted that Peary had reached the pole, so the only challenge left was to get there in a radically different fashion, in a manner suitable for the technological twentieth century: through the air. Once again it became a race between two people, Roald Amundsen of Norway and Richard Byrd of the United States.

In 1910 Amundsen had chartered Nansen's *Fram* to go to the North Pole, but without warning one day he swung her bow about, headed south and beat Scott to the South Pole in 1912. Now he would be the first to make the attempt to fly over the North Pole, setting off from the northern tip of Spitsbergen, halfway between Norway and the pole, in 1925 with five companions in two Dornier flying boats, the N-24 and the N-25. For hours they flew through mist and fog; then "suddenly the mist disappeared and the entire panorama of polar ice stretched away before our eyes—the most spectacular sheet of snow and ice ever seen by man from an aerial perspective."

But where were they? Whatever difficulties were encountered in navigating with a sled across the polar ice were magnified enormously in trying to fly to the North Pole with the equipment available in those days. Position was determined the same way, by taking a sextant sighting of the sun, but imagine the difficulty in doing so inside a bouncing, jolting airplane, compared to lying down in comparative comfort on steady ice. Trying to keep the instrument level with the horizon and the bubble centered while the aircraft bounced, pitched and yawed was an enterprise doomed to failure.

So Amundsen didn't try. When he had reached the vicinity of the North Pole according to his dead reckoning, he looked around for a place to land in order to take a more precise navigational fix and to make some geophysical measurements. He spotted an open lead, radioed his intentions to his companion ship, and his pilot set the N-25 down. As the ship touched water, one of its two engines quit; it was a harbinger of things to come.

The N-24, with an American, Lincoln Ellsworth, in command, was afraid to land in the same lead; there didn't seem to be enough room for two planes there. So they circled for ten minutes looking for another body of water large enough to land on, and finally found one a few miles away. As they taxied to a safe berth next to the ice, the mechanic cried out, "The plane's leaking like hell!"

So the expedition wasn't in great shape. Never mind. The first thing Amundsen did was to take a sextant sighting of the sun, and discovered that they were still 120 miles south of the pole. They must have been bucking headwinds without knowing it.

Suddenly a seal popped his head up beside the plane, looked the crowd over for a moment, then ducked down and swam away. The crew watched him go in amusement. If they had known what the future held, they would have shot him on the spot.

Instead the crews of the two boats, separated by high hillocks of ice which blocked their view, spent the next twelve hours trying to locate each other. When they finally managed to establish communication by signal lights and flags, they began to realize their predicament. The N-24 was leaking badly; the N-25, Ellsworth wrote, was "terrible to behold . . . she lay with her nose pointing into the air at an angle of forty-five degrees, among a lot of rough hummocks and against a huge cake of old blue Arctic ice about forty feet thick. . . . She looked as though she had crashed into this ice." Each plane had one engine disabled. "In short, we were badly wrecked."

It took four days for the crews to reach one another. By then Ellsworth had realized that his plane, the N-24, would never take off again. Their only hope lay in repairing the N-25, which was a dicey proposition. On preparing to leave Spitsbergen they had found they were 10,000 pounds heavier than the plane's lifting capacity, and so they had jettisoned as much as they could, including their long-range radio transmitter, much of their food supply and most of their repair equipment. So now they had little to work with, and with no long-range radio they couldn't signal their position to the outside world; they were as lost as Sir John Franklin had been seventy years previously. Also, they had food for only one month, even with strict rationing. "How we should have liked to have had that seal we saw on the first day!" Ellsworth lamented, but they saw no more seals, or life of any kind.

They slept in the plane, with only the metal skin between them and subzero temperatures. They set June 15, three weeks after their crash landing, as the date on which they must fly out or try to walk back to civilization. They knew that the latter choice was minimally above cutting their wrists and lying down to die; their only real hope lay in getting the N-25 back into the air.

By June 2 they had repaired the plane sufficiently to try, but by then the lead had closed and there was no way to take off. Day after day they labored incessantly to clear a space on the ice long enough and wide enough to use as a runway, but each time the ice moved and shattered behind them as they worked their way forward.

Ellsworth's diary, June 10: "The days go by . . . the future looks so helpless . . ."

On June 14 they managed to finish a runway of 500 meters and tried to take off, "But we only bumped along and the plane made no effort to rise."

The next day, June 15, the final day, they tried again. This time the N-25 bumped and bounced along, then took one final bounce into the air and clung there, its propellers clawing at the cold, thin atmosphere. Somehow they grabbed hold and pulled the plane a few feet higher, then a few feet more, and finally they were flying, their speed building to more than 100 miles an hour. They were on their way home.

Admiral Richard E. Byrd completes the triumvirate of twentieth-century American polar explorers. In the entire lexicon of polar exploration the word *fake* has been applied, rightly or wrongly, to only three people, and all three are American heroes.

Perhaps there is a better word than fake. A few years after his attempts to reach the North Pole, Byrd went to the opposite end of the world and tried to be the first to fly over the South Pole. In his group were three other pilots, and after establishing a base camp he set down the basic rules: they would fly further and further from base each day, exploring the region from the air, finally reaching the pole, but nobody, repeat *nobody*, was ever to fly further than Byrd had gone first. In other words, by direct order he was to be the first to fly over the pole.

One day after Byrd had made his morning exploratory flight two of the pilots, Dean Smith and Lloyd McKinley, were up in the air checking out the plane after routine maintenance. It turned out to be a bright, clear day, and so they decided to see how far south they could fly. They radioed back their intentions.

Immediately the reply came: "No. Return to base."

They looked at each other, smiled and repeated their message. The same reply came back. They repeated it one more time, adding that unless they heard a direct order to the contrary, they would do as they were suggesting. The reply came back: "This is a direct order. Return to base."

Smith and McKinley turned off their radio and flew south. They flew past all known regions, and after a flight of several hours saw in the distance a gigantic mountain. "We could see that it was a magnificent solitary Matterhorn of a mountain," Smith later wrote, "rising at least eight or ten thousand feet. This was far out into one of the blank spaces on the map. We kept on as far as we dared use fuel, then turned and headed back for Little America [their home base]."

Byrd greeted them seemingly without rancor when they returned and explained to him that their radio must have been faulty, for they had heard no order to return. He took

them inside, along with the rest of the group, for a de-
briefing. Smith tells what happened next: "Meetings of this
nature were held in a rectangular room adjacent to Byrd's
quarters: measuring about fifteen by twelve feet, it served
as library, staff room, game room, and office. We pulled off
our furs, spread our maps on the center table, and, excited
as children, told of our flight and our discovery.

" 'This Matterhorn peak, how far would you say it was
from the eastern end of the Rockefellers?' asked Byrd [re-
ferring to a known landmark].

" 'We flew on for at least forty-five minutes and were still
not more than halfway. I'd say at least a hundred and fifty
miles.'

" 'How precisely can you spot it on your map?' Byrd
now asked.

"McKinley and I compared notes and conferred at some
length. 'From our longitude here I'd say it lies pretty close
to northeast by east, call it sixty degrees. I'd put it somewhere in here,' and I drew a circle about thirty miles in
diameter on the map.

"Byrd spoke very seriously. 'This is most important. I
congratulate you gentlemen on confirming my discovery.
You have located this new land in almost exactly the place
where I saw it this morning.'

" 'You saw it this morning!' exclaimed McKinley. 'But
you didn't say anything about it after the flight.'

" 'No. I wanted to be sure before I announced it. But I
did mark it on my map. Wait, I will show you.'

"Byrd went into his room, closing the door behind him.
We all sat mute. I caught Balchen's eye. He shrugged and
rolled his eyes to the ceiling. Owen kept shaking his head,
gently. Gould looked amused.

"After about five minutes Commander Byrd returned,
spreading a map on the table.

" 'Here is the course of our flight this morning,' he said,
pointing to a penciled line. 'And over here is where I

marked the new peak.' He showed us a heavy cross, drawn with a softer pencil than the course of the flight itself. Sure enough, if transposed to my map his would fall close to the center of my circle.

" 'Now that you have seen the mountain, I feel justified in announcing my discovery. I have decided to call the area Marie A. Byrd Land in honor of my wife. Russ, you are authorized to report this to the *Times*. Please let me check your story before you send it.'

"The commander shook hands with Mac, Lloyd, and me. 'Congratulations on a splendid flight. This is a historic day.'

"McKinley and I walked together to the mess hall. 'It takes keen vision to be a great explorer,' he cracked. 'You and I will never be great explorers.' "

But back to the North Pole. The year after Amundsen's aborted flight he decided to try again to fly to the pole, though this time not in an airplane. They were unreliable, he decided. Instead he would use another modern technology: the dirigible.

Dirigibles, or blimps, had proved themselves in World War I when they were used to escort convoys across the Atlantic. Not a single ship was ever sunk by submarine when the blimps were along. More important to Amundsen was the fact that no blimps themselves had been lost. They had crisscrossed the Atlantic many times without accident; they were safe and reliable; they were the aerial vehicles of the future.

Nonsense, said Richard Byrd. The airplane was faster, he pointed out correctly. There was no argument there, but when he went on to claim that planes were safer he was on shakier grounds, and when he talked of their reliability he had his eye firmly on the future.

Looking back today, we can see that both men were right. Certainly the airplane was the aerial vehicle of the far future, but for the next decade the dirigible would rule the sky. With its rigid construction and onboard engines instead of Andrée's drag ropes and sails, the modern blimp was as far beyond Andrée's balloon as today's jetliners are beyond the Wrights' first plane.

Well, not quite, but they were the most dependable method of air travel available at the time. In 1929 the German *Graf Zeppelin* would fly around the world in only twenty days, touching down just three times along the way. Over the next decade she would make nearly 600 flights, crossing the Atlantic 139 times and amassing more than a million miles without incident. Her sister ships would carry thousands of passengers in comfort and safety; in twenty-five years of flying not a single life would be lost until May 6, 1937, when the *Hindenburg* reached Lakehurst, New Jersey after flying from Germany. It arrived in a thunderstorm, something struck a spark, and the flammable hydrogen gas erupted into flames. From this moment on the airplane ruled supreme.

But in 1926 the dirigible was Amundsen's vehicle of choice. He toured the United States to raise money to buy one, but he had the bad taste to publicly question Peary's claim to the pole, and by then Peary was an American hero and such talk didn't help Amundsen win audiences. In the end Lincoln Ellsworth donated $125,000, and the Norwegian bought an Italian airship which he named the *Norge.* It had been designed by Umberto Nobile, who was hired to go along as aircraft commander and pilot. On May 7, 1926, it was delivered to Spitsbergen and preparations began for the flight to the pole.

Meanwhile, Byrd was also in Spitsbergen getting his Fokker trimotor airplane, the *Josephine Ford*, ready for his flight. The Fokker was the Model T of its day, built by the Dutch firm for use by the earliest airlines all over the world. It was powered by three air-cooled engines developing 200 horsepower each, and could fly on only two of them.

That is, when it could fly at all. Byrd had arrived in Spitsbergen a week before Amundsen, but he was having problems with the plane. He intended to make a long flight, heading first to Peary Land and then to the pole before returning, but with the Fokker loaded with the supplies necessary for such a long trip it was simply too heavy, and when it landed after its trial flight it smashed its landing-gear skis.

Byrd was distraught. He was racing against time to beat Amundsen, and there was no wood on this treeless island with which to repair the skis. As he stood cursing and kicking the Fokker, a Norwegian air force officer named Bernt Balchen came up to him. Balchen, who would later accompany Byrd to the South Pole, said that he had been sent by Amundsen, who had heard about Byrd's trouble and had an idea. He showed the astonished Byrd how to fix the skis by using wood from the oars of a lifeboat, and when they were fitted onto the Fokker they worked perfectly.

Byrd probably could not understand this sort of behavior, but he accepted it. He thanked Balchen and Amundsen, climbed into his Fokker and roared off into the northern light before Amundsen could do so, even though he and his pilot, Floyd Bennett, had hardly had any sleep for thirty-six hours. They took off at forty-five minutes past midnight on the morning of May 9.

At 4:07 P.M. that same day they returned—successfully, Byrd proclaimed. They had changed their plans, he said, and flew straight to the pole instead of to Peary Land. On the way home they had intended to fly over Peary Land, but had developed an oil leak and so had come straight home.

Magnificent! The first flight over the North Pole. *The New York Times* trumpeted, ALL THE WORLD GIVES PRAISE TO BYRD FOR

HIS SUCCESSFUL DASH TO THE POLE! Separate articles covering the paper's first three pages were headlined:

NATION'S LEADERS LAUD BYRD'S FEAT

CONGRESS TO GIVE HIM CONGRESSIONAL MEDAL OF HONOR

BYRD'S OBSERVATIONS GRATIFY SCIENTISTS

FOKKER LAUDS BYRD'S FLIGHT AS BIGGEST AIR FEAT

FLIER'S WIFE IS JUBILANT

GOVERNMENT CHIEFS AND SCIENTIFIC MEN PAY TRIBUTE

The lead article told the world that "America's claim to the North Pole was cinched tonight when, after a flight of fifteen hours and fifty-one minutes, Commander Richard E. Byrd and Floyd Bennett, his pilot, returned to announce that they had flown to the Pole, circling it several times and verifying Admiral Peary's observations completely."

All in all, a perfect triumph. Except . . .

The Fokker's cruising speed was seventy miles per hour, and the distance from their base at Spitsbergen to the pole was a bit over 1300 miles. Therefore it would take nineteen hours for the round trip, plus an extra thirteen minutes for a couple of circles around the pole which Byrd said they had performed. They had left at 12:45 A.M. and had returned just after 4 P.M., an elapsed time of fifteen and a half hours.

Well, we had a tail wind, Byrd explained.

Both ways?

Well, sort of. We had a mild tail wind going north, which then "began to freshen and change direction soon after we left the pole." The *Josephine Ford* had made nearly a hundred miles per hour coming home.

And how did he know he had reached the pole?

We took a sextant sighting of the sun, Byrd answered.

From an airplane in flight?

No problem, Byrd said. Not for a competent navigator.

Well, maybe. But nearly twenty years later the British

Royal Air Force was sending its bombers to raid German cities. The conditions were similar, in that the Lancasters and Halifaxes were flying at night over a blacked-out continent, which meant there were no landmarks below to allow them to correct their navigation; Byrd was flying in daylight, but over featureless polar ice, again with no landmarks. After the war, the British found that not only did most of their bombers miss the industrial centers of the cities they were attacking, but that many of them missed the cities entirely. Bombs were dropped into fields and lakes, and when they did manage to hit a city it was often the wrong one. Not until the latter years of the war, when radar techniques were invented, was Bomber Command able to find its targets.

In 1926 there was no such thing as radar. If the Royal Air Force's best navigators, with all the improvements in aerial navigation that took place between 1926 and 1941, couldn't find entire cities on flights of a few hundred miles without landmarks, it certainly seems at least possible that Byrd missed the pole.

Was there any way to check his navigation?

Yes, there might have been. A tradition of every explorer since men first started long voyages over the horizon had been to carry their nation's flag and to plant it on whatever new territory they found. But Byrd didn't do this. As the *Times* reported, he "established an exploring record by not dropping flags." Why not?

He forgot. He was "too busy."

Too busy? Even though, being a firm patriot and in the pay of the United States Navy, he had taken with him more than a hundred American flags? His intention had been to drop them from the *Josephine Ford* and bedeck the North Pole in a spangled array of star-spangled banners. If he had done so the array would have been clearly visible to Amundsen, who was set to take off within a few days. There is no solid land at the pole, and the polar ice does drift, but the movement is on the order of a few miles per day at most, so Amundsen would have seen the flags within a few miles of the pole.

But Byrd *forgot*. He flew a plane that had been carefully drained of any excess baggage, a plane on which every ounce of equipment was measured and evaluated, a plane on which the hundred flags were carried only after careful deliberation—and then forgot to drop them. He circled the pole for thirteen minutes and forgot to drop his flags. He took pictures of the pole—pictures which could have been taken anywhere on the featureless polar ice—and didn't think of how lovely those pictures would look to his supporters back home with American flags covering the landscape?

Dennis Rawlins, the astronomer who doubted Peary, points out one possible reason for this otherwise incomprehensible inconsistency in the behavior of a man who never in his life missed a publicity opportunity. Byrd knew that Amundsen was coming after him, and he couldn't afford to have Amundsen report that he had seen no American flags when he circled the North Pole. Even worse, Amundsen might have reported that he *did* see the flags, not at the pole but out in the middle of nowhere. For this is where Rawlins suspects Byrd actually was: nowhere.

Did Byrd bring back any proof? No, not even evaluations of the magnetic variation, the same data that Peary had failed to record. His flight made a tremendous impression, dominating newspapers all over the world, but it was a useless venture in the annals of polar exploration whether he actually reached the pole or not. No new data of any type—meteorological, magnetic, or depth soundings of the ocean—were obtained. Byrd's observation that there was no continental land mass anywhere near the North Pole would have been a useful one had it not been preempted by Amundsen the previous year. So what did he accomplish? He flew somewhere near the North Pole—how close no one can know for sure—and then flew home again. Given the state of aviation science in 1926, it was a daring flight, but that's about all one can say for it.

Well, there is one thing. The last sentence of the *Times*'s lead article mentioned that Byrd had "verified Admiral Peary's observations completely." Interesting, but precisely which "observations" did he verify so completely? That the North Pole is covered with snow? What did the *Times* mean? Nothing else in the article referred to any such observations.

But an article in the *Times* the following day looked as if it might provide the missing information. Its headline read: OBSERVATION EXPERT PRAISES BYRD'S FEAT . . . RECALLS CHECKING OF PEARY DATA, WHICH AVIATOR HAS CONFIRMED. In the form of a telegram from O. H. Tittman, one of the committee that "verified" Peary's achievement, the article went on to ask: "Who can fail to be thrilled by Commander Byrd's great achievement? It is most gratifying that his observations confirmed those of another brave American, the first to reach the Pole." Then the piece goes on to talk about Peary, but not once does it say what his observations were that Byrd had confirmed, or what they could possibly have been.

What could Byrd have seen from the air that would confirm Peary's success? As a matter of fact, there *was* one set of data common to both explorers. Peary traveled to the pole by dead reckoning, which he explained as setting his course by magnetic compass and estimating the distance traveled. Byrd's Fokker carried three such magnetic compasses and, the *Times* reveals as an aside while praising Byrd's new sun compass, "all of them deviated eccentrically after reaching high latitudes. Bennett declared that when he was piloting the magnetic compasses were wholly useless . . ."

Aside from this one statement—that Peary's claimed method of navigation was "wholly useless"—no other observation from the *Josephine Ford* has the remotest relationship to anything Peary observed or claimed to have done.

Meanwhile, back at Spitsbergen, Roald Amundsen had readied his dirigible, the *Norge,* and two days after Byrd's flight he and his crew took off and sailed without event to the pole. After all the drama and trauma of a hundred years of tragic expeditions, the large white blimp sailed serenely over the ice and snow. "The sun shone brilliantly out of a sky of pure turquoise, and the whale-like shadow that our airship cast beneath us trailed monotonously across a glittering snow field." They sailed quietly for twenty-eight hours, riding smoothly on the wind, the propellers nudging them forward, until "the navigator who had been on his knees at one of the starboard windows since 1:10 with his sextant set on the height and declination that the sun should have at the Pole, corresponding to the given date, suddenly announced as the sun's image started to cover his sextant bubble, "Here we are! We are over the North Pole!"

They circled over it at 300 feet, leaning out of the gondola's windows, looking down at the site which had lured men like the ancient sirens, pulling them beyond their capabilities, dragging them to their doom on the frozen sea. They looked down and saw nothing but calm snow, ice, sunshine and a gentle breeze; they saw no sirens, heard no ghosts, felt no terrors. They circled slowly and dropped three flags—Norwegian, American and Italian—then sailed onward, heading south toward Alaska on the other side of the polar sea.

The original plan for the *Sovetskiy Soyuz* had been to emulate the *Norge* and sail from the pole to Alaska. But shortly before embarkation we received this message from the trip's organizers: "We are still involved with unbelievable bureaucracy with regard to permission of the vessel to

enter Nome. We are dealing with at least four or five different government departments, all of whom are moving at a
very slow pace . . ."

In the end, the *Soyuz* never did receive permission to
enter the Nome harbor. The problem was that the ship is
nuclear, and this single word transports us back into medieval society with attendant devils, plagues and evil vapors.
The guardians of cities rise up and stand at the city gates
with their swords crossed to ward off the devil, and with
shouts of "Unclean! Unclean!" they turn the poor vagrants
away.

It is hypocritical for American cities to be so inhospitable
to nuclear ships when our own navy comprises the world's
foremost nuclear fleet, and when we have spent so much
time, energy and money convincing foreign governments
that there is nothing to fear from allowing our nuclear submarines and aircraft carriers to dock. Perhaps we should
spend some of this money on educating our own citizens.
On the other hand, this is not just *any* nuclear ship, it's a
Soviet one, from those lovely folks who brought us
Chernobyl.

At any rate, Alaska is forbidden to us, and so we set sail
due south from the North Pole—after all, what other direction is there?—and head toward Provideniya, on the eastern tip of Siberia. On the way, however, we will run into a
bureaucracy which makes the American one look like a
child's puzzle of fewer than ten pieces, a bureaucracy so
convoluted that it chokes its society to death. The wonder
is not that the Soviet Union finally collapsed, but that it
lasted so long when it was so inefficient.

For the moment, though, we know nothing of this. We
plow our way through the ice toward Wrangel Island,
which has the world's largest concentration of polar bears,
and where the Russians have settled Chukchi and Eskimo
populations in an indigenous native culture. It should be
interesting.

*   *   *

The only interesting incident of Amundsen's flight over the
North Pole came after it was over, when Amundsen and
Nobile, who had designed the *Norge*, had a falling out. I
asked Taffy Mostyn, the Welsh-born Arctic historian who
has been transplanted to the University of Glasgow and
who compensates with a perversely classical Oxbridge accent, what the problem was. Doing a good imitation of
Terry-Thomas, he answered, "You know, I believe it was a
case of Nobile having the traditionally active Latin mouth.
He was hired as the pilot on the flight, but when he came
back he went around saying he had gone to the pole, and
oh yes, there were one or two other chaps along, but he
didn't quite recall their names. That sort of thing."

Actually it was a bit worse than this, according to Richard Montague, a journalist who covered several of the Arctic exploration stories and later wrote a book about aerial
exploration. He writes that on the trip from Italy to Spitsbergen, Nobile proved to be "conceited, stubborn and a
poor pilot," according to Hjalmar Riiser-Larsen, Amundsen's pilot on the previous trip and his choice to be the pilot
on this one.

The negotiations for the *Norge* had begun with the Italian
government proposing that Amundsen come along on
what basically would be an Italian expedition. Amundsen
had refused, and had ended up buying the airship. Now,
on the trip up to Spitsbergen, Nobile informed Riis-Larsen
that the airship would fly the Italian flag. Riis-Larsen refused, and Nobile threatened to walk off at the next stop,
leaving them all stranded. But when Riis-Larsen informed
him that he was capable of flying the *Norge* himself and
would be quite happy to see the little Italian leave, Nobile
changed his mind.

In Amundsen's autobiography he writes that Nobile
nearly caused them to crash several times during the voyage. Though he was officially the pilot he never touched

the controls except for three times. Once, taking over the elevator controls, he turned the wheel too much and the *Norge* tipped its nose over and dove toward the ground, coming out of it only when Riis-Larsen grabbed Nobile by the shoulders, threw him aside and righted the craft himself. The second time was a duplicate of the first. The third time Nobile took them up instead of down, and while no one was watching he took them so far up that the internal gas pressure, expanding against the reduced atmospheric pressure at that height, nearly ruptured the cells. Disaster was avoided when three of the Norwegian crew ran to the bow and their weight tipped the airship forward and down again.

Nevertheless, Nobile does deserve some credit for the successful completion of the world's first dirigible flight to the North Pole. He had, after all, designed the aircraft. Still, the plan, idea and preparation for the flight were all Amundsen's. Yet in interviews afterward Nobile described himself as one of the leaders as well as the pilot, neither of which he had been, and the dissension became acrimonious. When the world ignored his claims he took his complaint to the new leader of his country, Benito Mussolini.

Mussolini was eager for any chance to secure glory for Italy, so he sponsored Nobile's new plan for the first proper exploration of the North Pole. Nobile would design and build a new dirigible, the *Italia*, which would not only fly to the pole but would land there. It would carry men and supplies to set up a proper scientific base, and while the six men of the scientific group spent three weeks taking a series of meteorological and geophysical observations, the dirigible would explore by air the islands of the Canadian archipelago and bring back to civilization the first comprehensive survey of the polar regions, compliments of and bringing honor and glory to Il Duce's fascist government. What a hundred years of capitalist exploration had failed to do, fascist scientists would accomplish.

It was a grand plan, and it almost worked. In May 1928 the *Italia* left Spitsbergen for the pole, but without the six scientists of the landing party, who decided at the last moment that the preparations were inadequate and who went home. Still, the dirigible took off in bright sunshine, flew to the pole without any problems, hovered, took a few pictures and then headed back to Spitsbergen.

This was when the problems began. As we had experienced on the *Soyuz*, bright sunshine in the Arctic summer can turn to thick fog without a moment's warning, and that is what happened in 1928. The *Italia* was forced lower and lower to maintain visibility—radar was still a dozen or so years in the future—and moisture from the fog began to drip onto the air bag and freeze there. As the weight increased it became harder and harder to maintain altitude. Then ice began to freeze onto the propellers. This threw the balance off, and the props began to shake. The vibration broke off the ice, but some of the sharp fragments were spun into the gas bag, ripping holes in it. The crew scrambled through the superstructure repairing them as fast as they could, but as the ice continued to build up they fell behind and new holes appeared before old ones could be mended.

The winds shifted erratically, faster than they could be compensated for. With the pandemonium caused by the frantic patching of holes, the crew lost track of where they were. Now the elevator tab malfunctioned and they had trouble controlling their height. Then the rudder malfunctioned and they listed to port. The ice continued to build up, and they began to sink, tail first. Full power was applied, but the rudder failure meant that the power was wasted. Its nose pointed high, its propellers whirling, the *Italia* sank lower and lower, faster and faster, out of control.

It crashed onto the ice. The gondola split open and ten men were flung out onto the ice; six others clung to their seats and remained aboard. One of them, Arduino, reacted quickly, throwing out of the airship any supplies he could grab, dropping them to his companions on the ice below. In the next moment a gust of wind caught the now helpless *Italia* and flung it away into the northern wastes. The ten men strewed over the ice floe watched in horror as it lifted and sailed away, flapping in the wind, carrying with it their provisions and the six men who had kept themselves from falling out. Neither the *Italia* nor Arduino nor any of the others on board were ever seen again.

Of those left on the ice, two, including Nobile, had broken legs and another an arm. The others scrambled around, trying to gather the supplies Arduino had dropped and anything else that might have come loose when the airship crashed. They scoured the icy hummocks and returned with more than a hundred pounds of food, one tent, a sleeping bag, matches and fuel, a gun and ammunition, and best of all a radio, complete with long-range transmitter. One of the group was the *Italia*'s radio operator, and he immediately put the set together and began sending out an S.O.S.

But no one heard him. Back at Spitsbergen, as first the hours and then the days passed without the airship's return, the word went out that the *Italia* was missing. Biaggi, the *Italia*'s radio operator who now spent his time glued to the set, wondering how long the batteries would last, told his companions that everyone knew they were lost; he had picked up a radio broadcast all the way from Rome, telling the world that they had failed to return. But with the routine perversity of a malevolent nature, his own radio transmissions didn't reach Rome or anywhere else. As he listened hour after hour, day after day, he heard from all over the world the news that they were lost; as he transmitted hour after hour, day after day, he heard no reply. No one, it seemed, was listening.

That couldn't be true, his fellows argued. The radio messages they heard indicated that the whole world was aware of their fate, was arguing over where they might be and where rescuers ought to be searching.

Biaggi shrugged. The world might be listening for their S.O.S., but it certainly wasn't hearing anything. He went back to his set and began tapping out his Morse code message again and again and again.

Rescue ships were sent out. Reconnaissance airplanes scoured the skies from Franz Josef Land to Spitsbergen and all the way to Greenland.

Nobile took a series of sextant sightings of the sun and determined that the ice floe on which they were trapped lay near a tiny island named Foyn, only 180 miles northeast of Spitsbergen. But the search area they heard described on their radio covered nearly 25 percent of the earth's total area! It would take centuries for them to be found, and nobody seemed to hear their own transmissions giving their location: S.O.S.F.O.Y.N.C.I.R.C.A.

In desperation a week later, Nobile sent three men out to try to reach civilization and report the location of the others. Three days after they disappeared into the blowing snow, someone heard Biaggi's transmissions. A Russian peasant listening to a music broadcast picked up the message on his amateur set. He understood the S.O.S. transmission, though not the rest of it, but he knew—even peasants in the depths of Russia knew—about the great search for the missing *Italia*. He notified the leaders of his local Soviet and they notified Moscow, but Moscow said it was nonsense. All the great radio receivers in the most prestigious research establishments of the world were listening day and night, trying to pick up any message from the ether, and they had failed. Therefore there was no message; the peasant had heard nothing. Furthermore, Moscow said, the peasant's radio set was tuned to a frequency that was not that of the *Italia*'s radio transmitter, so the signal, whatever it was, could not be from the missing airship. They declined to notify the search parties.

But scientists at the Arctic Research Institute of the Soviet Academy of Sciences took the signal more seriously. One in particular, a Professor Samoilovich, pointed out that perhaps the transmitter on the ice was not the *Italia's* *main* transmitter, and perhaps it sent on a different frequency. Which would explain why none of the great laboratories had heard any messages; they were listening on the wrong frequency.

But why would an airship carry two transmitters working on different frequencies? Samoilovich shrugged. Who knew with the Italians? Then he pointed out that Foyn Island was right where the airship might have been blown from the pole.

A week later Moscow capitulated and informed Rome. Back on the ice, Biaggi heard the announcement that all search parties were now heading for Foyn. Ships and planes from Norway, France, Italy and Sweden were on their way.

Three weeks after the crash, the men huddled together on the ice saw one of the rescue planes. But it did not see them. As they watched in frustration it continued on its way and soon disappeared. Once again they were alone.

Two days later Roald Amundsen joined the search. He had bitter feelings about Nobile, but a stronger kinship with him and all the others lost in the Arctic. He joined the crew of a badly equipped French airplane and flew out from Spitsbergen. At this time the French had only two aircraft suitable for long-range exploration—barely suitable, that is, for neither had a radio powerful enough to send signals more than a few hundred miles. One of the planes had water-cooled engines and therefore was not suitable for flying in subzero temperatures, while the other was air-cooled and so not suitable for dusty regions. Naturally the French bureaucracy assigned the air-cooled plane to the tropics, where it was impossible to keep it flying, and sent the water-cooled plane to the Arctic, where Amundsen and the French crew flew it off to look for the *Italia* and were never seen again.

One month after the crash the survivors were sighted. The Italian airplane radioed back to base that he had spotted a single red tent in the white emptiness, and the image was spread across the world by wireless radio. People everywhere could imagine that single red spot in the whiteness, and cheered the hero who had found it.

But the tragedy hadn't yet ended; there was nowhere for the plane to land, so it dropped supplies by parachute and returned home. Most of the supplies, including all the food and fresh water, broke apart and fell into the water; the men on the ice floe recovered only shoes and sleeping bags. It took four more days before an airplane managed to land. The pilot, Lieutenant Lundborg of the Swedish air force, told Nobile he could take out only one man at a time and asked Nobile to climb aboard.

No, Nobile said. Take my men first. I will come last. But Lundborg insisted. His reasons are not known; perhaps he wanted the glory of landing back at Spitsbergen with the leader of the expedition; perhaps it was thought that Nobile would be more useful directing rescue operations from a safe haven. At any rate, Nobile consented to go only when Lundborg promised that the others would be taken off by immediate return flight. This decision was one the Italian would regret for the rest of his life.

That evening after Nobile and Lundborg landed safely in Spitsbergen the weather closed in. No more flights were made that day. Early the next morning Lundborg tried again, hoping to bring back the two other men who had suffered broken bones, but when he landed on the ice he cracked up. The plane was wrecked beyond repair, and now he was stranded there too.

For two weeks daily flights were attempted, but none of them succeeded in landing. As June ended and July rolled in, the weather began to warm up enough for the ice to start breaking up. Each day the ice floe the men were stranded on shrank a bit more; any day it might split right down the middle.

On July 6 a Norwegian pilot succeeded in landing and taking Lundborg off, but this was the only flight that succeeded in landing. By the next day the ice was too broken up and too small for any more flights to even consider the attempt. Things looked grim, but then the Russians arrived on the scene like John Wayne leading the cavalry. With trumpets blaring the icebreakers *Krassin* and *Malygin* bore down on Foyn.

With the *Krassin* taking the lead, the two ships began breaking through the ice pack. On the 10th of July their scout plane returned to report that he had spied the men. The *Krassin* shifted course and found them. However, it was not the main party of the *Italia*, but two of the three men who had left in an effort to walk back to Spitsbergen; the third man had died.

The exultation of rescuing the men soon turned to horror. Both were in pitiable condition, but Mariano was significantly worse off than Capitano Zappi, the leader of the little expedition. At least Zappi was dressed warmly, wearing two pairs of fur-lined boots, two pairs of warm socks, three pairs of trousers including one fur-lined, a fur vest and a knitted vest under a linen coat, a linen cap and a fur hat on top of that. Mariano had no boots at all; he was lying unable to move in a pool of half-melted ice. He had on only one pair of cotton trousers, one pair of soaked-through socks and two vests; he had no hat, no coat, no fur-lined trousers or fur-lined boots. His toes were frostbitten, gangrene had set in and he was raging with fever. When the two men were undressed the Russians saw that some of the clothing Zappi wore was the wrong size; it seemed to belong to Mariano.

Zappi said that they hadn't eaten for two weeks, but he was able to climb up the fifteen-foot ladder into the *Krassin*.

Mariano was unable to move, and was taken aboard on a stretcher. The medical officer reported that when both men were given enemas to clear out their intestines as part of the emergency medical treatment, Zappi's entrails indicated that he had eaten only a few days ago. But Mariano, too weak and feverish to talk coherently, was on the verge of starvation; he had probably not eaten for two weeks. (God takes care of those who help themselves. Zappi recovered; Mariano did not.)

Finally, a French reporter wrote that when Mariano was pulled aboard the *Krassin* delirious with fever, he moaned, "You can eat me, but not until after I die."

Upon hearing a statement like that, one's thoughts naturally turn to the third man, a Swede named Malmgren. What had happened to him?

Zappi reported that Malmgren had simply deteriorated faster than the other two. He had sunk into depression, become so weak that they had to drag him along, and finally had refused to move any further. "Leave me," he told them.

Zappi said that the two of them had walked on a bit, then sat down and waited. Malmgren refused to budge. "Take my food and go," he said when they returned to him, and finally they had done so.

To have left their companion was bad enough, but Mariano's begging not to be eaten until he was dead suggested another scenario. The world's fascination with the heroes on the ice turned to revulsion, and to disgust when it was revealed that Nobile had left his starving men and had been the first one to be rescued. Though he was not the most likable of men, for this he was taking a bum rap. He had insisted on staying behind with the others, and only accompanied Lundborg under duress. For the rest of the rescue operation, until the *Krassin* made its way to the main party and rescued them all, he was kept a virtual prisoner by the Italian commander in Spitsbergen, and when he returned to his country he was singled out by Mussolini as the scapegoat. Fascism could not fail; ergo, someone was at fault. It had to be Nobile, who was forced to resign his commission in disgrace.

Perhaps the worst loss in the *Italia* tragedy was the death of Roald Amundsen. Neither he nor any of the crew of the French rescue plane were ever found. There are still stories, Taffy Mostyn tells me, that somewhere he is living in peace and solitude. One hears that he has been seen in Mexico, or perhaps Antigua or the Lesser Tortugas. It is said that information about his supposed disappearance is contained in secret papers in the Royal Archives in Oslo. A new king of Norway has recently been crowned, the grandson of the king who reigned at the time of Amundsen's "death," and perhaps he will release these records, it is said.

I wouldn't hold my breath. Amundsen was simply one of those heroes too wonderful to die, whose loss we cannot accept. So I won't wait to have those secret Norwegian archives opened, but instead will go on believing that he is living happily with Amelia Earhart somewhere on a tropical isle where it never gets cold and there are no taxes.

The *Italia* incident was the last great tragedy of polar exploration. There was almost one more.

This afternoon we come across a small island, little more than a bare rock jutting out of the cold sea. It rises vertically out of the ocean, levels off into a flat plain, then climbs steeply again to disappear into a cloud of fog hanging around its temple. We stop to take a look. It is impossible to reach the island by small boat; the cliffs are unclimbable and the coastline is blocked with ice. But a helicopter shuttle is laid on, transporting us from the ship to the mesa midway up the island's height.

We all head for the afterdeck, pausing at the button board. This is a two-by-three-foot board with six rows of two-inch-diameter buttons mounted on hooks, standing by the passageway aft. There is one button for each passenger, and on each side is printed our room number. One side is painted red, the other white. As we head for the chopper or the boat to leave the *Soyuz* we turn our button from white to red. When we come back aboard we turn it from red to white. This is to ensure that nobody is left behind to die in the Arctic after an island visit. But the system is useless: twice before, after such visits, the Klaxon has boomed out a chiding from the captain, telling us that so-and-so had forgotten to turn his button back from red to white. Neither time did the helicopter return to the island to look for the supposedly lost soul; instead the crew simply turned the button and later informed the captain.

Huddled in our parkas, sweaters, boots and gloves, burdened with our life vests, each of us pauses to turn our buttons from white to red. The life vests are a nuisance. They are cork-filled rather than inflatable, so in effect they are always inflated. Wearing them on top of sweaters and a parka is like being a child again, dressed for the cold weather in clothing so bulky that you can't move. If someone behind you in the line speaks to you, you have to turn your whole body around to see them. I hate the vest, but it is required every time we leave the ship, whether by boat or chopper. This time I decide to take a chance on being sent back to my cabin and losing my place in line: I leave it behind. When I get to the front of the line there is one place left in the chopper and the guard waves me on without noticing that I'm not wearing it. Good for me.

As I climb aboard the chopper I find I have something else to worry about. The *Soyuz* has two helicopters. One is the small craft I flew on before, with room for two pilots and three passengers in the back seat. Today I am on the larger one, which was built as a KA-32 attack chopper, to take soldiers into battle. I half climb and am half pushed aboard, the door clangs shut behind me and I am in hell.

It is a small cabin, with room under battle conditions for

sixteen soldiers, or under normal conditions for perhaps a dozen thin people or six fat ones. With our parkas and everyone else's life vests on, we are all fat, and there are sixteen of us. There is no window except for one small square looking onto the back of the pilot's head. In the center of the room is the vertical rotor shaft, which starts to quiver and roar as soon as the door is slammed behind me. As it roars the whole cabin shakes and we are thrust violently against each other. We try to find handholds to steady ourselves but there is nothing but the bare walls and the stools we are sitting on. Suddenly the room lurches, and as we fall together in a wild scramble of arms, legs and bumping, cork-filled life vests the helicopter rises into the air like a roller coaster gone berserk.

A wave of claustrophobia envelops me, suffocating me, almost irresistible. It takes all my willpower to keep from breaking into uncontrollable screams. Instead I close my eyes and hug myself. I have never had such a violent attack before. I can't help thinking of my last flight, when we became lost in the fog. I know that just a few hundred feet above us is another fog. If we become lost in it . . . if we begin to sail in circles forever and ever . . . If the others become frightened and begin to scream I know I shall too; we will all be caught up here in this tiny shaking room screaming to be let out . . .

The room drops, bangs against something, stops shaking, and the rotor dies down. The door is opened from outside and I am pulled out. The others climb out after me; we are on the island. I glance at my watch. It has been less than ten minutes, and I inhale for the first time.

As always when landing on an island, we take off our life vests and drop them in a large pile; then we ramble away to investigate this strange polar rock. I want to be alone, so I head straight to the edge, on a radial line away from the landing spot. The drop is a vertical one, and it is dizzying but exhilarating to stand there. The sense of space after being confined in the chopper is overwhelming. I nearly want to spread my arms, leap over the side and sail off by myself like Superman. For the first time I understand how under certain circumstances it wouldn't take much for a person to jump off a building. But maybe the people who actually jump are feeling totally different. How would one know?

I wander along the edge for a while, and then head up the comparatively gentle slope toward the bank of fog. The climb is easy at first, but after a hundred yards it begins to get tiring. Still, it is a good feeling, this stiffening of the thighs as I force myself forward and upward. My breath is coming harder now, and I even have to unbutton the parka. But as soon as I pause to rest the wind comes whipping in and chills the sweat under my armpits, so I zip up again.

Sweat was more than a nuisance to the early Arctic explorers as they hauled their sleds over the ice in temperatures of 30 or 40 degrees below zero. It is just about zero degrees now, so my sweat doesn't freeze into a solid layer of ice in my clothing, breaking and cutting me every time I move. Also, I can stop whenever I want—which, as I climb, becomes every few minutes—instead of being forced to march and haul a couple of hundred pounds of weight for hours at a time, with death waiting if I falter. My climb is nothing at all like the horror faced by real explorers, but it gives me a touch of empathy.

I can't reach the fog. However hard I climb, however fast I push myself, it seems to recede before me as I approach, always hanging in the distance just beyond my reach. Finally I give up, sit down on a large white rock and look back on the scene below me. The people from the ship are tiny creatures, scattered in small groups around the central pile of life jackets which stands out in a bright red pylon. I think of Nobile's red tent, the one splash of color in a blank universe.

I drift off into reverie. When I return to this blank universe I realize that the pile of red vests is smaller than before. A group of people is waiting by it; the chopper comes down and opens its doors and they climb in and head off back to the ship. It's time to go back.

I don't want to climb back into that hellhole, so I decide to take my time. Let the others shove themselves in and go back; I will wait until there are only a few of us left. If we aren't jammed in together, it won't be so bad.

So I wait, and soon there are only a few left. I start back, but it's further than I think. As I struggle over the tundra I see the chopper come and go twice again, and now as I begin to run in my L. L. Bean Arctic boots, which are not built for running, it returns once more and I see that there are only six people waiting. I begin to shout and wave my hands, but their backs are to me, they are watching the helicopter, and the roar of the beating blades drowns out my voice.

The chopper settles down in the swirling dust, the people duck under the still-rotating blades and climb aboard, and the whole kit and kaboodle leaps off the earth, rises into the air and sails away.

Suddenly it is very quiet on the island.

By the time I reach the landing point it is empty. There are no life vests anymore, no pile of red, and I realize that if I had taken my vest it would still have been here and the crew would have realized that someone was still on the island. My only hope now is the red button back on the board at the gangway entrance. The crew will see it and know that I am still here. Or they will see it and think the Russian equivalent of "One more jerk who forgot to turn his button." Then they will turn it for me, the Klaxon will sound, the captain will chide me for being careless and the *Soyuz* will sail away through the ice-encrusted ocean.

I look around. There are no trees on the island, no wood

with which to build a fire. I could set fire to my parka—
perhaps it would generate enough smoke for someone on
the ship to see—but I don't smoke and so have no matches.
Cigarettes are detrimental to your health, but so is being
caught on an Arctic island without matches.

From where I stand I can't see the *Soyuz*; it is cut off by a
rise in the plain beyond which lies the sea. If I run to the
edge, jump up and down and wave my arms, perhaps
someone will see me. But I realize this is a vain hope, for
the sun is behind me and the entire island will be within its
glare.

Not to panic, I tell myself. Sooner or later someone will
miss me. Surely by tomorrow morning my roommate will
see that my bed hasn't been slept in.

But there are one or two other beds on board which are
not regularly slept in. Liaisons have been made. Perhaps he
will think I got lucky.

Not to panic, not to panic. I look around. There is no
shelter on the island, nothing but the tundra, nothing to
keep me from the wind, which now is perversely blowing
harder and colder. The sweat which poured off me during
my last headlong run down to the landing spot is now
freezing under my arms, around my belly and in my shoes.

Then I hear voices. I'm beginning to hallucinate already.
It turns visual; up from behind the rise of the plain comes a
red-hooded head, and then another and another. It's like
the scene in *Lawrence of Arabia* when out of the shimmering,
blinding desert a figure begins to appear in thin air, slowly
solidifying into a real person. Two persons, then a third, all
in their red parkas, with their red life vests slung over their
shoulders.

They climb up the slight incline to where I'm standing,
chatting and talking among themselves, nodding and saying hello to me; we all stand there together, and then in
another minute or two we hear the helicopter returning.

Nansen survived in the Arctic wilderness for a year and

a half; I was here alone for about three minutes. But in both cases it turned out all right. In fact, better than all right; there are only four of us returning on the chopper's last trip, so there is plenty of room and no cause for panic.

When I get back to the ship I notice that my button has already been turned over from red to white.

That evening I bump into Dr. Nishtar in the bar, and he wags his finger in my face. "You are a naughty boy," he says, sounding like Gandhi. "You neglected to turn over your button."

"No, I didn't," I start to say, but he laughs.

"Oh, yes. You cannot fool me. I returned on the last helicopter, and I saw that your button was still red. I turned it over for you. So you have me to thank that the good captain does not announce your disgrace for forgetting." He laughs again.

"There was one more flight," I tell him. "I was still on the island."

Still he laughs; he will never believe me.

AUGUST 7

The ice is as thick, perhaps even thicker, than it was at the pole. Though we are heading south, we are moving toward the geometric center of the permanent ice pack. The ship rocks and shakes continually as it batters its way through. The lecture after breakfast is totally unintelligible; it's like sitting in a tin house during a meteorite shower; the banging, shaking and continuous thunder drown out everyone's words.

After the lecture, as we are streaming out of the theater, there is a sudden calm. The Klaxon announces that the ship is going to stop and that we will be able to disembark. When we go out on the deck, it looks as if the *Soyuz* has been grounded. The gangplank is lowered and we bundle up, go down and walk around. A volleyball net is set up in the snow, people stamp around on either side of it packing down the snow and a game begins. Someone has brought along a scuba outfit; the crew help chop a hole in the ice and a couple of people go down into the black water. I guess it is something to tell the folks back home about.

At 12:15 we go back on board, the *Soyuz* backs away from its berth, takes a running start and goes crashing through the ice again. At lunch we eat very carefully, timing the bringing of food and drink to our mouths with the motion of the ship. Put your spoon in the soup, hold the bowl with your left hand . . . Crash! We break through the ice . . . Quickly lift the spoon to your mouth and gulp it down before the bow rises for another breakthrough.

There is a rumbling shudder and the ship stops again. Everyone looks around in puzzlement, and perhaps with the beginning of apprehension. We can't be having another party on the ice already. And we can't be stuck in it, can we?

For several long moments there is absolute silence. After ten days of continual ice-breaking, the lack of motion is eerie; somehow the ship seems dead. Then the Klaxon blares out, "Attention please! In some moments there will be a new motion of the icebreaker. Don't be afraid."

Now the stern begins to sink and the bow rises higher and higher; it feels like we're in an airplane trying to take off. Everyone grabs at the table to hold on, and then we lean forward again; the bow begins to sink faster and faster, comes crashing down with a roar and an awful thunder, and the ice cracks beneath us. What happened was that we ran into the thickest ice yet, too thick for the normal weight of the ship to crush. So we took on water, a thousand tons of it, in the stern. This sank the stern and raised the bow high over the unyielding ice; then within a minute or two we pumped the thousand tons forward into the bow, bringing it crashing down to crush the heavy ice. The ship rolls a bit and shakes itself like a puppy, the ice shatters and breaks away, and we sail on.

In the dining room the soup has spilled all over the table. The waiters come running quickly to mop it up and replace it.

Why did they do it? Standing on the bow of the *Soyuz* as we leave the frozen inferno behind, I find it hard to understand why Cook, Peary and Byrd all told equivocal stories about reaching the North Pole. Even without this accomplishment all of them were great explorers and brave men who pushed the frontier of human experience to new limits. Why weren't their very real accomplishments enough?

The answer, I think, is different for each of them. At first glance Cook is the hardest to understand. His lies destroyed him, ruined his life, led to prison and to social disgrace. Without his lies he would have been a respected figure. Probably no other explorer in history, with the single exception of Amundsen, has explored so much territory in both the Arctic and Antarctic regions. If he had been content with this, he would have lived to become an elder statesman instead of spending his declining years in jail and writing vitriolic letters to newspapers defending his honor. If he had been content to be known as the first man to circumnavigate Mount McKinley, which he certainly was, and had not also claimed to have climbed it, which he certainly did not, his whole life would not have started to unravel. If he had told the truth about his 1908 Arctic journey, which was undoubtedly a remarkable one, instead of insisting that he had reached the pole, he would be honorably remembered as one of our great explorers. Why did he self-destruct?

Because he was, as suggested earlier, a naïf waif, a child in grown-up's clothing. Just as children believe adults when they are told ridiculous stories about Santa Claus, animals that talk and mermaids who sing, Cook believed whatever other people told him. Undoubtedly this is why he ended up in jail; he believed what he was told about oil under the lands for which he acted as agent. He believed others as children believe, and he expected others to believe him, just as children expect it. A child can become rigid with anger when his story about brushing his teeth is not believed and he is sent back to the bathroom; though he knows he is lying, it is still an insult not to be believed. It *could have* been true; he *might* have brushed his teeth. In the same manner Cook embellished his tales to make them more interesting, and then nearly came to believe them himself. They *could have* been true; he *might* have reached the pole. So he became furious when others did not believe him, even though deep down he knew that he was lying. Along with his fury he had a childish stubbornness, inevitably linked with his childish charm.

Peary was a more complex man, but the explanation for his behavior is probably just as simple. His life was devoted to reaching the North Pole, and he couldn't accept his final failure. No matter that he undoubtedly came much closer than anyone before him: *nothing short would suffice.* In particular, it would have been unbearable for him to get close to the pole and then have to listen for the rest of his life while Cook told how *he* had attained it. So he gave in to temptation, and then had to stick by his story.

Byrd was neither a child nor a monomaniac, but simply Richard Byrd of the Virginia Byrds, a man entitled to success by virtue of his birth, his family, his karma. He pushed himself to the limits of his courage and beyond it—on some of his flights into the unknown he was later described by companions as cowering in terror, and yet he drove himself on and on—because he was expected to surmount the normal range of men. It would not have been suitable for him to have turned back short of the pole because of an oil leak, only to have a Norwegian reach it a few days later, just as it would not have been suitable for a new mountain to have been discovered in Antarctica by someone other than himself. Hence he claimed the mountain and the pole because they were his birthright.

So who was the first person to reach the North Pole? For the South Pole there is no ambivalence: Roald Amundsen and Robert Scott raced across Antarctica in 1912, and Amundsen won. But for the North Pole the answer becomes a matter of distinctions. Cook was the first person to claim it, but few people still honor his claim. Peary and Byrd still have their supporters, but I think that the weight of opinion and evidence is firmly against them. Amundsen, then, was the first person to *see* the North Pole, just as he was the first to reach the South Pole, but in the case of the north he never stood on it, merely sailing over it in the *Norge*. Eleven years later, in 1937, a Russian airborne team came within thirty miles, and in 1958 the American nuclear submarines *Nautilus* and *Skate* reached the pole under the ice; neither surfaced and no one got out. The following year the *Skate* returned and broke through the surface, and for the first time in history men stood on the North Pole.

But getting there by nuclear sub somehow doesn't satisfy the Peary-Cook demon. Getting there on foot is required, and the first person to do this was Ralph Plaisted, an American who snow-mobiled there in 1968. But he too didn't quite fulfill my admittedly vague criteria, for he needed a gas-combustion engine, and once at the pole was met by an airplane and flown home. The first person to get to the top in the old-fashioned way was Wally Herbert, my shipmate on the *Soyuz*, who led a dogsled expedition there in 1969 and reached the pole exactly sixty years to the day after Peary claimed to have attained it.

When I was a boy in Atlantic City I used to sit on our porch and play chess with my grandfather. I haven't played much since, but today a chess tournament is announced, the competition to be between teams from the guests and the crew, and I volunteer. After lunch we troop down to the crew's lounge, where five or six men are waiting for us. We pair off and introduce ourselves. "David Fisher," I say.

"Mischa Oblensky," my opponent says, smiling broadly, and we sit down on opposite sides of the small chess set. We try to talk, but he speaks no English and my Russian is limited to a few words. He is a pleasant-looking, peasant-looking, thickset young man with a great mustache and thick, high hair. He has given me white, and I move first: king's pawn two to four.

Next I try a gambit which I don't really expect to work, and it doesn't. It's a sucker play, allowing me to bring my king's bishop across the board in one direction and my queen diagonally in the other, both focusing on his bishop's pawn. Then with one deft swipe I would take his pawn with my queen for checkmate.

He smiles as if at a good joke, and blocks the entire maneuver by moving his knight's pawn forward one space. He probably hasn't seen that opening since *he* was a kid playing *his* grandfather.

From there on it gets worse. Somehow I am on the defensive immediately, using every move to react to him rather than beginning a campaign of my own. At one point I carelessly miss a challenge to my queen and move my knight instead. He shakes his head and shows me the danger. But I have missed it, and I gesture to him to take my queen. No, no, he insists by gesture and a vigorous shaking of his head, and reluctantly I move my queen out of danger.

I manage to hold him off for nearly a half hour before he apologetically uses the one English word he knows: "Checkmate." I don't see it at first, but quickly he demonstrates, moving the pieces around so fast that I have trouble following him. But he's right; I could make four or five more moves, but the game is over. After we shake hands he reaches into his pocket, brings out a small pin with the word "Murmansk" on it and presents it to me. I have nothing to give him in return, but he insists I take it.

Afterward the tourist team meets in the lounge. To my astonishment one of us actually won a game.

In the bar lounge after dinner I am talking about Peary with Wally Herbert when we are interrupted by the slight static which precedes an announcement; then the Klaxon suddenly booms with a heavy Russian accent: "Attention, please. At twelve midnight you must change your clothes."

We all look around at each other and there is silence for several moments. Then the static once more, and the Klaxon sounds again, this time with someone else's voice: "Attention, please. At twelve midnight you must change your *watches*. One hour forward, please."

We are traveling through a world where time is meaningless, but in several days we will be reentering normal life. We left on Murmansk time and will be returning again on the other side of the earth, with a twelve-hour time difference. To adjust to this we begin resetting our clocks one hour each day.

We are heading for Wrangel Island and the Eskimo settlement, but we run into problems. Back in January the organizers had received permission from the USSR State Committee for Nature Preservation for this trip. But today a message comes from Moscow that we may not proceed to Wrangel. Our captain talks to our KGB representative, who tells him not to worry; it's simply a conflict between the USSR bureaucracy and that of the Russian Republic, which has authority over Wrangel. These two groups are always bickering, he says. He gets on the radio, and within hours another message comes through. This is from C. Vashanov, chairman of the Russian Republic State Committee for Environment and Nature Preservation, who "by way of exception gives permission for the *Sovetskiy Soyuz* nuclear icebreaker to visit Wrangel Island with a call at the Ushakovsky settlement. . . . You are advised to remit 300,000 rubles on special account of the preserve in Mys Schmidta settlement . . ."

So everything is okay, except for the extra 300,000 rubles. But it is agreed to pay them, and it all seems settled until just before midnight when another radiogram is received.

This is from V. S. Revyakin, chairman of the Committee for Environment and Rational Use of Natural Resources of the Supreme Soviet of the Russian Republic, and it tells us that the Committee for Environment and Rational Use et cetera "strongly objects to visits of Wrangel Island Preserve. Please be advised that the letter of the USSR State Committee for Nature Preservation has no legal validity . . ."

Our KGB man is awakened. He reads the radiogram and shrugs. "This is very bad," he says, and goes back to sleep.

AUGUST 8–11

---‑‑ ·ıⅡ‖ıꞏ ‑‑‑

We are passing the 81st parallel now, on the 150th meridian, heading for eastern Siberia. There has been another flurry of radio conversations between us and the various committees for nature preservation et cetera of the USSR and the Russian Republic, but our KGB man was right: the Revyakin committee is the strongest, and what they say goes. Actually, he explains to us, it's just today that they happen to be the strongest. A year ago it was the USSR State Committee for Nature Preservation that had the ultimate authority, and who knows what will happen next year? But right now it is the Supreme Soviet of the Russian Republic that holds the cards, and so we won't be going to Wrangel. (Of course we have no idea just how high those cards are, and that within a few weeks the consequences will run far beyond the question of authority over Wrangel. We simply marvel that the KGB man is able to keep track of who pecks who in the Soviet barnyard; still, it is his job, after all.)

The temperature has warmed up to 3 degrees centigrade, and water drips everywhere from the ice that has been coating the ship. The sea ice is slushy, but there are still occasional giant chunks which we break through.

Wally Herbert gives a lecture on the Peary-Cook controversy. He is sure that neither of them reached the pole.
Peary is a hero of his, but a flawed one—a combination of
saint and sinner. He points out many coincidences between
Peary's life and his own, such as that he reached the pole
on the same day of the year, April 6, that Peary claimed he
had sixty years earlier. He attaches a mystic significance to
this.

That's what Wally Herbert is, a mystic, and his stories are
wonderfully enjoyable. He knows how to spin a yarn; his
lectures are by far the best on board. Later, as I have lunch
with Sue Ann and Ralph Teller, I realize that I didn't see
them there. Ralph is the one who is convinced that the
Japanese tried to invade California in 1941. He seems to
have forgiven me for doubting it.

"I didn't see you at the lecture this morning," I say.

He shakes his head. "Wouldn't be seen dead there."

I turn to Sue Ann quizzically. She smiles and twirls her
finger around her head, as we used to do when we were
kids to indicate that someone is crazy. "Ralph's crazy?" I
ask her.

"Herbert's crazy," Ralph says. "The man's a psycho. No
point listening to him."

"Well, he's *been* here," I argue. "Probably knows better
than any of us what it's all about."

Ralph shakes his head. "All he can think of is that Peary
didn't go to the pole. He's nuts."

"He makes a good case."

"That's the point! People like that can always convince
you; they're good speakers and they know more about it
than you do. Doesn't pay to listen to them."

Ralph is also sure that cold fusion is real; he showed me
an article in *Fortune* about Stanford Research Institute, who
say they get out more energy than they put in. I pointed out
that there are a whole bunch of researchers who haven't
been able to duplicate those results, but Ralph knows what

he wants to believe. He has a proper outlook on life: if someone wants to tell you something you don't want to know, why should you listen to him? The guy is either right or wrong; if he's wrong you're only wasting your time if you listen to him, and if he's right he's just going to irritate you. Life's too short for that.

During the night we pass through the 77th parallel, heading southeast for the New Siberian Islands, where the De Long expedition met its fate. I wake up feeling something is different, and lie in bed trying to figure out what it is. Then I realize: we are not crashing along any longer, but are sailing smoothly. I get out of my bunk to look out the open porthole, and there is no ice out there. We are moving through open water for the first time in nearly two weeks.

After breakfast I go up to the bridge. There are always half a dozen or so passengers up there; the crew doesn't seem to mind our wandering around. One of us points out to starboard: "There's a ship out there."

We all go over to look. Yes, there's definitely something out there. One of the men has a pair of binoculars, and he passes it around. It is definitely a ship, a freighter of some sort. But there is no reason for a freighter to be in these waters. Where could it possibly be going?

The crew is paying no attention. I look again through the binoculars. It's a funny sort of freighter; its superstructure is weird, almost as if it were on stilts.

Someone asks the captain about it. "No," he says, and smiles. We look at each other, wondering what he means. His English isn't good. I try again. "What kind of ship is that?"

"No." He smiles again and turns away.

"It's military," Jackie S. says. "We're not supposed to see it. I bet he'll get in trouble for letting us get this close. We'd better not say anything about it."

This opinion makes sense to most of the passengers, who

nod wisely and say no more, looking at the ship only out of
the corner of their eyes, pretending to see nothing. But Gil
Fortune, who flies his own plane back home, has gone to
the other side of the bridge and is looking into the radarscope. I join him. He smiles as I come up, the same smile
the captain gave us, and I recognize it; it is not a smile of
embarrassment for letting us see a military secret, but one
of secret knowledge. "Take a look," he says.

I know what I'm going to see. I watch the radar beam
circle 360 degrees around the ship, and there is nothing
there—no radar reflection, which means no ship. I know
this, but I find it hard to believe. I go back to the starboard
window and look again; there it is, clear as day. Back to the
radar, and there it isn't.

It is funny how technological we have become; I don't
hesitate for a moment in believing the radarscope instead
of my own eyes. If the radar doesn't see it, it's not there. It
is an Arctic mirage, the sort of thing that fooled Peary into
thinking he had discovered new lands.

Mirages form when light travels through air of varying
density. We see objects when light from them reaches our
eyes, and we make the unconscious assumption that this
light travels in straight lines, which it ordinarily does, and
with this assumption the brain interprets the signals from
the optic nerve and tells us that there is a pretty girl to port,
or a strange freighter to starboard. But light doesn't always
travel in straight lines. If you put a yardstick into still water, the stick appears to bend sharply at the water's surface;
this is because the water has a higher density than the air,
and the light is refracted into a new direction when passing
from one medium to the other. In the Arctic, the cold sea
water chills the air above it so that there is a layer of high
density air along the sea surface. Light from distant objects
can follow this layer, which acts much like a mirror, and
something far beyond the horizon can suddenly appear in
front of you. This is called a *superior mirage*, and is in a

sense the opposite of the more familiar *inferior mirage* which is seen in deserts or on hot roads in summer, when a layer of air warmed by the hot ground leads to the appearance of water in the distance. In the inferior mirage the reflecting layer is below the observer's eyes; in the superior mirage it is above it. This difference gives a different image; in the superior mirage one often sees a true image and an inverted one superimposed. This is the reason for the queer-looking superstructure on the freighter. We are seeing two images of it, one lying upside down on top of the other.

These Arctic mirages are so incredibly distinct that one would swear they must be real. But your image in a mirror is just as distinct, and there isn't anyone there, is there?

One of the most famous of Arctic mirages is Crocker Land, which Peary "discovered" on his 1906 expedition when he stood on the northern shore of Greenland and saw "snow-clad summits of a distant land" above the far-off horizon. He had no hesitation in claiming and naming this new land. Seven years later Donald MacMillan, who had accompanied Peary on his last North Pole expedition, set off to find and explore it:

"April 21st was a beautiful day; all mist was gone and the clear blue of the sky extended down to the very horizon. Green [one of the expedition crew] was no sooner out of the igloo than he came running back, calling in through the door, 'We have it!' Following Green, we ran to the top of the highest mound. There could be no doubt about it. Great heavens! what a land! Hills, valleys, snowcapped peaks extending through at least one hundred and twenty degrees of the horizon. I turned to Pee-a-wah-to anxiously and asked him toward which point we had better lay our course. After critically examining the supposed landfall for a few minutes, he astounded me by replying that he thought it was poo-jok (mist). E-took-a-shoo offered no encouragement, saying, 'Perhaps it is.' Green was still con-

vinced that it must be land . . . [but] . . . as we pro-
ceeded the landscape gradually changed its appearance
and varied in extent with the swinging around of the sun;
finally at night it disappeared altogether."

By early afternoon we reach the first land of the New Siberian group, Bennett Island, the smallest and most northerly
one, and now we see ice again; the rocky island is surrounded by it. Its western end is shrouded in a low-lying
fog, its upper levels covered with a permanent ice cap. The
Klaxon tells us that the Zodiac landing boats can't reach the
island because of the heavy ice, but they are going to circle
it for two hours. The scout helicopter has reported a mass
of walruses sunning themselves in one of the coves. Everyone interested in going to have a look should report to the
aft deck immediately.

No, thanks, I decide. Two hours pitching, rolling and
freezing in a motorized rubber raft is a bit much just to see
a bunch of old walruses. I can see them anytime at a faculty
meeting back home.

For those who don't want to torture themselves in the
Zodiac, the helicopters will fly to the island. Thanks again,
I decide, but no thanks. The fog is still hanging over the
island, and if I have learned anything it is that these Arctic
fogs have a will of their own and like to move around.

But no one else seems to be nervous, and the choppers
begin shuttling people to a small plateau halfway up to the
glacier. An hour later the fog has dropped low enough to
cut off the plateau, and everything stops moving. Visibility
aboard ship is reduced to fifty yards. I am standing on the
foredeck trying to see the island, the Zodiac or the helicopter, but nothing is visible. We are isolated in a gray vac-
uum. There is not a sound to be heard; the sea is dead calm
and the fog shuts off sound as well as sight.

The Zodiac boats were due back from their two-hour trip
about now, but they haven't returned. There is no way they

will be able to find the ship in this pea-souper. It's like the London fogs you read about in Sherlock Holmes stories, a perfect setting for a murder. I am glad I didn't go in either the Zodiac or the chopper. What will they do if the fog doesn't lift for hours?

But ten minutes later it begins to clear, and soon the day becomes lovely again. Bright sunshine burns through the mist and dispels it. The first sounds to break through are the screaming chirping of the seventy zillion or so red-necked phalaropes that inhabit the island's cliffs; the next sound is the chugging of a Zodiac as it sights us and pulls alongside. Two minutes later the first chopper arrives from the island.

Dinner tonight is Russian-style. We have all been complaining that the food is generic European; we are on a Russian boat and would like a taste of *their* food. At first the crew insists on thinking we are kidding them; then they think we must be trying to be kind, and we can't convince them that we mean it. Who would want Russian food if they could have European? they think. But finally we persuade them, and they lay on a Russian evening.

It's fantastic. The waiters and waitresses are dressed in peasant clothing, which is a bit touristy, but the first things they bring out to the tables are pitchers full of vodka. From then on everything is lovely, though I don't seem to be able to remember much about it. I do have a recollection of an entertainment after dinner, with the crew singing Russian folk songs and doing a pantomime of sorts; then there was Cossack dancing, with everyone clapping and shouting like mad; later still I have an even vaguer recollection of someone—one of our older and more dignified male passengers—running around stark naked, being chased by a large Russian peasant woman.

I stagger along the deck to get some fresh air and try to sober up, but it's no use. The air is fresh and seems mildly tropical, but the vodka is too strong. I check the thermometer and find it has warmed up to nearly 4 degrees centigrade, which is balmy enough but not really tropical: It's the vodka that does it.

A lovely light pervades the universe. There is not a cloud in the sky, a few scattered icebergs, mostly empty sea. Sleep; I must go to sleep.

I wake at 3 A.M. to feel the old bump-and-grind motion; we are crunching through ice again. Outside the porthole it is bright daylight already, with the sun shining on solid pack ice once more. I go back to sleep, and wake up at 8 A.M. freezing cold, the coldest I've been yet. I can't bear to get out of bed, with the wind rushing in through the open window, but it is either that or die here under my quilt. My roommate isn't here and his bed hasn't been slept in, so it's up to me. I make a dive for the porthole, and then get straight back under the covers.

Once the window is shut the heating system takes over, and soon it is too hot to stay in bed. Over breakfast I find out that there was a wild party all night. One of the young ladies stops by the table where I am sitting with one of the married men and discreetly pushes something into his hand. He looks down and quickly stuffs it into his pocket, but not before I see that it is his underpants.

In the afternoon we helicopter ashore on the next island, Gukera Henrietta. This is the island discovered by the doomed De Long expedition, and which was used as a scientific outpost by the Soviets from the Second International Polar Year in 1932–3 until it was abandoned in 1959. They spent those twenty-two years taking meteorological data, with the scientists spending two years at a time here, until finally the government decided that such activities weren't worth much and were too frivolous for a serious society to keep paying for. Which is true, in a sense; if anyone asks what use these data are going to be, you can't give an answer. Like the time Michael Faraday learned how to create electricity by whirling a ferrous disk through the poles of a magnet, the forerunner of today's dynamos which generate all our electrical power the world over. His first little apparatus generated only enough electricity to make the needle on his voltmeter move the tiniest fraction, and when he demonstrated it to the prime minister, Sir Robert Peel, the P.M. looked dubiously at the flickering needle and naturally asked, "Of what use is this?" Poor Faraday had no answer. He could only reply, in effect, "I don't know, but I'll wager that someday you'll tax it."

This is the bottom line on basic scientific research; you never know how things are going to turn out. The British Antarctic data, for instance, was of no earthly use for many years, but has since saved millions of lives.

The British research team in Antarctica was established in 1957, as part of their contribution to the International Geophysical Year. One of the sets of meteorological data they began to accumulate was atmospheric ozone concentrations, even though at the time nobody cared much about the subject. "Of what use is this?" the prime minister might have asked, and the answer given would have been no better than Faraday's.

But as the British gathered their data throughout the 1960s, they noticed that there seemed to be a distinct downward trend in the figures. This didn't make any sense, but they continued to measure the concentration every year, and by the late 1970s and early 1980s they were convinced that there was a distinct and continual lowering of the ozone year by year. Still, the data were just about at the limits of their precision, so they couldn't be sure. They didn't report their results because of this imprecision, because there wasn't any reason they could think of why the ozone should be depleted in polar regions more than in any other part of the earth, and because of an impressive high-tech American experiment which gave contradictory results. In the late 1970s an American satellite, *Nimbus 7*, was put into orbit around the poles carrying a fully automated ozone-detection instrument. For the next several years the *Nimbus* data were published regularly, and showed no ozone depletion.

But by 1982 the Brits were measuring depletions up to 20 percent, well beyond any reasonable source of error. It looked as if a hole were developing in the ozone layer. However, the American work still didn't show any such effect. The British team simply didn't know whether to believe their own data or the more sophisticated American satellite data.

They managed to get funding for a more sensitive instrument, and by 1983 it too showed the ozone hole, which by now was even bigger than before. The following year the hole had grown to a 30 percent depletion factor, and when another group in the Argentine Islands a thousand miles away got the same result they began to be convinced that they had something real, so finally they published their results.

When the Americans read the report they naturally wondered what kind of grass the Britishers were smoking, because their own much more sophisticated instrumentation aboard the *Nimbus* satellite didn't show anything like the ozone depletion . . .

Then suddenly they realized what they had done: they had programmed their satellite with an erroneous assumption. Since the instrument was totally automated, it would fly around the world taking measurements continually, and would provide too many data for anyone to analyze. So the American scientists had told the computer in advance to ignore any data that lay outside normal limits. By the time the satellite was launched there had been many ozone measurements made around the world, and they all agreed within about 10 percent. In order to look for small variations within this 10 percent range, the Americans made the assumption that anything beyond this range would be due to one of those occasional but unavoidable errors that crop up in any measurement and should be ignored. They told the computer to store such data, but not to bother them by reporting it.

So the *Nimbus* instruments saw the ozone hole and told the computer about it, but obediently the computer didn't tell the scientists. As a result the Americans went blithely on their way without ever knowing that the ozone layer was being destroyed, until a group of old-fashioned British scientists out in the field, freezing their toes off in Antarctica, discovered what was happening.

When they saw the British report the Americans ran back to their computer and told it they wanted to see *all* the data, and when they did they saw the hole staring up at them, grinning like a deadly Cheshire cat.

For technical reasons having to do with ice particles in the atmosphere, the Antarctic ozone hole was a harbinger of things to come all over the world. It showed us that we were producing substances harmful to the ozone, and we quickly found out what they were: the chlorofluorocarbons in aerosol sprays and refrigerants. This had already been suggested, but without any clear sign of a real effect few people had been willing to believe the scientists who were sounding the alarm. Now, with the ozone depletion clearly shown in the Antarctic, people and governments all over the world began to listen. By the early 1990s several agreements had been formalized to reduce the atmospheric CFCs, although it is too late for many people; the ozone depletion already under way will let in ultraviolet light that will cause skin cancers, cataracts and melanomas, and it is estimated that upward of a million people will die unnecessarily because of the CFC production of previous decades. But if the British Antarctic team hadn't found the ozone hole when it did, it might have been several more years before the effect of ozone depletion was discovered in more temperate latitudes. This time delay would have caused the deaths of several million more people.

Increasingly our scientific effort is directed toward high-tech remote sensing techniques such as satellite observations, but just as with the British Antarctic team's detection of the ozone depletion, there are still important measurements to be made which must be done on the spot. In fact, on this very day—August 9, 1991—a team of three research vessels is scheduled to depart from Tromsö, Norway, to follow in the wake of the *Soyuz* and carry out a series of oceanographic and atmospheric experiments. Sweden's *Oden*, Germany's *Polarstern* and the United States's *Polar Star* will head toward the pole on an eight-week cruise dedicated primarily toward understanding the Arctic's role in the climate variations that are threatening the planet. The danger is particularly potent up here. Even a moderate temperature rise might melt enough ice to expose warmer water underneath, and this in turn could accelerate global warming all over the earth. According to the computer models, the temperature trends predicted for the coming decades will result in even higher temperatures in the Arctic than elsewhere. While initial rises of 2 to 3 degrees are feared for the temperate latitudes, an increase of more than 12 degrees centigrade is being predicted for the polar regions, and such a temperature could cause catastrophic effects worldwide.

To examine these possibilities, today the three nations are beginning the first comprehensive scientific study of the Arctic seas ever undertaken. They will drop permanent recording buoys which will continually log and transmit temperatures, salinity and the chemistry of the waters at various spots. They will dig up from the seafloor sediments rich in fossils, through which they will be able to study both the chemical and climatic history of the region to see how the one has varied with the other in the past, which will give us a clearer picture of how they might vary in the future. They will drill right through the sediment into the hard rock below to bring up samples to be analyzed in labs like my own, where I will measure isotopic variations in some of the gases trapped in the rocks, and from these data will try to reconstruct the atmospheric and magmatic history of the earth. They will take air, colloid and dust samples, and they will sample the plankton, forams and diatoms; all these will be analyzed, compared, correlated and factored, and perhaps out of all this—together with the background data provided by the Soviet scientific station that labored for more than twenty years here on Henrietta Island—will come a new understanding of the oceanic, atmospheric and geologic relationships that have shaped the past and will continue to shape the future of this spinning, lonesome planet.

AFTERWORD

PROVIDENIYA
AUGUST 12–16

––––––––––––––––––––––– ‖‖‖‖ –––––––––––––––––––––––

The fog was so thick when I woke that it was streaming in through the open porthole. As I lay in bed watching it, my roommate John woke up. It was the first time on the entire voyage that we had awakened at the same time. He told me that last night at the bar he was talking to Mike, the cruise's organizer, and the scuttlebutt was that Aeroflot was talking about going on strike. While our flight out from Provideniya back to the States would be on Alaska Airlines, the local air traffic controllers would probably go out with the airline workers even though it was illegal, which meant that we wouldn't be able to get out of Provideniya.

This doesn't sound bad. Provideniya is the Soviet Union's easternmost city. It lies on the very tip of Siberia, facing Alaska across the Bering Strait, and is said to be populated by an indigenous Eskimo population mixed with Russian colonists. The idea of spending a few days in Siberia appeals to me.

At dinner I got into a discussion with Ralph and Sue Ann Teller and Paul and Mary Westin about greenhouse warming. None of them believes in it. "It's not a question of belief," I said. "It's a question of evidence and experiments that—"

"It's all theory," Ralph interrupted. "If it was true you'd have evidence to prove it."

I started to describe the evidence we already have—the known increase of carbon dioxide and methane, and the infrared absorption spectrum of those gases—but when I got into the array of experiments being started that very day on the other side of the North Pole by the *Oden*, *Polarstern* and *Polar Star*, they all guffawed and shouted me down.

"That's what it's all about," Paul Westin said. He is a fat lawyer from St. Louis. His wife is at least twenty years younger, plump rather than fat, and he obviously adores her. I'm not as sure about her feelings toward him. At the beginning of the voyage I thought she was looking for a part-time bed partner, since every time we talked she winked at me. Later I noticed her winking at every man she talked to; later still I realized she winked at *everyone*, male or female; it's simply a nervous tic. Still, she doesn't seem to take him seriously, which he makes up for by taking himself very seriously indeed. "Getting federal money to do your experiments and pay your salaries, that's what all you guys are up to. Sucking the tax tit. Begging your pardon," he said to the ladies.

Ralph agreed. "It's a simple question," he pointed out. "Is the world getting warmer or not? If it were, you could do a simple experiment and prove it. Instead you've got three ships sailing all over the world doing all these other experiments, costing millions of dollars. I don't blame you," he interrupted himself, apparently fearing that I would take offense. "I don't blame you at all. Get the money while it's good, that's what I say."

The others all chimed in. Sure, that's what they'd do, too, but don't expect a bunch of sophisticated, intelligent people like *us* to swallow your scare stories, okay?

The problem these people have is that they believe science works the way they were taught in high school: You have a theory, you test it with an experiment, and the experiment either proves or disproves it. They remember being told that when Einstein invented relativity it was tested by an experiment having something to do with the stars; the experiment proved he was right, and that's the end of it.

"That's not the way it worked," I said. "The first experiment *disproved* Einstein, but it was later found to be wrong. Experiments are hard to do and full of possible errors. What about the Symmes holes?"

"What are Symmes holes?" they asked, and I had them hooked. "The only really important result of Byrd's North Pole flight," I told them, "was that it disproved the Symmes theory of polar holes." We had another cup of coffee, and I told them about these holes.

In 1818 Captain John Symmes of the United States Cavalry announced that he had deduced that the inside of the earth was hollow, filled with concentric spheres on which unknown races lived, and could be reached by openings in the earth's surface at the North and South Poles. He traveled around giving speeches and asking for volunteers to accompany him and money to pay for an expedition to the North Pole to find these "Symmes Holes" and peek inside. In 1823 his request went all the way up to Congress, where it gathered twenty-five votes before dying, as he himself did a few years later.

However, by this time the theory had a life of its own. In the next fifty years at least two books were written supporting it, and several variations prospered on their own. It was to these theories that Congressman Macon was referring when, objecting that Peary could not possibly have reached the pole, he wrote into the Congressional Record that "it is contended by scientists . . . that the thing they call the

North Pole is a hole that extends into the interior surface of the earth. . . ." With such support, thousands of people flocked to Symmes prophets with enthusiasm and, more importantly, with money for the promulgation of the faith.

And why not? The world is full of slightly paranoiac people who want to believe that there is more in heaven and earth than is dreamt of by our scientists and poets—as indeed there is—and who also want to believe that they themselves are capable of such dreams. So they know that Kennedy was killed by the CIA (or by the Mafia, or by Marilyn Monroe or Lyndon Johnson or Bobby), that the universe was created in six days, that Ollie North is a hero and that the world is either flat or hollow inside.

In fact the idea has a prestigious history, as pointed out by Martin Gardner in his lovely book *Fads and Fallacies in the Name of Science*. In 1721 Cotton Mather defended the idea, which was evidently proposed originally by Edmund Halley, friend of Newton (who, incidentally, was described by a contemporary as nothing but a "drunken sea captain") and discoverer of the laws of cometary motion based on Sir Isaac's laws of motion. Halley wondered if perhaps the aurora borealis might be composed of luminous gases escaping through polar holes. In 1913 a further variation suggested that what we perceive through our blurry telescopes as the ice caps of Mars are actually openings into its luminous interior, and that strange northern beings such as mammoths and Eskimos are simply creatures that have come up through the holes to see what is out here, and haven't been able to find their way back home.

Then in 1926 Richard Byrd flew over the North Pole and didn't see any hole. The adherents to the various theories of Symmes Holes fell away in droves, the priests stopped lecturing, and the fad died away.

"You see what I mean?" Ralph asked triumphantly. "That's how it works. You have a theory—like big holes at the poles—and you do an experiment, like fly over the pole and take a look, and it either proves the theory or disproves it. That's exactly what I mean."

"Except that the experiment was flawed," I sprang my trap. "Byrd *didn't* fly over the pole. He missed it by at least a hundred miles. So the hole *could* have been there and he wouldn't have seen it. But everybody believed him, and so they disbelieved the theory."

Westin was confused. "But the theory's wrong, isn't it?" he asked.

"Sure, but the Byrd experiment didn't *prove* it was wrong even though everyone thought it did."

"So what's the difference? It's either right or it's wrong. And it's wrong. I mean, what the fuck? Excuse me, ladies."

"That's not the point. The point is that experiments can be erroneous, so just because a single experiment agrees with a theory, that doesn't make it right, and if it disagrees, that doesn't make it wrong. That's why we need so many experiments to find out if the earth is getting warmer, and how much warmer it's going to get, and how fast it's going to warm up, and what the consequences will—"

"What do you mean, Admiral Byrd didn't fly over the North Pole?" Ralph asked. "Everybody knows he did." He laughed, finished his coffee, and stood up. "You're quite a kidder, Fisher," he said, slapping me on the shoulder. "Quite a kidder."

Outside it is dark for the first time since we left Murmansk, and I see the stars once again. It is not a deep night; toward the west it looks as if it was just after sunset, and the sun will probably be up by the time we go to bed.

On August 14 we sailed around the northeast corner of Asia and passed through the Bering Strait. It had gotten warmer during the night, and though there was a strong breeze we could walk around the deck without our parkas. Sweaters and jackets were still necessary, but it felt wonderfully warm. There wasn't any ice outside, neither in the sea nor on the handrails and steps. The ocean water had turned dark blue instead of the forbidding black of the far north. We were now at 67°50′ N, 171°45′ W, heading for Big Diomede, an island known to be a haven for walruses, seals and polar bears. We didn't have permission to land there, but since we hadn't landed on Wrangel the organizers decided to try for it. It isn't a protected area, and therefore permission to land wasn't subject to the approval of a dozen different committees back in Moscow; it is purely under the control of the local Border Guard.

These seas are breeding grounds for whales, and we stood around on deck all day looking for some. Every half hour or so there would be a shout or a call on the Klaxon: "Spout sighted off the port bow!" Everyone would run over to that side of the ship, lean over the rail and scan the seas with binoculars. Once in a while we would see the spray rising in a vertical leap and a couple of times we even caught sight of a huge tail flashing in the sunlight, but that was all. Except about midday when a strange odor was noticed, growing stronger by the minute. Then a cloud of birds was seen whirling around a huge black object floating on the surface, and we drew closer and found a dead whale, stinking to high heaven, with every bird in the region flocking to it, digging a chunk of bloody meat from the huge hole which its fellows had dug in the carcass, and flying home in triumph with it.

Toward evening, out of the mist rose Big Diomede, an extraordinary sight appearing out of nowhere, looking rather like Bali Hai in the movie version of *South Pacific*, except that this island was solid and real. Then with no warning the mist closed in again and the island thawed, resolved itself into a dew and disappeared. It was like watching the world dissolve.

We cruised around the island while the radios crackled and our KGB man talked to the Border Guard ashore. The captain had talked to Moscow and got their permission to land, even though it wasn't necessary, and our KGB man pulled his rank and told them we had permission from every conceivable source, but in the end they simply wouldn't let us land. The commander said no, and finally we had to accept that that was simply that.

So we continued along the far eastern coast of Siberia, passing Cape Dreshnev, which had an abandoned lighthouse, and Cape Peek (pronounced pe-ek). A Soviet coast guard cutter came alongside, looked us over and waved us on. The coastline was magnificent, with cliffs rising a thousand feet straight out of the water. We nosed around Peek and inched our way southwest along the coastline, and by August 15 we reached Arakamchechen Island, where we were allowed to land. It is several miles square and is inhabited by about five hundred walruses and one Russian, who lives in a wooden shack and counts the walruses every spring. He made us a pot of tea and was happy to chat. We complimented him on the weather, which was sunny, warm and beautiful.

He laughed. "No sun," he said, proud of his English, as he had every right to be. "Snow. All year snow." He gestured around the whole island. "Snow, snow, snow." He nodded vehemently, and laughed.

I left the group talking to him and wandered off up a slope and down the other side. I came around a curving hillock and suddenly saw before me an Arctic version of Stonehenge. Situated near the edge of the grassy plain a few yards from the cliffs which fell to the sea, overlooking the whole vista, was a circle of twenty-foot-high, ghostly white spars reaching up to the sky. In the midst of all this nothingness they were startling, and I came up to them silently and circled around.

"Rather interesting, wouldn't you say?"

I turned around. Taffy Mostyn, our Welsh historian,

stood behind me, sucking on his pipe and looking up at the structure.

"What is it?" I asked.

"Oh, the same old thing, you know. Stonehenge and all that. Whale ribs, actually. Reverence for the beasts and heaven and the gods."

"Is it new?"

"Heavens, no. They don't do this sort of thing anymore. Much more likely to revere Johnny Carson or Geraldo. No, no, this is thousands of years old." He strode away.

I didn't believe him. I touched the whale ribs; they were firm and solid, not chipped or eaten away by the weather. I was tempted to chip off a piece and bring it home for radiocarbon dating, but we had been thoroughly indoctrinated in the sanctity of the pristine Arctic we were visiting —we had been told to leave no garbage or debris behind, and to take nothing out with us—so I didn't.

Somewhere around his ninetieth birthday, George Bernard Shaw wrote that he regretted nothing he had ever done in his life; he regretted only the things he hadn't done. But I didn't break off a piece, and soon the rest of the group came up, we all went back to the ship, and by the next morning we had reached Provideniya.

"Nature, conventionally grand, rising in tree-covered hills above the sea and the town," Graham Greene wrote when he steamed into Freetown harbor and caught his first sight of Africa, "was powerless to carry off the shabby town." Siberia is different; nature manages quite definitely to carry it off, dignifying this shabbiest of towns. The harbor of Provideniya covers nearly 300 degrees, and is a scene of calm, majestic beauty. In the distance the conventionally grand hills rise into towering, overpowering mountains topped by an enveloping mist, and the town lies nestled protectively at their foot. From where we sit at anchor we can see a few scattered buildings, and one tall chimney breathing out wisps of black smoke which dissipate in the steady breeze. After the harsh, vertical islands of the polar seas this is a gentle refuge; in comparison to the bustling cities we come from it is a quiet haven.

We stood on deck soaking it in as the hours passed and the rumors began to fly. There were problems; we weren't going to be allowed to land; a confusion had arisen in Russia and no one knew what was allowed and what was not; the airlines were on strike, so we couldn't leave . . .

Then the Klaxon announced that all passengers would begin disembarking in half an hour. We all ran back to our rooms to pack.

A small, dirty cutter took us from the *Soyuz* to the landing dock, and we clumped up wooden steps to the small shack that served as the customs station. It was closed, so we simply walked around it and into the town. As far as the authorities were concerned we had left port at Murmansk, so even though we had traveled from one side of the world to the other we had never left the Soviet Union at all. To them it was as if we had taken a cruise from New York to Baltimore.

We climbed another flight of wooden steps and were in the center of Provideniya; in those few steps we went through the looking glass into a 1940s movie, a world of black and white. The sky was still blue, but it was far away and lent nothing but contrast to the scene below. A drab, gray and dispiriting scene, without a hint of color. One central block of the main road was paved, and was full of potholes. Thirty yards to either side of the center of town the roads became dirt. The local tourist chief, Mishna, was there to meet us with three buses whose combined ages must have topped a hundred years.

He took us on a tour of the town. He was a young man, perhaps in his early thirties, with a quiet manner, a thick walrus mustache and a sad smile. It seemed incredible that anyone living here should have any sort of smile, and we saw no other that day. Driving in our little buses up a curving dirt road was the scariest part of the entire polar trip; I thought we were going to tip over and fall into the gorge below.

We asked Mishna about the smokestack in the harbor. The town gets its electricity from the generator powered by a motor bought from the United States fifty years ago, he told us, and that was the source of the smoke. "You are lucky today. Usually there is a—what do you say?" He gestured with his hands, one on top of the other. "The cold air below and the warm air above?"

"An inversion?"

"Yes, inversion. The waters come cold into the harbor from the north, and this makes a cold layer of air which is trapped by the mountains. So no wind can blow in from the sea, and this keeps the smoke in the harbor. Usually you cannot see the sky. All is black above. And below." He laughed. "Usually you cannot see to the end of Provideniya. Today is the bestest day we have been having all year." He offered his little smile under the walrus mustache. "It will not last long."

Indeed it did not. The inversion must have been building even as we spoke, for as he took us through town we noticed that each time we caught a glimpse of the tall chimney in the harbor the smoke was getting thicker and thicker.

We drove by the "Provideniya Hilton," as Mishna called it, a square gray building, the only hotel in town. It is impossible to describe its squalor. "Do you want to go inside?" he asked. No one did. I once had a room in New York for $2.50, and that place looked better than this. The thought of spending a few days in Provideniya while the airlines are on strike was looking less attractive all the time.

There is a movie theater, but it is closed. There is a television station, but it lost power several months ago. There is a restaurant, but it is closed. Is anything open? Mishna takes us to the local hospital for Down syndrome: mongoloid babies. "It is one of the largest in the world," he tells us.

"Do patients come from all over the Soviet Union?"

"Oh, no. Who would want to come here? All from Provideniya."

Why are so many mongoloid children born here? Mishna doesn't know; it has always been so.

"Fetal alcohol syndrome," I suggest. "Is there a lot of drinking here?"

"Pardon? Drinking?"

"Alcohol? Vodka?"

Mishna laughs. "Oh yes, of a certainly." He spreads his hands. "What else is there to do? All winter it is very boring here."

We are standing in the central square, looking around the town on its pleasantest day of the year, trying to imagine spending the long, dark winter here, pregnant. Of course they drink. What else is there to do?

The hospital is their triumph, and as we leave Mishna tells about their failure. The local schools are open to the Eskimos, and arrangements are made to house the children until they graduate. Then they are supposed to return to their tribes. It is a well-meant program intended both to educate them and to preserve their way of life. But the children refuse to return to their tribes; once they have had a taste of life in this metropolis, they don't want to go back home. Their native life is so miserable that even Provideniya is preferable.

Leaving Provideniya was worth the entire cost of the trip. For the rest of my life, whenever the world falls apart or my health fails, when my money runs out or the roof leaks or the car breaks down on a lonely road in the rain, I will think of the seven hours spent in the Customs Detention

Shed at Provideniya Airport and will be happy I am no longer there.

Earlier we had rebelled against going to the airport several hours before our charter flight from Alaska was due, and had grumbled when told that it was necessary because one couldn't count on the speed and efficiency of the Soviet customs force, but after touring with Mishna even sitting in an airport seemed preferable to wandering any longer around the town.

We were wrong. We drive from town on a long, dusty, bumpy road around the perimeter of the harbor to the airport. As we circle it we look back and see the town disappearing minute by minute as the smoke particles from the chimney bounce against the low ceiling of the inversion and fall back onto the town, blanketing it with a thickening layer of gray ash. By the time we reach the airport the sky over Provideniya has been clogged up, the cork has been put back in the bottle, and the Brigadoon of Siberia has ended its one bestest day of the year.

The airport is not a bustling center of international travel activity, and the customs people don't show up unless there is a reason to. They had been told we were coming, but evidently didn't believe it until we showed up. At that point a telephone call was put in for a customs official. He arrived after a half hour or so, and immediately began checking us in. This consisted of examining our customs declaration, which listed everything we had brought into the Soviet Union and everything we were taking out, and all our luggage. It was no big deal; he was averaging about six minutes per passenger. Still, there were a hundred passengers, which meant six hundred minutes, or ten hours to get us all through customs.

But after a while another agent showed up, and an hour later still another, and pretty soon the "International Departures Lounge" was filled with passengers who had cleared customs. There was nothing for us to do now except wait. And wait and wait.

Several of us began to wander around the lounge, which was a large, bare room with benches around the walls, to look for the amenities. *An* amenity. Anything. Finally Jacqueline Smith went up to the Border Guard who was supervising us and asked where the bathroom was.

He laughed. Jackie S. is not used to having to ask for bathroom facilities, nor to being laughed at for whatever reason. She bristled, and insisted that she wanted to use the bathroom. The rest of us thought the guard had laughed because he didn't understand English, but now he asked her seriously, "You want use bathroom?"

"Yes."

"You want bath?" He had heard Americans were weird, but hadn't believed it.

"I don't want a *bath*," Jacqueline said testily. "I want to *use* the *bathroom*."

The guard didn't know what to say; clearly his English teacher hadn't prepared him for this. Nor did Jackie S. know what to say; clearly her etiquette teacher hadn't prepared her either. It was an impasse until Tess Mannix stepped up and said, "We'd like to use the toilet."

"Ah!" In a flash it had all become clear. The Border Guard, a rosy-cheeked lad of about twenty, now knew what to do. "Your question will be answered," he said officiously, and turned and left the room. We saw him outside conversing with another guard, and when he returned he announced, "Your question will be answered." But that was that.

During the next hour several more people besieged him, and to each he gave the same reply. Finally the outside guard came in and whispered to our man, who went up to Jackie S. and told her to come with him. She followed after him, relief in every pore in her face; when she returned five minutes later the relief was replaced by horror. "Don't even bother," she said to Tess, the next woman in line.

"What's wrong?" Tess asked.

Jackie could only shiver.

"Is there any toilet paper?" Tess asked.

Jackie laughed shrilly and hysterically. One of the other women proffered a small pack of Kleenex. "I always carry Kleenex when I travel. You never know," she said. Tess took it and followed the guard. Evidently Kleenex was the least of the problems, however, for when she returned her face was as white and horror-stricken as Jackie's had been.

I could hardly wait for my turn, and to tell the truth, it was something to see. The amenities at Provideniya airport consist of one large unisex room with no ventilation or anything else—in fact, with nothing but a gaping hole in the center of the floor. It is true that the floor slopes gently down toward it from all angles so that in theory all wastes directed toward it should eventually slide into it, but something must have gone wrong, for the floor was coated with a thick film of slime centuries old, consisting of fecal and urinary components intimately mixed into a slurry of filth that makes even the New York subway look and smell good. I knew now why Jackie had laughed when asked about toilet paper: that indeed was the least of her worries. Taking advantage of my equipment to its fullest I stood as far as possible from the hole, aimed in its general direction and hurried out as quickly as possible.

A couple of hours later the Alaska Airlines jet arrived and we clambered aboard, pissed delightfully in its fragrant "bathrooms," ate its wonderful airline food and less than an hour later set down in Fairbanks.

Of which the less said the better. It has one decent bookstore, a great porno shop and that's about it. I went to the 7-Eleven, bought a Slurpee, and next morning flew home.

* * *

I still think occasionally about Provideniya. It reminds me of Los Angeles, a region of incredible natural geologic beauty, raped and reduced to a gray, smoggy ugliness by man. When I was a kid I remember being told that certain sexual acts were crimes against nature. Not so; *this* is a crime against nature.

But perhaps we should be glad we have places like Los Angeles and Provideniya, where the consequences of atmospheric pollution can readily be seen. Perhaps they will serve as warnings. I hope they are warnings only, not coming attractions.

BIBLIOGRAPHY

Andrée, Salomon. *Andrée's Story*. New York: Viking, 1930.

Bartlett, Robert A. *The Log of Bob Bartlett*. New York: Putnam, 1928.

Beattie, Owen, and John Geiger. *Frozen in Time*. New York: Dutton, 1988.

Berton, Pierre. *The Arctic Grail*. New York and London: Penguin, 1988.

Branch, W. J. V., and E. Brook-Williams. *A Short History of Navigation*. London: Brown, Son & Ferguson, 1942.

Churchill, Winston S. *The River War*. London: Eyre & Spottiswoode, 1940.

Cook, Frederick A. *To the Top of the Continent*. New York: Doubleday, Page & Co., 1908.

————. *My Attainment of the Pole*. New York: Mitchell Kennerly, 1913.

————. (F. J. Pohl, ed.). *Return from the Pole*. New York: Pellegrini and Cudahy, 1953.

Ellsworth, Lincoln. *Search*. New York: Brewer, Warren & Putnam, 1932.

Franklin, Sir John. *Narrative of a Journey to the Shores of the Polar Sea*. London: J. M. Dent & Sons, 1910.

Gardner, Martin. *Fads and Fallacies in the Name of Science.* New York: Dover, 1957.

Hakluyt, Richard. *Principal Navigations . . . of the English Nation.* London, 1598.

Henry Hudson, The Navigator. London: Hakluyt Society, 1860.

Henson, Matthew A. *A Negro Explorer at the North Pole.* New York: Walker, 1912.

Herbert, Wally. *The Noose of Laurels.* New York: Atheneum, 1989.

Kane, Elisha Kent. *Arctic Explorations in the Years 1853, '54, '55.* Philadelphia: Childs & Peterson, 1856.

M'Clintock, Francis Leopold. *A Narrative of the Discovery of the Fate of Sir John Franklin and His Companions.* Boston: Ticknor and Fields, 1860.

McKee, Alexander. *Ice Crash.* New York: St. Martin's, 1979.

MacMillan, Donald. *Four Years in the White North.* New York: Harper, 1918.

Malaurie, Jean. *The Last Kings of Thule.* New York: Dutton, 1982.

Maxtone-Graham, John. *Safe Return Doubtful.* New York: Scribner's, 1988.

Mirsky, Jeannette. *To the Arctic!* Chicago: University of Chicago Press, 1934.

Montague, Richard. *Oceans, Poles, and Airmen.* New York: Random House, 1971.

Mountfield, David. *A History of Polar Exploration.* London: Book Club Assoc., 1974.

Nansen, Fridtjof. *Farthest North.* New York: Harper, 1898.

Parry, J. H. *The Discovery of the Sea.* Berkeley: University of California Press, 1974.

Payer, Julius von. *New Lands Within the Arctic Circle.* London: Macmillan, 1876.

Peary, Robert E. *The North Pole.* New York: Frederick A. Stokes, 1910.

————. *Northward over the Great Ice*. New York: Methuen, 1898.

Perry, Richard. *The Jeannette*. Chicago: Coburn & Newman, 1884.

Poe, Edgar Allan. "MS. Found in a Bottle," in *The Portable Poe*. New York: Viking, 1945.

Rand, S. B., "Peary and his Campaign for the Pole," *McClure's Magazine*, Vol. 18 (1902), pp. 354–63.

Rawlins, Dennis. *Peary at the North Pole: Fact or Fiction?* New York: R. B. Luce, 1973.

Robinson, Bradley. *Dark Companion*. New York: McBride, 1947.

Smith, Dean C. *By the Seat of My Pants*. Boston: Atlantic Monthly Press, 1961.

Stefansson, Vilhjalmur. *Arctic Manual*. New York: Macmillan, 1944.

Sundman, Per Olof. *The Flight of the Eagle*. New York: Pantheon, 1970.

Taylor, E. G. R. *The Haven-Finding Art*. New York: Elsevier, 1971.

Weems, John Edward. *Peary, the Explorer and the Man*. Boston: Houghton Mifflin, 1967.

NOTES

‖‖‖

SOVETSKIY SOYUZ

3–5   *"I saw that we had passed upon"*: Kane, Vol. I, pp. 358–62.

JULY 27

18   *"Item, that no blaspheming"*: quoted in Maxtone-Graham, p. 29.

19   *"took into his hand"*: from Hakluyt, quoted in Mirsky, p. 27.

19   *Willoughby had sailed on:* Mountfield, p. 27.

23   *the polar luxury tourist cruise:* The following can be found described in Maxtone-Graham, pp. 262–64.

JULY 28

28–29   *"The 15th, all day and night"*: from Hudson, quoted in Rawlins.

33   *The century's most suspenseful:* The following can be found described in Beatty and Geiger, Mountfield, Berton, Maxtone-Graham, Mirsky, and M'Clintock.

37–38   *"The man was very communicative"*: John Rae, quoted in Mirsky, p. 155.

40   *The following spring*: M'Clintock pp. 211ff.

40   *M'Clintock soon found*: Peary, 1910, p. xxi.

41   *"28 of May, 1847"*: M'Clintock, p. 256.

41   *"April 25, 1848"*: Quoted in Mirsky, p. 134.

42   *"The best hunters"*: Franklin, p. 357.

JULY **29**

44   *A hundred and twenty years ago*: Taken from the accounts of Perry, pp. 661ff, and Mirsky, pp. 174ff.

44   *"No water was to be seen"*: von Payer, quoted in Perry, p. 663.

45   *"as we sat"*: von Payer, quoted in Perry, p. 664, and Mirsky, p. 175.

46   *"All spring"*: von Payer, in Mirsky, p. 177.

46   *"as we were leaning on the bulwarks"*: von Payer, in Perry, p. 668.

46–47   *"There before us"*: von Payer, in Mirsky, p. 177.

47   *"Snow and rock"*: von Payer, in Mirsky, p. 177.

49   *"The spray of its surf"*: von Payer, in Mirsky, p. 179.

51   *Several years earlier the* Jeannette: The following can be found described in Perry, pp. 737–823 and Mirsky, pp. 196–99.

52   *"Occasionally"*: Quoted in Mirsky, p. 197.

52   *"People beset in the pack"*: Quoted in Mirsky, p. 197.

55   *All of which gave Fridtjof Nansen*: The following can be found described in Nansen, Mirsky, pp. 201–13, Maxtone-Graham, pp. 127–64, Berton, pp. 489–600, and Mountfield, pp. 127–32.

57   *"If I am to be perfectly honest"*: Nansen, p. 211.

58   *"We found large expanses"*: Nansen, p. 372.

58–59   *The sweat "condensed"*: Nansen, p. 376.

59   *"Ridge after ridge"*: Nansen, p. 387.

60–61   *"Look sharp? I should think so"*: Nansen, p. 472.

64   *a land "which I believed"*: Nansen, p. 570.

65   *"On one side the civilized"*: Nansen, p. 572.

66   *"they had a lump or two . . ."*: Jackson, quoted in Mirsky, p. 211.

JULY 30

73–74 *"The cold had certain effects"*: Smith, pp. 215–16.

74–81 Andrée's story is taken from Andrée and
83   Sundman, and from Berton, pp. 498–511, Mirsky, pp. 305–10, Mountfield, pp. 133–34, and Maxtone-Graham, pp. 165–83.

86   *"When I was out"*: Kane, Vol. I, p. 392.

JULY 31

92   *"smooth and unbroken"*: Quoted in Maxtone-Graham, p. 18.

93   *"Polar exploration is the cleanest"*: Quoted in Maxtone-Graham, p. 12.

93   *On one of his early voyages:* From Macmillan, p. 17.

94   *"All sailors are somewhat like children"*: Quoted in Mountfield, p. 75.

AUGUST 1

99–100 *"To all, the time was"*: Churchill, p. 142.

101   *A Royal Navy surgeon:* Maxtone-Graham, pp. 63–64.

101   *It is an insidious disease:* Stefansson, p. 314.

102   *"The gums of many"*: Quoted in Maxtone-Graham, p. 30.

102   *"to the consistency of cheese"*: Stefansson, p. 314.

102–03 *"It is to the advanced state"*: Quoted in Berton, pp. 412–13.

105–12 *On May 19, 1875:* The following can be found described in Nares, pp. 674–85, Maxtone-Graham, pp. 55–73, Berton, pp. 414–32, and Mountfield, pp. 115–16.

106 *"More bother with these wretched dogs":* Kane, p. 64.

106 *"Don't feed them":* (Quoted in) Maxtone-Graham, p. 59.

109 *"If I was asked what":* Kane, Vol. I, p. 394.

110 *"December 2, Saturday":* Kane, Vol. I, p. 432.

113 *"It was about half an hour":* Kane, Vol. I, p. 274.

AUGUST 2

126 *"I should then see the discovery":* Quoted in Branch and Brook-Williams, p. 15.

127 *In the seventeenth:* Parry, p. 27.

128 *The Spanish captain's error:* Branch and Brook-Williams, p. 13, and Taylor, p. 253.

129 *"The Board of Longitude was":* Branch and Brook-Williams, p. 16.

129 *Fourteen years later:* Branch and Brook-Williams, pp. 17, and Taylor, pp. 261–62.

AUGUST 3

142 *where Peary first made his appearance:* The following account is taken from Peary 1898, Rand, Weems, Herbert, and Berton.

142 *"Tall, erect":* Quoted in Weems, p. 52.

143 *"In situations requiring":* Quoted in Weems, p. 64.

143 *"the untiring energy":* Quoted in Weems, p. 67.

144 *"birthplace of the New World":* Quoted in Weems, p. 65.

144–45 *"I am after the Pole":* Rand, p. 358.

146 *"the dirtiest campaign":* Quoted in Rawlins, p. 246.

148 *"has brought my name":* Quoted in Herbert, p. 65.

149   *"It was evident"*: Peary, 1898, Vol. I, p. 346.

151–52   *"My Darling"*: Quoted in Herbert, p. 103.

154   *"I shall never see"*: Quoted in Berton, p. 520.

154   *"If a sledge"*: Peary 1898, Vol. II, p. 574.

155   *The meteorite was sold*: Berton, p. 521.

156   *"Why didn't you tell me?"*: Robinson, p. 135.

157   *"You will have been surprised"*: Quoted in Berton, p. 522.

158   *"My dream of sixteen years"*: Quoted in Berton, p. 530.

163   *In 1903 Cook set out*: The following account is taken from Cook, 1908, Herbert, and *National Geographic*, Jan. 1907, pp. 49–58.

165   *"I owe much"*: Peary, 1898, Vol. I, pp. 45, 424.

165   *"We are glad to welcome"* and following speeches: *National Geographic*, Jan. 1907, pp. 49–58.

AUGUST 4

174–75   The remarks of Congressman Macon are from the *Congressional Record*, Quoted in Rawlins, Weems and Herbert.

175   *Things were different in 1908*: The following account is from Peary, 1910; Cook, 1913; Berton; Herbert; Maxtone-Graham; and Weems.

175   *"The lure of the North!"*: Peary, 1910, p. 10.

176   *"Going through St. Peter"*: from Bartlett, pp. 177–78.

177–78   *"the final and complete"*: *National Geographic*, Jan. 1907, p. 57.

179   *"My dear, dear Father"*: Quoted in Weems, p. 204.

179   *"A cheer that echoed"*: Peary, 1910, p. 25.

179   *"An indescribable blending"*: Robinson, p. 210.

180   *Peary's cabin*: Peary, 1910, p. 31.

181   *"Rip 'em, Teddy!"*: Peary, 1910, p. 105.

181–82 *"unknown and uninhabitable"*: Cook, 1913, p. 155. Following quotes are also from Cook, 1913.

182 *"He held out"*: Robinson, p. 213.

183 *"I believe in you"*: Peary, 1910, p. 27.

183–84 *"This house belongs"*: Cook, 1953, p. 218.

184 *"How do we spend"*: Kane, Vol. I, pp. 169–73.

186 *"I can still see"*: Peary, 1910, p. 224.

186 *"Sometimes, in opening"*: Peary, 1910, p. 251.

187 *"The next march"*: Peary, 1910, p. 265.

187 *"After breakfast"*: Peary, 1910, p. 268.

188 *"The last march"*: Peary, 1910, pp. 287–88.

189 *"As we approached"*: Cook, p. 466.

191 *At the end of the month*: Described in Herbert, pp. 296–97.

192–93 *"With bated breath"*: Cook, pp. 222–23.

193–94 *"Terror gripped my heart"* and following quotes: Cook, pp. 225–84.

196–98 *"Bounding joyously"*: Cook, pp. 281–84.

198 *"Cook has handed"*: Time, March 30, 1936, p. 4.

198 *"Both Ah-we-lah"*: Cook, p. 225.

198 *"the great tormentor"*: Malaurie, p. 234.

199 *"They were all as children"*: Peary, 1910, p. 333.

200 *"The documents"*: Outlook, January 1, 1910.

200 *In his picture of the "First Camp"*: Mirsky, p. 301.

201 *Brooklyn Standard-Union*: Berton, p. 606.

AUGUST 5

211 *"had the Eskimos build"*: Peary, 1910, p. 248.

212 *"The distance which we traveled"*: Peary, 1910, p. 211.

213 *"As true as the needle"*: MacMillan, p. 243.

214 *"was glad to see"*: Peary, 1910, p. 226.

215 *"The northerly wind"*: Peary, 1910, p. 268.

215 *"The first thing"*: Peary, 1910, p. 287.

215 *But A. E. Thomas:* Herbert, p. 238 and Rawlins, p. 155.

216 *eight men voted for Peary:* Berton, p. 619.

217 *who proposed that Peary:* The following is quoted in Herbert, pp. 345–53 and Weems, pp. 290–93.

218 *In 1988 the society published: National Geographic,* September, 1988, pp. 387–413.

219 *the "end of a historic controversy": National Geographic,* January, 1990, p. 44.

222 *Scientific American:* June, 1990, p. 25.

222 *In the spring of 1991: St. Louis Post-Dispatch,* June 18, 1991.

AUGUST 6

227 *"suddenly the mist disappeared":* Ellsworth, p. 91.

228 *"terrible to behold":* Ellsworth, p. 95.

230 *A few years after his attempts:* The following can be found described in Smith, pp. 198–99.

234 *Byrd was distraught:* Montague, p. 11.

234 *New York Times,* May 10 and May 11, 1926.

239 *"The sun shone brilliantly":* Ellsworth, p. 138.

241 *Nobile proved to be:* Montague, pp. 10–11.

241 *In Amundsen's autobiography:* Quoted in Montague, p. 17.

246 *Two days later:* Mountfield, pp. 241–42.

248 *The icebreakers* Krassin *and* Malygin: The following is drawn from Montague and McKee.

AUGUST 8–11

269 *"April 21st":* MacMillan, pp. 80–82.

AUGUST 12–16

283 *In 1818 Captain John Symmes:* Gardner, pp. 20–22.